Alexander Macalister

Zoology of the Vertebrate Animals

Alexander Macalister

Zoology of the Vertebrate Animals

ISBN/EAN: 9783337815141

Printed in Europe, USA, Canada, Australia, Japan

Cover: Foto ©ninafisch / pixelio.de

More available books at **www.hansebooks.com**

HANDBOOKS for Students and General Readers.

ZOOLOGY

OF THE

INVERTEBRATE ANIMALS

BY

ALEX. MACALISTER, M.D.

*Professor of Zoology and Comparative Anatomy in the
University of Dublin.*

Specially Revised for America

BY

A. S. PACKARD, Jr., M.D.

*Professor of Zoology and Geology in
Brown University.*

NEW YORK
HENRY HOLT AND COMPANY
1879.

EXPLANATORY.

This Series is intended to meet the requirement of brief text-books both for schools and for adult readers who wish to review or expand their knowledge.

The grade of the books is intermediate between the so-called "primers" and the larger works professing to present quite detailed views of the respective subjects.

Such a notion as a person beyond childhood requires of some subjects, it is difficult and perhaps impossible to convey in one such volume. Therefore, occasionally a volume is given to each of the main departments into which a subject naturally falls—for instance, a volume to the Zoölogy of the vertebrates, and one to that of the invertebrates. While this arrangement supplies a compendious treatment for those who wish, it will also sometimes enable the reader interested in only a portion of the field covered by a science, to study the part he is interested in, without getting a book covering the whole.

Care is taken to bring out whatever educational value may be extracted from each subject without impeding the exposition of it. In the books on the sciences, not only are acquired results stated, but as full explanation as possible is given of the methods of inquiry and reasoning by which these results have been obtained. Consequently, although the treatment of each subject is strictly elementary, the fundamental facts are stated and discussed with the fulness needed to place their scientific significance in a clear light, and to show the relation in which they stand to the general conclusions of science.

Care is also taken that each book admitted to the series shall either be the work of a recognized authority, or bear the unqualified approval of such. As far as practicable, authors are selected who combine knowledge of their subjects with experience in teaching them.

PREFACE.

THE STUDENT who would acquire a satisfactory knowledge of the principles of Zoology is recommended to commence by learning the elementary principles of General Biology; and having mastered these he should then study the groups of the Invertebrates as here detailed, coupling his study with a practical examination of such common types as are easily to be obtained. A jellyfish, or a hydra, an earthworm, an oyster, a snail, a cockroach and a lobster, are forms everywhere procurable, and, if examined, will give the student a good general idea of the structure of Invertebrate Animals. It must be borne in mind that without some such practical study, no amount of reading will suffice to convey accurate and adequate ideas of animal organisation.

ALEXANDER MACALISTER.

CONTENTS.

CHAPTER I.

Nature of Animals—Processes of Life—Tissues and Organs —Symmetries of Animals . . . . PAGE 1

CHAPTER II.

Classification of Animals—Method of naming—Resemblances of Relationship and of Adaptation—Mimicry—Parasites—The Seven Sub-kingdoms of Invertebrate Animals—Each Animal has a Life History, not a mere Growth—Rudimental Organs—Tendency to Individual Variety 6

CHAPTER III.

Conditions of Distribution in Time and Space—Freshwater, Marine, and Terrestrial Life—Methods of Study of Zoology 13

CHAPTER IV.

Sub-kingdom 1. Protozoa: Rhizopods—Amœbæ—Sun-Animalcules—Gregarines and Radiolarians . . . 18

CHAPTER V.

Infusion-Animals—Luminous Animalcules—Summary of the Forms in Sub-kingdom 1. 25

CHAPTER VI.

Sub-kingdom 2. Sponges 28

CHAPTER VII.

Sub-kingdom 3. Cœlenterate Animals: Hydras—Sea-Firs, Medusæ 32

CHAPTER VIII.

Sea-Anemones—Corals—'Dead Men's Toes'—Sea-Pens . 41

CHAPTER IX.

Sub-kingdom 4. Echinodermata: Stone-Lilies—Feather-Stars—Starfishes 47

CHAPTER X.

Sea Urchins—Sea Cucumbers—Summary of Forms included in Sub-kingdom 4 52

CHAPTER XI.

Sub-kingdom 5. Worms: Turbellarians—Tape-Worms—Flukes—Round and Thread-Worms 57

CHAPTER XII.

Wheel-Animalcules—Spoon-Worms—Leeches. . . 66

Contents.

CHAPTER XIII.

Bristled-Worms — Earth-Worms — Summary of Normal Worms 70

CHAPTER XIV.

Aberrant-Worms—Moss-Polyps and Tunicated Animals . 74

CHAPTER XV.

Sub-kingdom 6. Mollusca or Soft-bodied Animals: Class 1. Arm-footed Molluscs; Class 2. Bivalves . . 78

CHAPTER XVI.

Class 3. Head-bearing Molluscs: Whelks, Snails, &c. . 84

CHAPTER XVII.

Class 4. Cuttle-Fishes—Nautili and Squids—Summary of Characters of the Classes of Mollusca 90

CHAPTER XVIII.

Sub-kingdom 7. Jointed Animals or Arthropoda . . 96

CHAPTER XIX.

Class 1. Crustacea: Crabs, Lobsters, Shrimps, &c. . 98

CHAPTER XX.

Class 2. Spiders, Mites, and Scorpions . . . 108

CHAPTER XXI.

Class 3. Myriopoda, Centipedes, and Gally-Worms . 112

CHAPTER XXII.

Class 4. Insecta: Insects—General Characters and Structure 115

CHAPTER XXIII.

Orders of Insects whose Metamorphoses are Imperfect—Aphides, Bugs, Straight-winged Insects and Dragon-Flies 123

CHAPTER XXIV.

Insects whose Metamorphoses are complete . . . 127

INDEX and GLOSSARY 137

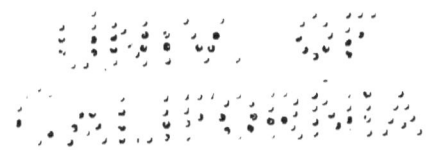

INVERTEBRATA.

CHAPTER I.

GENERAL CHARACTERS OF ANIMALS.

Physical Conditions of Life.—An animal, chemically considered, consists of a few elements[1] united into extremely unstable combinations, which are at every moment undergoing chemical change. The constituent materials are constantly becoming grouped into more simple and stable compounds, and in that state they are either eliminated or retained in an inactive condition, while other materials from without are being taken in, and so modified that they replace the molecules removed by the previous decomposition. As long as life lasts, these conditions of waste and repair continue; so that the particles of the bodies of al lanimals are in a state of constant change.

The food of animals contains carbon, hydrogen, nitrogen, and oxygen, which must be grouped into complex molecules before the animal can use them for his nutrition. Combinations of the requisite complexity can be derived only from previously organised

[1] Carbon, hydrogen, oxygen, and nitrogen.

materials either animal or vegetable. In most vegetables the forces concerned in assimilation are sufficient to break up originally stable compounds, such as carbonic acid, and to induce the elements to combine into the unstable combinations of which living textures consist.

The process of repair in animals has three stages, 1st, the taking in of material as food; 2nd, the changing of food into a substance capable of forming part of the living organism, *i.e.* blood; and 3rd, the laying down of this assimilated material in the tissues of the body of which it thus becomes a constituent, replacing the losses sustained by each organ in each discharge of its function.

For the life-processes of animals oxygen is necessary, and special structures, called respiratory or breathing organs, are often provided for taking it in. The carbonic acid formed from the waste of the tissues is usually got rid of by these organs.

The material with which the vital properties are connected is of the same nature in all animals and is called protoplasm. The simplest animals are mere masses of this substance, which in them discharges all the functions needful for the maintenance of life; the more complex are built up of aggregations of particles of the same material, or of substances derived from it in the course of growth. Each of these constituent particles or *cells*, as they may conveniently be called, usually consists of a mass of protoplasm surrounded by an envelope of some material derived by chemical action from protoplasm. Cells continuously grouped make up tissues, and a group of tissues which performs any special duties in the life of an animal is called an organ.// While there are thus varying degrees of complexity among animals, yet the parts of a simple animal have to perform as many essential functions as those of a more complex animal, the increase in complexity of an organism being correlated not with an increase in the number of essential functions but with the need for the more perfect fulfilment of existing duties. Increase in complexity thus results from division of labour, and, with each increase, the sphere of the functional activity of each part becomes narrowed. For example, in jelly-fishes one set of cavities act as organs of digestion and of circulation, while in higher animals these functions have separate organs, and even subsidiary portions of these great functions have for their accomplishment distinct parts.

Functions.—Three sets of functions are discharged by organs in the body of an animal: namely, 1st, those of Relation; 2nd, those of Nutrition; 3rd, those of Reproduction.

The organs appropriated to the functions of Relation are those which connect the animal with its environing conditions, informing it about its surroundings, and enabling it to avoid disagreeable or to court agreeable external influences. These organs are of two kinds: (A) those of sensation, such as the skin, or organ of touch, and the special sense organs (eye, ear, nose, tongue), and (B) those of motion, which may be of three kinds, (*a*) inconstant processes of protoplasm called *pseudopodia* (fig. 8), (*b*) minute, constant, hair-like processes having the power of waving to and fro, called *cilia*, or (*c*) contractile cells and fibres in bundles called *muscles*. The first kind occur in the lowest animals and in naked protoplasmic particles; the second in infusorial animals (fig. 14); the third in all but the simplest animals. Connected with the organs of relation we find a system of fine white threads called nerves, whose endings occur in these organs, and whose starting-points are central clusters of nerve-cells, called *ganglia*. These threads convey the variously received stimuli from the sense organs to the ganglia, and carry the command for motion from the ganglia to the muscles.

The function of Nutrition is discharged by four sets of organs: 1st, those of feeding, consisting of a cavity or stomach, for the reception of the food, with glands appended thereto, which secrete fluids to assist in assimilation; 2nd, organs of circulation, which carry

FIG. 1.

Euplotes Charon, a ciliated infusorium showing the stages of division.

the assimilated matter, or blood, through the body for the nutrition of the tissues; 3rd, organs of respiration, by which oxygen is taken in; and 4th, organs of excretion whereby the waste products are eliminated.

General Characters of Animals. 5

There are three stages in the contest between waste and repair which is characteristic of life. In the first, repair is in excess of waste, and individual growth proceeds until a definite limit, constant within certain bounds for each species, is reached. When this is attained, excess of nutrition still continues but tends to become separate and independent; by such discontinuous modes of growth, the third set of functions, or Reproduction, is accomplished. Of this there are three chief forms: (A) either the whole body of the parent may split into two or more, each becoming a perfect animal like its parent; this process is named *fission*. (B) In the second mode of reproduction a small portion of the body of the parent animal enlarges and becomes detached as a bud, which develops directly into an organism like its ancestor; this is called *gemmation*. (C) In the third mode small particles called eggs arise from the tissues of the parent, and on being fertilised, are capable of developing into new individuals; this is called *ovulation*.

FIG. 2.

The second stage of existence having for a time continued, the organism reaches a third stage, in which waste exceeds repair, and as, by degrees, the assimilated material becomes insufficient to keep up the processes of life this stage terminates in death.

Gemmation in the common *Hydra viridis*.

Summary.—Animals consist for the most part of protoplasm, are constantly undergoing waste, and being built up by the assimilation of food. They differ from plants in being usually capable of locomotion (though this has exceptions), in being only capable of assimilating organic matter (except in the case of water and oxygen), and in having their cell-walls composed of nitrogenous matter, while in plants non-nitrogenous matter abounds. Higher animals are strongly differentiated from plants; the lower forms are often of doubtful position. Animals may be simple or complex, complexity depending on division of labour, and the consequent specialisation of function in organs which become differentiated from each other. The chief functions are Relation, Nutrition and Reproduction, the latter taking place during the stage when individual growth has ceased and while as yet repair exceeds waste.

CHAPTER II.

ORGANS AND CLASSIFICATION OF ANIMALS.

Method of Study.—The first branch of zoology necessary to be studied is the anatomy of the organism, and the best method of study is the examination of some of the commoner types of each class. As many of these are small, and optical assistance necessary, the student should provide himself with a good pocket lens. For dissection, the instruments required are, a scalpel, a fine-pointed pair of dissecting forceps, and several sharp-pointed needles fixed in wooden handles and with their extremities ground flat, so as to cut as well as tear. As many small animals can be most easily dissected under water it is convenient to have a shallow

Organs and Classification of Animals. 7

wooden tray lined with sheet lead for the purpose, while it often facilitates dissection to have a thin sheet of cork weighted with lead, so as to retain its position at the bottom of the fluid upon which the various parts may be pinned down. To preserve animal organs the best materials are, spirits of wine, or a weak (2 per cent.) solution of bichromate of potassium.

The study of the forms, nature and relations of organs to each other and to the organism in general,

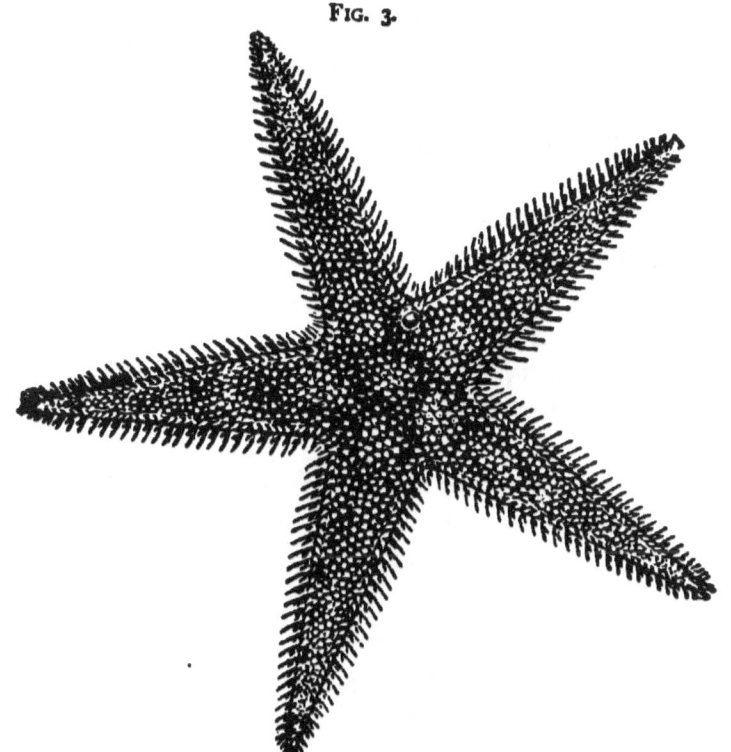

FIG. 3.

Common orange Star-fish *(Astropecten aurantiacus)*.

and the laws deduced therefrom is known as Morphology; the study of the uses of parts is called Physiology.

Morphology.—Groups of organs are generally symmetrically disposed in animals; either they are arranged in order around a central point in one plane, or else each individual consists of a succession of similar segments, as in a centipede. In the first case the symmetry is said to be radial as in the star-fish (fig. 3); in the second the segments are each made up of two symmetrical halves, and the symmetry is said to be bilateral.

In a perfectly symmetrical animal all the organs should be proportionally developed, but as the varying conditions of animal existence often require the more extensive performance of some duties than of others, we always find that some organs are larger, others smaller. In fact animals are so perfectly fitted to their surroundings that could we know all the conditions under which a given animal existed, we could form a good conception of its structure and *vice versâ*.

The Embryo.—To understand the true relations of structures in animals it is necessary to watch the growth of the organism from the earliest stages of its production in the egg until it attains its adult condition. The embryo is not a simple miniature of the full grown animal, but reaches its perfect state by undergoing a series of changes, which follow each other in a definite order. In this process, parts and organs start into being which were before unnoticeable, and some of these have only a transient existence fading off into nothingness. Thus the common acorn shell emerges from its egg as a little free-swimming larva (fig. 4), with eyes and feelers, but these totally vanish in the adult (fig. 5); such organs are known as *provisional* organs, and occasionally they

Organs and Classification of Animals. 9

leave traces behind when their functions have ceased, like the cord-like obliterated embryonic blood-vessels in mammalia. In some animals, during their development, organs spring into being for a shorter or longer period, but never perform any function and either vanish

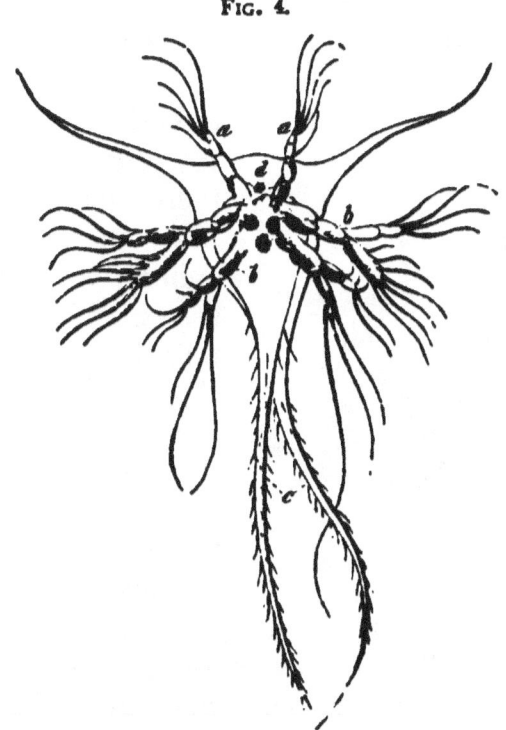

FIG. 4.

Larva of common Acorn-shell (*Balanus porcatus*), showing antennæ (*a*), limbs (*b*), and eye (*d*).

or remain permanently in an undeveloped condition; such organs are called *rudimental*, and they are always such as in some kindred form discharge an important duty. Thus most cuttle-fishes have a groove in their body during their embryonic life, which closes in and forms a cavity wherein the internal shell is secreted; but the octopus or sea-spider, a closely allied form, has a similar groove which vanishes, leaving no trace behind. Instances of the kind might be multiplied, as there is scarcely an individual form in the higher sub-kingdoms which does not in its life history exhibit instances of provisional and rudimental organs.

Characters Essential and Adaptive.—In each animal we can divide the characters into two groups, essential and adaptive; the former of these are those whereby we can learn the relations of animals among themselves, and these are of primary importance in classification; the latter show the relations of the animal to its surroundings, but these in the adult often so overlie the essential characters as to obscure them. A study of the embryogeny of the animal will enable us to understand its relationship, for the adaptive characters are of later origin than the essential and may be traced as they are becoming superinduced. Thus among the parasitic mites of the genus Pentastoma, we could not know the true relations of the worm-like adults if we were not acquainted with the limb-bearing larva.

FIG. 5.

Adult form of *Balanus porcatus*.

Classification and Nomenclature.—The animal kingdom is a vast assemblage of individuals, and we require to arrange these in larger categories for purposes of study. Those individuals which are so far identical in structure as to lead us to believe that they are descended from common parents we speak of as belonging to the one species. *Species* is thus our unit in systematic zoology, but as two individuals are seldom absolutely identical in all respects specific distinctions must be more or less arbitrary. A group of allied species embodying the same structural ideas is called a *genus*. An assemblage of allied genera is a *family* ; a group of related families make up an *order* ; while related orders make up a *class*, and the several classes included in the animal kingdom are united in certain primary categories called *subkingdoms*. Systematic zoologists give a Latin name to each of these, and for convenience each species is designated by a Latin word to which is prefixed the name of the genus. The specific name is generally an adjective, the generic is a substantive, and should be written with a capital letter. Thus the dog is called by zoologists *Canis familiaris*, Canis being the generic, familiaris the specific name. *Canis aureus* is the jackal, *Canis lupus* the wolf. That species in a genus which most strikingly embodies the generic characters is the type of the genus. We also speak of the type of a family, of an order, or of a class, the type being that species which displays most clearly the characters of the group ; and for convenience we attribute certain characters to ideal types to illustrate truths in classification.

The type genus usually gives its name to the family , thus the dog-family is called Canidæ.

Homology.—In comparing animals, the most important resemblances are those which depend on common relationship to the types of the class to which they belong. These likenesses are called resemblances of morphological type. Thus if we compare a dog and a crow, we find in both a skeleton, a brain, a skull, four limbs, a heart &c., and we refer them both to the vertebrate type, inasmuch as they both embody the ideas of structure characteristic of vertebrate animals. Each part in one is said to be homologous with the corresponding part in the other, the wing with the fore leg, &c. Homology is thus identity of structure irrespective of function, and parts are homologous which represent the same parts in the ideal type of the class. Such resemblances are the bases of classification.

Analogy.—Likenesses of parts may also depend on similarity of function; thus the wings of insects and the wings of birds are used for the same purpose, and have certain resemblances. These similarities are called resemblances of analogy, and they tell us nothing as to the nature of the organs compared.

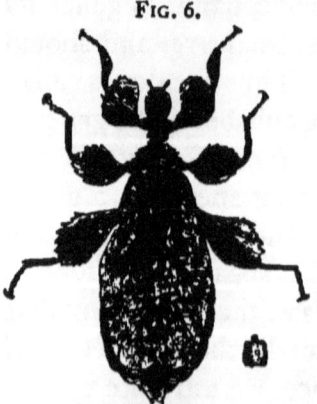

FIG. 6.

Leaf insect (*Phyllium siccifolium*).

Mimicry.—Animals of definite geographical areas often resemble each other in some respects; thus they may be mostly similar in colour, mostly white, or spotted, or striped, or brightly coloured. Sometimes animals mimic in shape or colour the leaves and twigs on which they live (fig. 6), or the prevalent colour of the herbage. Thus the Kakapo

Classification and Distribution of Animals. 13

or ground parrot of New Zealand, which can hardly fly, is in plumage like the mottled green vegetation among which it lives. The ptarmigan and other birds become white in winter, so as to become inconspicuous among the snow. Sometimes an insect mimics in appearance another of different nature living in the same district. In such cases the insect imitated is one which, from its disagreeable secretions or sting, is not a favourite prey of insect-eaters. Hence the mimicry protects the imitator, who is usually rarer than the insect imitated.

Organs which are homologous consist of homologous parts; and as this is not the case in organs resembling each other only in function, we must be careful to discriminate morphological from physiological likeness.

In animals which consist of successive segments in a chain, like centipedes or lobsters, each segment is composed of parts similar to those of its neighbouring joints. Such parts are said to be serial homologues, as for example the fore and hinder limbs of quadrupeds.

CHAPTER III.

CLASSIFICATION AND DISTRIBUTION OF ANIMALS.

Sub-Kingdoms.—THE animal kingdom includes eight sub-kingdoms. In these we observe a certain progressive increase in complexity, from one end of the series to the other; but they do not make a linear series, as the highest organism of each is in no degree related to the lowest organism of the next sub-kingdom, being usually much more advanced and specialised, so that in point of complexity the sub-kingdoms overlap each other.

The first sub-kingdom, Protozoa, includes those animals which have neither body-cavity nor nervous system, and are single celled.

Sub-kingdom 2. Polystomata, includes sponges, which have an internal cavity with a three layered wall, one outlet, and usually many inlets, but no differentiated organs, though consisting of many cells.

Sub-kingdom 3. Cœlenterata, includes jelly-fishes and sea anemones, having a stomach cavity and a body cavity as an outgrowth therefrom, and a radiate symmetry.

Sub-kingdom 4. Echinodermata, includes starfishes and sea-urchins, with a body cavity separate from the stomach, a nervous system, and a system of water-tubes which are agents in locomotion.

Sub-kingdom 5. Vermes, includes worms which are bilaterally symmetrical, and composed of successive similar segments, with no jointed limbs, and with a water-vascular system which has no locomotory function.

Sub-kingdom 6. Mollusca, includes oysters, snails, &c., possessing soft bodies enveloped in a leathery mantle, no jointed limbs, a circulating system, often an external shell and often an unsymmetrical nervous system.

Sub-kingdom 7. Arthropoda, includes crabs, lobsters, spiders, and insects, which have bodies made up of successive joints, with a symmetrical nervous system, an external skeleton and jointed limbs.

Sub-kingdom 8. Vertebrata, including fishes,

Classification and Distribution of Animals. 15

reptiles, birds and quadrupeds, which have an internal skeleton, a brain and vertebral column. This one sub-kingdom includes the most complex of animals whose structure requires more minute examination than does that of the other sub-kingdoms. We will in the present volume consider the seven invertebrate sub-kingdoms.

In comparing these sub-kingdoms, we speak of forms as being high or low in organisation according to the degree in which special parts are appropriated for the discharge of special functions. We also notice that no organ appears for the first time in animals in a state of complexity, but on the contrary, there is always in lower forms a prophetic foreshadowing of it in the modification of some part already existing.

Distribution.—Every species of animal is limited to a definite geographical area. Thus the earth's surface may be divided into regions, each characterised by special inhabitants, and the collected animals of any region we speak of as its fauna. As a rule, life increases in amount in any country with increasing, and diminishes with diminishing temperature. Thus the fauna of a tropical exceeds that of a temperate region. The number of animals is also larger when the difference between the winter and summer temperature is small, than in a country with the same mean temperature but with a greater range between maximum and minimum. Moisture is also favourable to animal life, and the fauna of a moist exceeds that of a dry region, other things being equal.

Many animals live in places from which light is excluded, as in caves ; these have rudimental eyes, and are white or colourless. Many large caves, like those of Kentucky, Adelsberg &c., have thus peculiar blind faunæ.

Sometimes the presence of one animal prevents the diffusion of others; thus in Africa the tzetze fly renders whole tracts uninhabitable by oxen and deer, which are destroyed by its poisonous bites.

The fauna of a limited area of a continent usually exceeds that of an island of equal size in its number of specific forms; and the fauna of an island lying near a continent resembles that of its neighbouring continent. Oceanic islands or those isolated by very deep straits have often remarkable faunæ of their own, *e.g.*, the Galapagos and New Zealand.

Tropical species are, as a rule, more limited in range than are those of temperate climates, and simpler animals are usually more widely distributed than are the more complex.

Fresh-water inhabitants are the fewest specifically, and as a rule are simpler in organisation than allied forms inhabiting other media. The fourth sub-kingdom has no fresh-water representatives; the second has only two, and the third only five species living in this medium; while the others are not very numerously represented in fresh-water.

The sea is the home of nine-tenths of the invertebrates (if we exclude insects), and there are also definite ranges of extension to be noticed in the cases of marine species. The conditions limiting specific life in the sea are depth, currents, and temperature.

Terrestrial animals are the most specialised, and

Classification and Distribution of Animals. 17

have organs in a more concentrated condition than in their aquatic allies.

Parasitism.—Some animals pass their lives within or on the bodies of others, and this condition induces striking alterations in structure. In some cases the intruder collects its own food independently of his host, being thus only indebted to him for house room ; of this nature are the sponges which live rooted on crabs, or the barnacles on the skin of the whale. The second series of intruders are fellow commoners with their hosts, feeding on the food which their entertainer collects ; while in a third class the parasite is a pensioner on the body of his host, feeding on his substance. Such forms are true parasites.

In all these conditions there is a diminished necessity for locomotion and for food-capture on the part of the parasite ; so the organs of motion, of sense, and of nutrition retrograde, but as the parasitic condition involves difficulties in the continuance of the species, the organs of multiplication are enormously increased in size and complexity.

Extension in Time.—Species of animals have limited ranges in time as well as in space, for they are dependent on the constancy of physical conditions for their specific longevity, and such alterations in these as are constantly occurring will tend to extinguish species ; hence the history of life in the past is a continual record of the dying out of types of life.

CHAPTER IV.

SUB-KINGDOM I : PROTOZOA.

General Characters.—The constituent animals of this sub-kingdom are animals of extreme simplicity, consisting for the most part of undifferentiated protoplasm. None of them possess a nervous system, sense organs, nor a body cavity, nor do we find differentiated organs present in any of them.

Among these there are five chief types forming five classes.

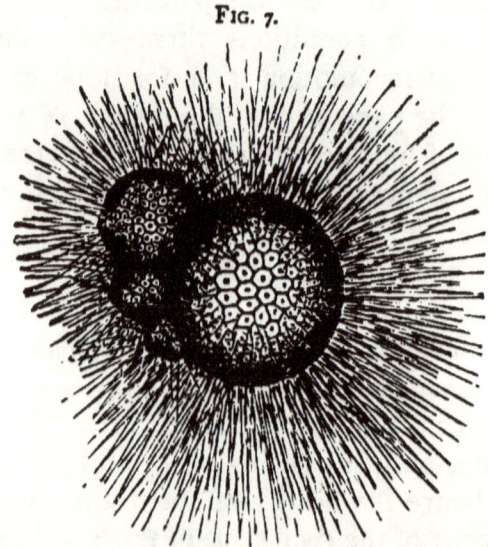

Fig. 7.

One of the minute Foraminifera, *Globigerina bulloides*, magnified seventy diameters.

Certain forms, called Monera, are even simpler than the Rhizopods, as they not only want the power of house-building but have no nuclei, and are thus the simplest conceivable living beings, mere specks of living jelly (fig. 9). Of these naked forms, some authors make a separate class under the name Monera.

Class 1. Rhizopoda.—In the fine white sand on the sea-shore or in the mud of the sea-bottom there are to be found minute calcareous shells of varying forms, ranging from $\frac{1}{300}$th to $\frac{1}{10}$th of an inch in diameter. Each shell consists of many separate chambers, arranged either one after another in a straight line or in a single or double spiral, or even grouped in more complex fashions. Each chamber is separated from its neighbours by a partition which is pierced with one or many holes whereby the several chambers communicate with each other. The shell-substance is either white and porcelain-like, or glass-like and more brittle, and pierced not only in the partitions but over its whole surface by numerous holes. On account of these perforations these little shells are called Foraminifera (hole bearing).

The animals which build these wonderful houses are exceedingly simple in their structure. The interior of each chamber in a fresh state is filled with protoplasm which is jelly-like, highly contractile on being irritated, and not only extends through the holes in the shelly wall but coats the outside of the shell with a glairy external living layer. This layer has no definite uniformity of outline, but is constantly changing its shape by sending into the surrounding water radiating protoplasmic processes which are inconstant, rapidly retracted, disappearing by being taken into the homogeneous matter of the animal's body, and coalescing when they touch each other. To these the name *pseudopodia* (false feet) has been given.

These little creatures live on any minute organic particles with which they come in contact, and their mode of feeding is simple; when the ray-like pseudopodia touch a particle of which they seem to approve as a prospective meal they converge around it, and

Fig. 8.

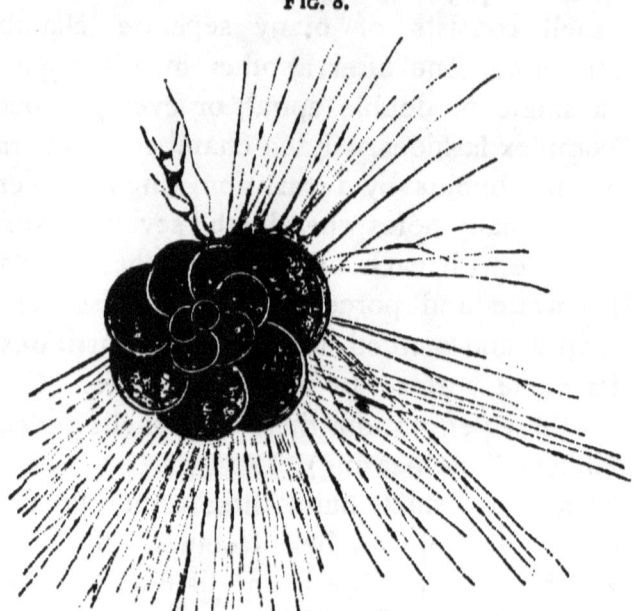

Rotalia Veneta, a Rhizopod, showing the pseudopodia.

touching each other coalesce, and draw the particle within the body proper, in which it is digested. As these creatures are homogeneous or nearly so, any one spot is as suitable for the protrusion of pseudopodia or for the taking in of food as another, but usually the processes are most numerous opposite the holes in the shell.

As the protoplasm includes its food in the manner described, foreign particles and fine granules become enclosed in it derived from the undigested parts of the food. Sometimes drops of water or of thin fluid may be seen in the protoplasm like little bubbles; these are called *vacuoles* (fig. 14), and they with the granules circulate actively in the body mass; obscure condensed points or nuclei also exist, and the name of the class is derived from the root-like spreading of the pseudopodia.

Mode of Growth of Rhizopoda.—Those Rhizopods that separate lime from the sea-water to form shells, begin the process while they are young single masses, and they increase by budding, each bud forming on the newest end of the last bud; consequently the perfect animal consists of a rod-like or spiral set of chambers, each chamber being a new, undetached bud. Some buds become quite separate and grow into new individuals. In a few cases each bud becomes detached, so that the animals always remain of one chamber.

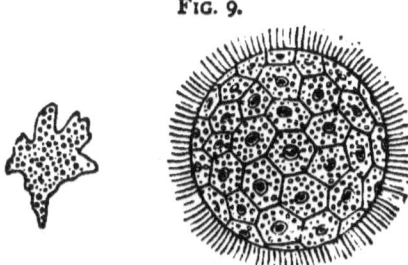

Fig. 9.

Two forms of Protozoa. *Protamœba primitiva*, the simplest living animal; *Magosphæra planula*, a compound form.

Shell-forming Rhizopods are occasionally aggregated in great masses and sometimes at great depths in the ocean. Such seems to have been their habit in past times, and many of the chalky limestones consist of the accumulated shells of Foraminifera.

Invertebrata.

Class 2. Protoplasta.—In the slowly running waters of ditches, or in bog pools, are found curious creatures in many respects reminding us of the naked Rhizopods. These amœbæ as they are called, are little masses of protoplasm, moving and taking food by means of pseudopodia. On close inspection many particulars will be noticed, in which they differ from those simple creatures which we have already examined. Thus their pseudopodia are blunt, and do not freely coalesce, on touching each other; the granules and vacuoles are not uniformly distributed through the protoplasm, but are for the most part in the central region, while the outer protoplasm is firmer. We also notice a denser central spot in the body, to which the name *nucleus* is given, as can be seen in each component mass of Magosphæra (fig. 9); and one or more little clear spaces may be seen occasionally to contract and expand alternately. Thus in the group of organisms of which amœba is the type, protoplasm has become partly differentiated, that is, some parts have assumed characters which the simple protoplasm did not possess. On account of this first trace of the development of tissue we call this group of

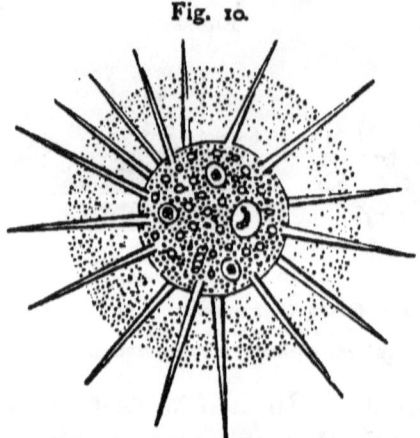

Fig. 10.

Heliophrys variabilis. One of the Sun animalcules showing the pseudopodia, nuclei, vacuoles, &c.

animals *Protoplasta* (first tissue). The amount of this differentiation is in some scarcely recognisable, while in others, the sun animalcules or *Heliozoa* (fig. 10), there are many nuclei, and each of the fine ray-like pseudopodia exhibits distinctly an inner axis of the granule-holding protoplasm and an outer layer of firmer material. These animals multiply by division, and in modes of feeding, &c., they resemble the Rhizopods, with which they are often united.

Class 3. Gregarinæ.—A group of curious parasites, the *Gregarinæ*, manifest a similar process of differentiation taking place in their life-history. These minute creatures are found in the digestive canals of beetles, earthworms, &c., and in their mature states they appear as elongated bodies with a firm outer wall which never becomes protruded, and consequently does not allow of the formation of pseudopodia (fig. 1, A, B). This outer stratum may itself consist of two layers; while internally the protoplasm contains a solid nucleus. At a certain stage in its existence the adult Gregarine becomes almost globular and quiescent, loses its nucleus, and its internal material becomes aggregated into many boat-shaped bodies, contained within the firm outer layer through which they eventually burst; each of these boat-like bodies (fig. 11 c) consists of a rigid outer case and an inner

FIG. 11.

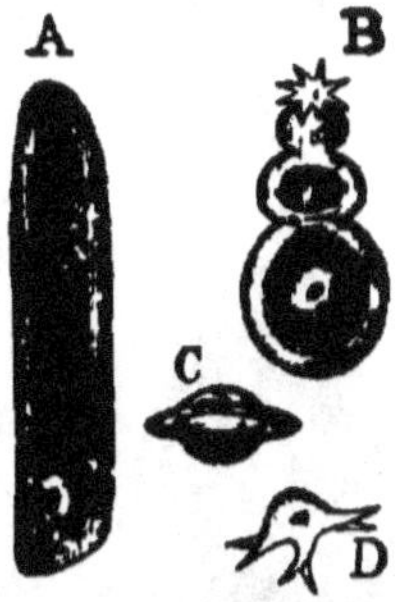

A. Gregarine from the Earthworm. *Monocystis lumbrici.*
B. Gregarine from the dragon-fly. *Pixinia rubecula.*
C. Boat-shaped body or Pseudo-navicella.
D. Amœbiform body set free from Pseudo-navicella.

particle of protoplasm. The former soon gives way, and the inner portion, freed from external restraints, moves actively by pseudopodia like a Rhizopod (fig. 11, D). On reaching a suitable nest this amœboid particle undergoes further development, and becomes a Gregarine like its parent. In size these parasites range from the $\frac{1}{50}$th to $\frac{2}{3}$rds of an inch.

Class 4. Radiolaria.—On examining the material brought up from ocean bottoms, there are frequently found small and beautifully sculptured shells, differing from those of the Foraminifera in that they consist of silica, not of lime, and hence they are comparatively indestructible by maceration in acids, by which process they can be isolated from the mud wherein they are found. In pattern these shells frequently consist of symmetrical, radiating rods, united by a variously patterned interweaving of threads of silica, the whole making a network often resembling flower-baskets, disks, and perforated spheres, hour-glasses, or helmets.

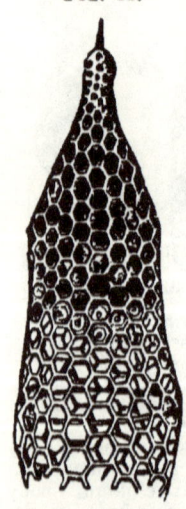

FIG. 12.

Flinty Shell of a Radiolarian *Eucyrtidium lagena*.

The animals which form these exquisitely ornate little shells are found to be comparatively simple, and in many respects allied to the Rhizopods, as they send out fine thread-like pseudopodia, from the surface layer. The deeper protoplasm is enclosed in a central membranous capsule, perforated with holes, and it contains fat, cellular masses, pigment and often a central vesicle or sac with striped walls; curious

Protozoa. 25

yellow cells are found scattered through the body in almost all species.

In size these Radiolarians are from $\frac{1}{2}$ to $\frac{1}{600}$th of an inch in diameter, the larger forms, however, are not single individuals but clusters united into compact colonies, each component individual having its own central capsule. Most of these are found floating on or in the waters of the sea. Some oceanic forms have no skeleton, and are described under the name sea-glue (*Thalassicolla*).

Some allied forms, destitute of central capsule and of yellow cells, are found in fresh-water bog pools in this country.

CHAPTER V.

SUB-KINGDOM I : PROTOZOA—*continued.*

Class 5. Infusoria.—If we place under the microscope, water in which animal or vegetable matter has been infused for six or seven days, especially in warm weather, we see that the fluid contains minute, actively moving creatures ranging in size from $\frac{1}{25}$th to the $\frac{1}{2400}$th of an inch in length. They are mostly oblong in shape and their rapid locomotion is due to the action of fine vibratile cilia which clothe, either the whole

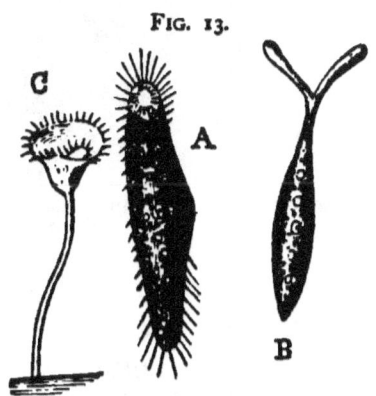

FIG. 13.

Three Ciliated Infusoria.
A. *Oxytricha gibba.* B. *Trachelocerca biceps.* C. *Vorticella citrina.*

surface, or else special areas of it; sometimes a few of these processes are rigid and act like little feet, or else they are all equal and fine, invisible during their active exercise owing to their rapid rate of motion.

The outer layer of their body is a firm cuticle which covers a differentiated protoplasmic lamina con-

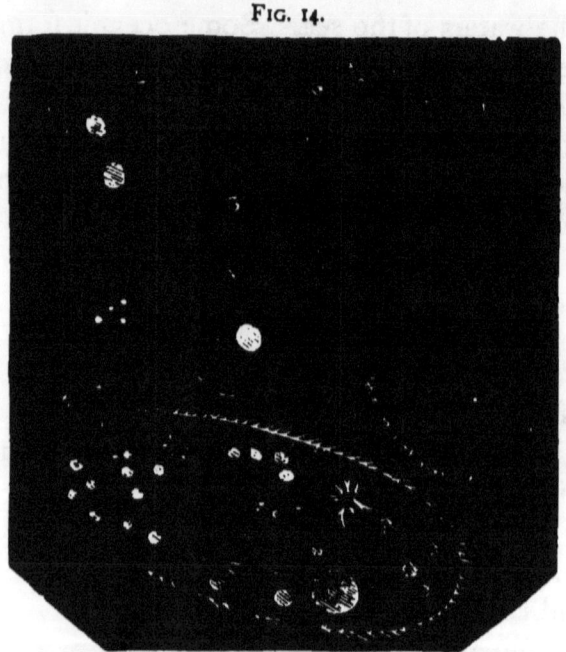

Fig. 14.

Paramæcium aurelia, an infusorian, showing the contractile vesicles (v), cilia and vacuoles (a).

taining one or more clear spaces or *contractile vesicles*, which when watched can be seen to expand and contract regularly, pulsating like a heart. Within this layer is a more fluid mobile protoplasm containing granules, vacuoles and a pair of singular solid bodies called respectively nucleus and nucleolus.

Protozoa.

Near one end of the body there is usually a funnel-shaped mouth opening into the inner protoplasm, where digestion takes place, as in Rhizopods; the undigested particles are ejected at a spot where the outer wall seems deficient, and which sometimes is a distinct opening.

These animals multiply either by fission like most of the other Protozoa, or else the nucleus breaks up into egg-like masses which seem to develop into new infusoria. This condition is preceded by the formation of a mucous mass around the animalcule, which becomes quiescent, losing its cilia.

The Vorticella, or bell animalcule (Fig. 13, c) is a common form fixed by a slender footstalk, which on

FIG. 15.   FIG. 16.

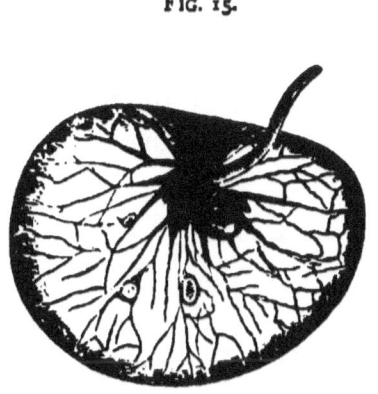 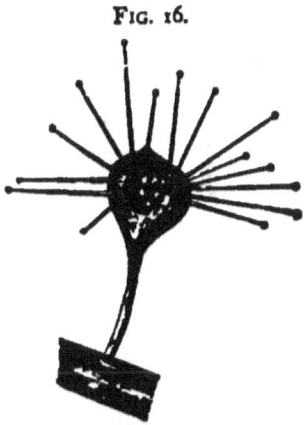

Noctiluca miliaris, a marine luminous animacule, showing its flagellum.   *Acineta mystacina.*

irritation instantly contracts into a spring-like spiral and the ciliary crown around the mouth of the bell becomes introverted. Another common form, *Ophrydium*, has an outer gelatinous envelope, and as division proceeds, this keeps the broods together so that they sometimes form masses of more than an inch in diameter, which are often found floating on standing water. The commonest forms are the slipper animalcule (fig. 14), the boat-like animalcule or *Euplotes* (fig. 1), and the hay infusion animal or *Colpoda*, but almost every infusion has its own form of animal.

Several groups of microscopic animals are allied to the Infusoria. Some of these are called *monads* and are mouthless nucleated bodies with one long cilium. Another of these is Noctiluca (fig. 15), a globular creature about $\frac{1}{80}$th of an inch long, with a short obtuse vibrating *flagellum* or filament and a mouth, but whose interior consists of netted protoplasmic threads whose meshes are filled with water. These organisms are among the commonest of those to which the sea owes its phosphorescence.

Other minute forms, called Acinetæ (fig. 16), are small, stalked masses whose surface is studded with radiating, retractile tubular suckers, through which they suck the juices of their prey.

CHAPTER VI.

SUB-KINGDOM II : SPONGES (POLYSTOMATA).

Metazoa.—All animals above the Protozoa possess an internal body-cavity, the wall around which is made up of three primary layers, often with difficulty discriminable in the lowest forms ; and there is either one terminal mouth into the cavity, or, as in the case of the sponges, many lateral pores communicate therewith.

Polystomata.

Characters of Sponges.—The common toilet sponge is a representative of a group of animals whose affinities are not easily understood. On examination with a magnifying glass it will be found to consist of irregularly branching and re-uniting threads of a highly elastic material, so arranged that the interspaces between the finer branches appear as pores or canals, which, from the nature of their walls, freely communicate with each other.

On examining the surface of a sponge, some large holes will be seen, which, on being cut into, are found to be the extremities of wide spaces or tubes; these divide within the sponge-mass into smaller canals, which again divide and subdivide until finally they end in the fine canals whose terminations are the minute surface pores between the superficial fibres of the mass. The walls of these spaces are themselves full of small pores in the interstices of the fibres which form the substance. This horny mass is really the sponge skeleton, having the same relation to the sponge animal that the spicules of Radiolarians bear to the soft parts of those creatures.

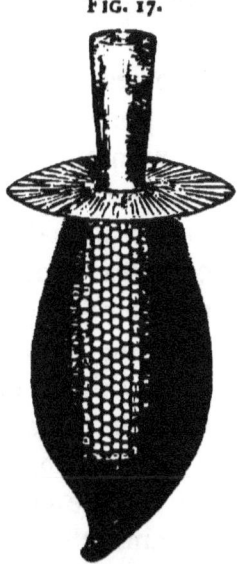

FIG. 17.

A calcareous sponge.

We can most easily understand the nature of a sponge animal by examining such simple forms of the group as may be found encrusting sea-weeds or stones on our own shores. These are nearly cylindrical, rooted by a flat protoplasmic expansion below (fig. 17), and have a single wide opening above, which is named the *osculum*. Its walls are pierced by numerous fine apertures or *pores*, which open directly into the central cavity. The wall consists of a cluster of Monad-like cells, provided with a collar, each sending out a pseudopod. In the wall and around each of the lateral pores are needle-like spicules of carbonate of lime usually united in threes, and arranged in a radiated manner. Sometimes they are in pairs or in twos. Others are like anchors, with two flukes.

As in most sponges the wall of the body-cavity below each mouth is thick, not simple and membranous, the pores elongate into canals. Most sponges also grow in tufts or clusters arranged so close together that the outer pores of the neighbouring, and closely united animals communicate with each other; thus a complex canal system grows up, according to the degree of thickening of the wall and coalescence of separate elements of the clusters, as well as by the superaddition of interspaces, which are often branched, between the separate individuals or elements.

In a living sponge, currents of fluid set in through the minute pores on the surface, setting out in large streams through the oscula; thus there are many mouths and few outlets. These currents are kept up by the waving of the flagella which bedeck the protoplasm masses that line the canals and cover the skeleton, and as these currents traverse the canals the small organic particles which they carry in are taken up by the cells of the wall in the same manner as food particles are swallowed by Rhizopods.

Spicules.—The skeleton of most sponges consists not only of the horny material with which we are familiar in the toilet sponge, but of spicules of silica of various shapes embedded in the horny mass, resembling pins, needles, clubs, crosses, anchors, hooks, wheels, &c. In others, siliceous spicules alone make up the skeleton, which has no horny matter. There is a calcareous skeleton in another group.

Reproduction and Classification. — Sponges multiply by division, either natural or artificial. That is, if we cut up a living sponge into many small pieces, each can grow into a perfect sponge. Other modes of growth or reproduction are by continuous budding, by the formation of free buds, usually arising in autumn and growing in the ensuing spring, or else by the formation of eggs which have been found in summer in many forms, and which develop in the following year Sponges are classified according to the material of the skeleton and the shapes of the spicules. Thus there are calcareous, horny, and siliceous sponges. The last class is the largest and includes some remarkable forms, such as the boring sponge (*Cliona celata*), which pierces holes in old oyster shells on our sea-shore, and is known by its pin-shaped spicules. The remarkable Neptune's cup (*Raphiophora*) is closely allied, though very dissimilar in shape and size. *Hyalonema*, the glass-rope, from Japan and Portugal, has long twisted siliceous spicules. *Euplectella*, the exquisite Venus's flower-basket, from the Philippines, is now well known as an ornament, and exhibits a most wonderful interweaving of siliceous spicules. *Spongilla*, the common green fresh-water sponge of lakes and rivers, is a familiar form, and each autumn it will be found to display the formation of winter gemmules or free buds. *Halichondria* (Chalinula) is the common sponge found on our sea shores, and *Sycandra* is the compressed white calcareous sponge found pendulous from rocks, or adhering to sea-weed near low-water mark.

CHAPTER VII.

SUB-KINGDOM III: CŒLENTERATA. CLASS I. HYDROZOA, JELLY-FISHES.

General Characters of Hydra.—The common *Hydra* (figs. 2 and 18), an inhabitant of our stagnant pools, is the type of the third sub-kingdom of animals. This voracious creature rarely exceeds half an inch in length, and possesses a cydrical body having the mouth at one end and a sucking disk for voluntary attachment at the other. Around the mouth are six, seven, or even ten slender contractile arms, capable of rapid motion, and about as long as the body, or even longer; these can be seen actively engaged in seizing prey and dragging it into the central mouth (fig. 18 T). The body is composed of two membranes, an outer and an inner; the former, which is called *ectoderm* (outer skin), making up the whole outer surface, the latter (called *endoderm* or inner skin) lining the interior

FIG. 18.

Hydra aurantiaca, the orange hydra, showing its tentacles and reproductive organs.

of the body, which consists of a simple stomach cavity from which the effete matters are ejected by the mouth.

On watching the process of feeding we notice that the arms exercise a power over living prey far greater than we could anticipate from their size; and on close inspection these *tentacles* (as the arms are called) are seen to be covered with minute oval sacs, whose outer thin walls (fig. 19 B), are easily burst by pressure, and when this occurs a long whiplash-like filament (C) which lay coiled within the cell, is suddenly projected, thus rendering the tentacle a formidable organ for seizing prey, their action being either mechanical, or by virtue, possibly, of some poisonous fluid.

The cells of the outer layer in *Hydra* have, projecting inwards or towards the endoderm, slender thread-like contractile processes, acting like muscular fibres. The ectodermal cells resemble nerve cells, and hence to this stratum the name *neuro-muscular cell-layer* is given.

FIG. 19.

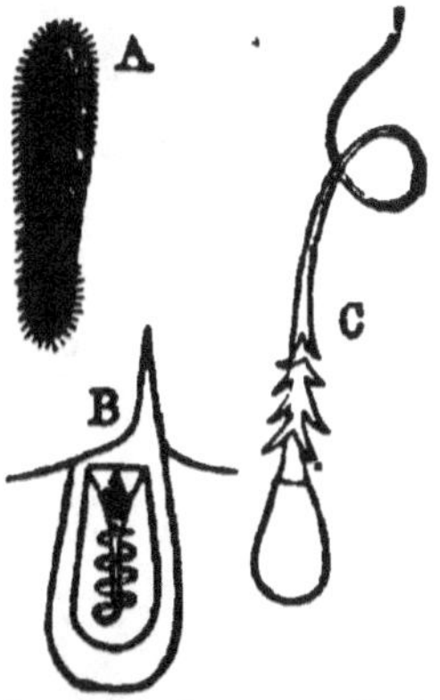

A, Planula or earliest stage of a hydroid on its emission from the egg. B, Thread-cell undisturbed. C, the same with the filament protruded.

Reproduction. — Hydras in early summer send off from near the base of the body small buds (fig. 2), which grow rapidly, each developing a mouth at its free end, together with a crown of tentacles, then, being detached, it assumes a separate existence. Sometimes a second crop of buds arises from the first bud before it has detached itself from its parent.

Later on in the season, eggs form within the Hydra, beginning as modified cells of the inner layer. These

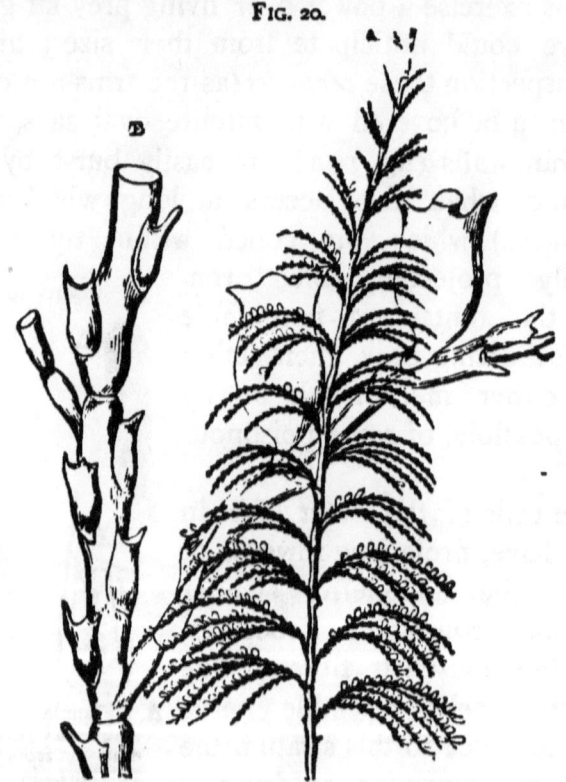

FIG. 20.

Sertularia abietina, one of the sea-firs; *a* natural size, *b* magnified. The figure shows the stem, or cœnosarc of the colony, with its polypites.

burst through the surface (fig. 18, *o*), become free, and in spring they shed their outer layer and proceed to develop into new Hydræ, which in course of time give rise to buds.

Sub-Class 1: Hydroida.—All the lower cœlenterate animals are built on the pattern of the hydra, they only differ in the details of their organisation and arrangement. In many of the marine forms, the hydra-like animals are grouped in clusters or colonies on a branched common axis or stalk (fig. 20). In each of these colonies every hydra-like organism is called a *polypite*, and the common stalk of the colony is called the *cœnosarc*.

These colonies we find on the sea-shore as branching tree-like growths on sea-weeds, often exceeding six inches in length, and some of them are known as 'sea-firs.' Each group begins its existence as a single polypite, rooted by that extremity of its body which is opposite to the mouth. From this root a stalk of cœnosarc grows upwards, and on this stalk new polypites form, each like a hydra in structure. New polypites arise as outgrowths from, and are structurally continuous with the common stem of the colony; and so the stomach of each is continuous with the tubular centre of the stalk. On this account there is a community of nutrition in the colony, a few actively-feeding polypites being able to make up for the laziness of others, which participate in the nourishment taken in by their more active neighbours.

Medusoids.—In these colonies some polypites are set apart for the production of eggs for the multiplication of individuals (fig. 21, C, D). Such polypites are much altered in form, and they frequently become detached from the stem and float about freely often as little jellyfishes about the size of a pea; they are called *medusoids*. With a fine muslin surface-net in any of our seas, many forms of these little creatures may be captured, especially in summer or autumn;

each appears somewhat umbrella-shaped, and the margin of its disk or swimming bell is adorned with

Fig. 21.

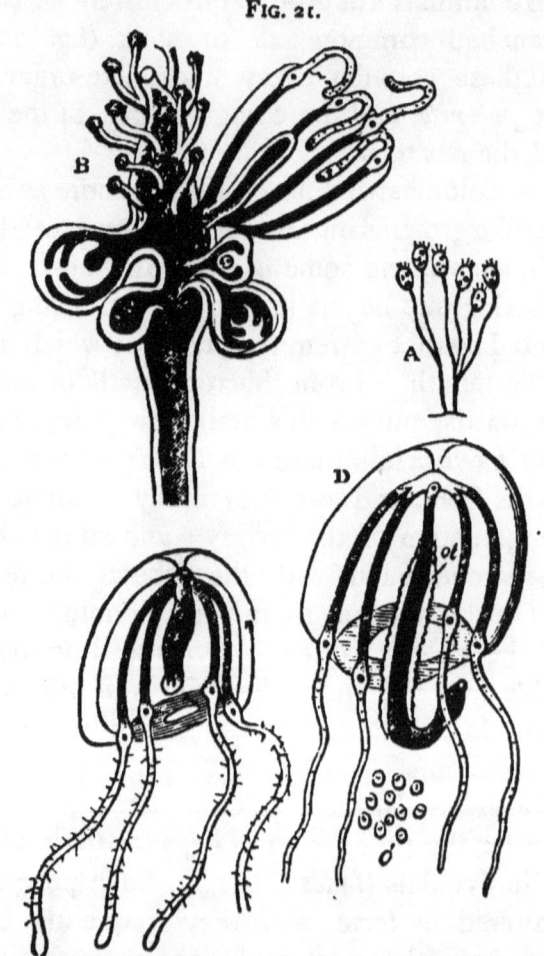

Different stages of Medusoids: A, rooted hydroid colony, natural size; B, polypite magnified, showing tentacles and swimming bells; C, D reproductive swimming bells, detached and free-swimming.

little, naked, coloured specks supposed to be eyes, and also with marginal tentacles. A central mouth exists on the under side of the swimming bell, opening

Growth of Hydroid Colonies. 37

into a stomach, from which four tubes radiate to the margin of the bell, where they are united by a circular

FIG. 22.

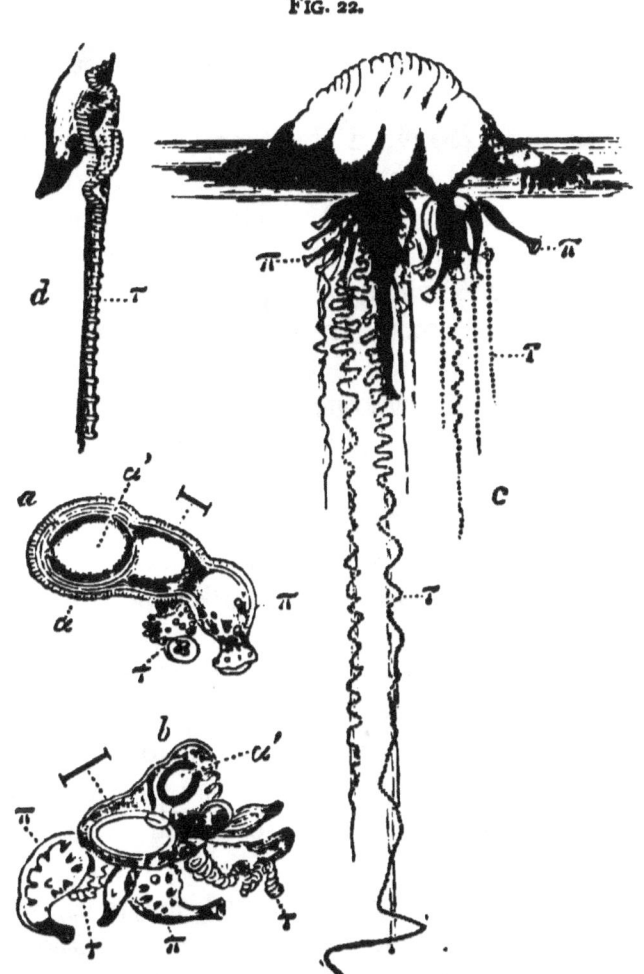

Physalia or Portuguese Man of War : *a, b, c*, three stages of growth ; *a'*, air-sac or float ; π polypites, τ tentacles.

canal, in the walls of which, or within the wall of the stomach, the eggs are formed.

Unlike as this jellyfish may appear to be to Hydra, it is in reality a polypite modified by a widening and thickening of the body wall at the base of the tentacles, and an elongation of the mouth into a central stalk. These free-swimming jellyfishes are thus not distinct animals, but only detached parts of hydroid colonies, and the eggs produced by them first give origin to small ciliated, infusorium-like bodies (p. 25), called planulæ (fig. 19, A) which after a short period of freedom settle on stones or shells at the sea-bottom, and develop into primary polypites and the common stem of a new colony, from which some buds becoming specialised and detached form in turn medusoids. There is thus an alternation of generations, the progeny of the egg resembling, not the immediate egg-producer, but the form which preceded this.

Divisions of Hydroida.—Of fixed Hydroids there are three orders: 1. simple forms, such as Hydra; 2. compound colonies whose stalks, polypites, and medusoids are naked (fig. 21); 3. compound colonies whose stalks and polypites are covered with a horny casing as in the true sea-firs (*Sertularia*, fig. 20).

Sub-Class 2: Siphonophora.—Floating on the sea there are frequently found colonies of hydroid polypites, not unlike those of the sea-firs in structure, but whose common stem instead of being rooted, swims by means of enlarged and altered polypites, whose stomachs are undeveloped, and whose bodies are dilated into swimming bells. From these, the cœnosarc extends, supporting both the nutritive and the reproductive polypites. Some possess in addition a sac filled with air which acts as a float and aids the

Jellyfishes. 39

swimming bell in locomotion. This is seen in the Portuguese Man of War (fig. 22), whose purple crested air sac and long tentacles are well known to sailors, and which, by their large thread-cells, inflict dangerous stings on those who incautiously touch them. These

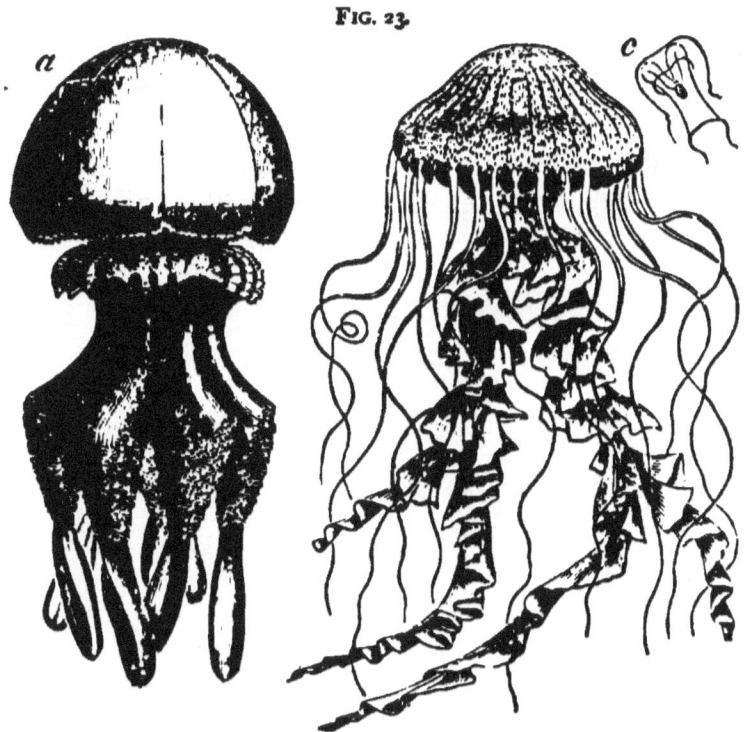

FIG. 23.

Disk-bearing Jelly-fishes; *a*, Rhizostoma; *b*, Chrysaora.

swimming and floating colonial Hydroids are called Siphon-bearers (*Siphonophora*).

Sub-Class 3: Discophora.—The large jellyfishes whose translucent bodies are so often thrown on the shore by the receding tides, are the representatives of a sub-class characterised by possessing single polypites depending from the centre of a large disk or umbrella varying from an inch to three feet in diameter. The mouth of the polypite is surrounded by lobate tentacles (fig. 24), and from the stomach there pass eight or more branching radial canals which are united peripherally by a circular canal. The eggs are produced in pouches of the stomach-cavity, and each of these on ripening emits a ciliated germ like an infusorium (fig. 24 *b*), which after a brief locomotory existence settles down on some solid body at the sea bottom (*c*), and develops a hydra-like animal with

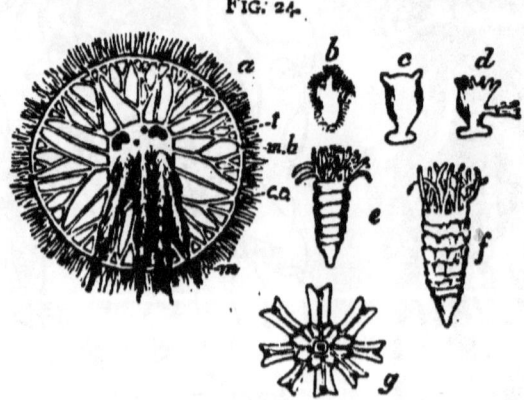

FIG. 24.

Medusa aurita in different stages of life ; *a* perfect adult form reduced $\frac{1}{13}$; *b, c, d* hydra-like stage; *e, f* strobila stages ; *g* one of the disks separated from *f*, and growing into adult form.

branching canals which, elongating, forms a little rooted colony (*d*). Each of these hydra-like forms becomes marked with transverse furrows (*e*) which, deepening, dip into the interior of the body dividing it into a vertical 'pile of saucers,' of which each discoidal segment becomes free as a new medusa. This is a good example of alternate generations.

Jellyfishes and Anemones. 41

In the common *Medusa aurita*, whose disk can easily be recognised by the four, ring-like, violet ovaries, there are marginal tentacles and also little pigment spots and clear vesicles (eyes and ears) symmetrically disposed around the disk, each covered by a little lobe of the umbrella margin. There is no trace of a marginal membrane or veil, such as exists around the mouth of the bell of hydroid medusæ.

Thread Cells and Nervous System.—The stinging power of these 'sea nettles' is due to their armature of thread cells.

When a hydroid is cut in pieces, each piece becomes a perfect animal if a portion of the margin is preserved, but if not, reproduction is very uncertain.

In these medusoids we meet for the first time with an area of sensitive tissue acting like a nervous system, and connected with the margin of the disk. If this be preserved motion continues to take place, whereas if the margin be cut away motion ceases.

Many medusæ are phosphorescent, emitting light from the whole surface, especially from the margin of the disk.

Ctenophora.—In one interesting little group, a fourth sub-class, called *Ctenophora*, there are eight radial rows of comb-like plates armed with cilia, which act as rowing organs. In these there is a certain amount of bilateral symmetry.

Summary.—The Hydræ and jellyfishes which constitute the class Hydrozoa possess a central stomach cavity into which a single aperture of entrance leads. They are also armed with thread-cells and possess a body wall of two layers.

CHAPTER VIII.

ACTINOZOA. SUB-CLASS I. ZOANTHARIA: SEA ANEMONES.

Structure of a Sea Anemone.—In many of the rock-pools around our shores there are to be found the exquisite forms which are the types of this class, and which, like animated flowers, may be seen expanding their sensitive petal-like tentacles in search of the materials that constitute their prey. On the retreat of the tide those that are left uncovered by the water contract, and appear as little, rounded, firm, gelatinous masses, attached to rocks and stones by means of a flat suctorial disk.

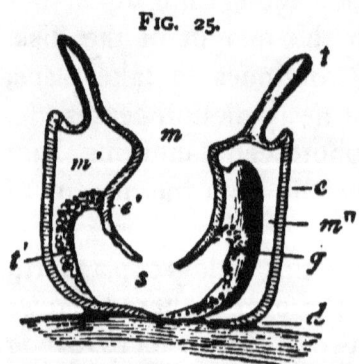

FIG. 25.

Vertical section of common Sea anemone, *Actinia mesembryanthemum*.
m mouth, *m'* primary mesentery *m''* secondary mesentery, *e* ectoderm, *e'* endoderm, *t* tentacle, *t'*, ovary, *d* disc of attachment, *s* body-cavity.

The body of one of these when expanded is somewhat cylindrical, having a free extremity which bears the mouth, and an attached end, which is usually capable of voluntary detachment. This extremity is sometimes called the foot. On making a transverse section the body appears like a double tube; the outer tube is the body wall, the inner bounds the stomach, and between them is the body cavity into which the stomach-sac opens below by a narrow aperture.

Sea Anemones. 43

The body-cavity extends upwards into the hollow tentacles, each of which is in fact a tubular prolongation continuous with this cavity. In life, when the body is expanded, the space between the stomach and the body wall contains sea-water which also inflates the tentacles, but on irritation the contraction of the outer wall drives out this fluid, which escapes in minute jets through the terminal pores at the extremities of the tentacles.

The body cavity is divided by vertical partitions which pass inwards to the outside of the stomach-wall, and thus divide the outer chamber into a series of smaller compartments which radially surround the stomach, below which they all communicate with each other. There are five or six such large partitions extending for the whole length of the body wall, which are called *primary mesenteries*, and between them are smaller partitions in equal numbers, called *secondary mesenteries*, between these, there are often still smaller *tertiary mesenteries*, twice the number of the primaries, and in some related forms other orders of intermediate partitions exist, still farther sub-dividing the body cavity, but each set shorter than its predecessors.

The outer surface of a sea anemone, and especially of the tentacles, is richly covered with thread cells, which, when burst, are sometimes thrown off as a continuous slough. This can be seen when an anemone is imprisoned in a bottle of sea-water, and in the same condition we notice that as the water becomes less able to support the life of the creature from its loss of oxygen and of material for food, that the body becomes enormously swollen by the inordinate amount of water which the anemone takes in.

Multiplication.—Sea anemones occasionally multiply by division, but, in general they increase by the development of eggs, in the thick cord-like edges of the mesenteries. These eggs are emitted by the mouth, and from them arise minute, ciliated embryos which become saccular.

Anemones can be multiplied also by artificial division, and if an anemone be cut horizontally the mouth end still continues to eat, and finally develops

FIG. 26.

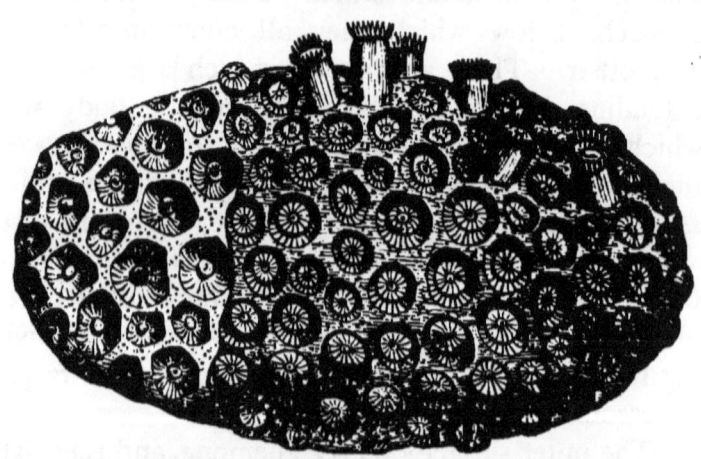

Caryophyllia fasciculata, a sclerodermic coral. The left side of the figure shows the coral denuded of soft parts; on the right the animal matter is shown, while at the upper part several of the polypes are seen projecting.

a foot, while the foot end may (but seldom does) continue to live and may ultimately develop tentacles. One experimenter produced by his sections an anemone with a tentacle-armed mouth at each end.

Corals and Coral Building.—Most sea anemones

Coral Builders. 45

are solitary ; a few only form colonies by continuous budding, and by the formation of a uniting cœnosarc. In sea anemones proper, there is no deposition of an indurating material, but in tropical seas a closely allied group of animals abstract lime from the seawater, and lay it down in one of two ways, either in the animal's tissues, or else in the centre of the cœnosarc, and *around* the body, *outside* the foot of each separate polyp. Hard masses thus formed are called *corals* ; and all the reef-building corals, the Madrepores and Oculinas, are examples of the former kind, or tissue-depositions. The deposit may be in the body wall, in the mesenteries of the polyps, or in the cœnosarc. Growth in these colonial forms takes place either by the formation of buds which remain continuous and may spring from various parts of the original stem, or else by fission, but in this case the new polyps remain connected together. Owing to these different modes of growth there is much variety of shape and structure among the hard parts of different corals. Large masses of coral, which are called reefs, are usually found in the seas of such climates as have a winter average temperature over 60° F. and where the water is clear, and not mixed with mud or fresh water. They abound chiefly between the depths of 1 and 50 fathoms, and vary in form according to the shape and condition of the sea-bottom.

A few of the coral-building animals are solitary, like the little *Caryophyllia* of European seas. Some of the commonest forms of corals brought to this country from the tropics are the mushroom-shaped lamellar *Fungiæ*, the richly perforated Madrepores, and the brain-corals, or *Mæandrinæ*.

Sub-Class 2. Alcyonaria.—The sea often casts on the shore large, yellowish, gristly masses, known by the fishermen as 'dead men's fingers,' but technically named *Alcyonium*, which are types of the second sub-class of Actinozoa. On placing this *Alcyonium* in sea-water the surface sends forth from each pore a little crown of tentacles. These are seen to be in circlets around the mouths of minute polyps, and they differ from the tentacles of sea-anemones in two respects; first, they are in multiples of four, usually being eight in number, and, secondly, they are pinnately fringed, that is, evenly toothed and lobed around the margin, each little tooth having a hole at its tip: otherwise the organisation is of the same type as that of a sea anemone. Minute calcareous spicules are abundantly scattered through the mass, and in some allied forms, these, together with hard horny matter, make up a continuous, coral-like, foot-secretion in the axis of the cœnosarc, as in the fan-corals or *Gorgonias*. In the precious red coral of the Mediterranean, this axis is of stony hardness; and in *Isis*, calcareous and horny joints alternate with each other in the central axis of the stem, thus combining firmness and flexibility. The red organ-pipe coral of the Indian Ocean, with its table-like partitions and its green polyps, belongs also to this group. The feather-shaped sea-pens, which are nearly related to the Gorgoniæ, are not rooted, but have the extremities of their stems buried in sand.

Recapitulation.—All the animals which make up the sub-kingdom Cœlenterata show a radiated arrange-

Echinodermata. 47.

ment of parts, the bodies being formed of a series of symmetrical segments around a central axis. In all of them, the body wall of each individual animal is made up of two membranes, an outer and an inner; all are aquatic, and, with about four exceptions, marine. They all have a central stomach, a mouth at one pole, surrounded by tentacles which are armed with *thread-cells*, these latter being almost universal in the sub-kingdom. When a nervous system exists it is as an obscure ring, and is related to the margin at the base of the tentacles.

The two great classes of Cœlenterates, Hydrozoa and Actinozoa may be contrasted thus : the former have.but one internal cavity; the latter have a central stomach cavity surrounded by a separate, though communicating body cavity, and the egg-producing organs open into this second space.

The two great sub-classes of Actinozoa are—

A, Those with simple tentacles in multiples of 5 or 6 : Sub-class 1, Zoantharia.

B. Those with pinnate tentacles in multiples of 4 : Sub-class 2, Alcyonaria.

CHAPTER IX.

SUB-KINGDOM 4. ECHINODERMATA : ENCRINITES
AND STAR-FISHES.

General Characters.—Sea-urchins, star-fishes, and sea-cucumbers make up a natural assemblage of animals, called *Echinodermata* on account of the spiny skins found in most species. They display a radiating symmetry, but either in the larval or in the adult condition there are traces of a bilateral disposition of parts. A body cavity is always present, containing within it the digestive organs, and the stomach cavity never communicates with this surrounding space in the perfect or adult animal, as it does in the Cœlenterates. The Echinoderms possess a nervous system of radiating

Fig. 27.

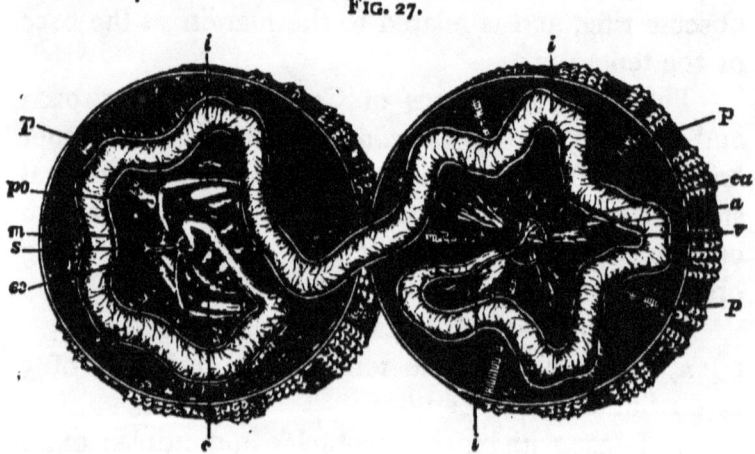

Section of the purple Sea Urchin (*Strongylocentrotus lividus*): *a*, anus; *œ*, œsophagus ; *i*, intestine ; *s*, one of the rods of the tooth apparatus ; *m*, muscles of the jaws , *p*, vessels of the sucking feet ; *po*, extremity of the water vessel ; *ca*, ocular plate ; *v*, ovary.

threads, united by a ring of nerve-matter around the mouth, and some of them exhibit pigment masses, which are supposed to be simple eyes containing the ends of nerve fibrils embedded in them. Calcareous matter is deposited in the skin, either in the form of spicules, or of plates which, by being jointed together, build up a shell or outer 'test' for the body.

When one of our common Echinoderms is put into a vessel of sea-water, locomotion can be seen to take

Feather Stars and Stone Lilies. 49

place by means of numerous little tubular processes which project through holes in the surface of the shell each of them ending in a little sucking disk. There are five pairs of rows of these feet in most species, and these, by attaching themselves and then contracting, draw the body of the animal along. Each of these *pedicelli*, or little feet, as they are called, is hollow, and contains sea water, and there are five long tubes in each Echinoderm, which pass meridionally, and by fine vessels convey the fluid into the pedicelli from a tubular ring which surrounds the mouth. To the tubular system which supplies the little feet, the name *Ambulacral* system is given. This arrangement of water-vessels connected with locomotion is peculiar to echinoderms. The sub-kingdom consists of four chief classes.

CLASS I. **Encrinites (Crinoidea)**.—These animals abounded in former times in the seas of our globe, but they are now for the most part extinct. The name is derived from the resemblance of many of the fossil forms to the flower of a lily, the infolded arms having a petal-like appearance. With a few exceptions, they are not, in their adult state, free and capable of locomotion, as are all other Echinoderms, but are fixed on a jointed calcareous stalk. Though when first hatched from the egg all Crinoids are free-swimming ciliated bodies, yet very soon they settle down, develop a stalk, and become rooted (fig. 28). There is a central mouth, surrounded by a circle of movable arms, which are often branched, and between these arms are little plates pierced by holes through which the ducts from the egg-producing organs open. In general

E

appearance these Crinoids look like star-fishes fixed on central jointed stalks, and they are furnished with feathery ambulacral feet on their upper surface, which as they cannot serve for locomotion seem to act as gills for breathing. The commonest of the living Crinoids

FIG. 28.   FIG. 29.

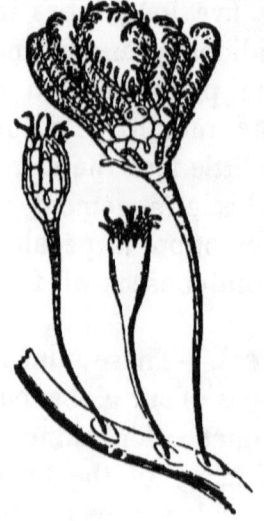
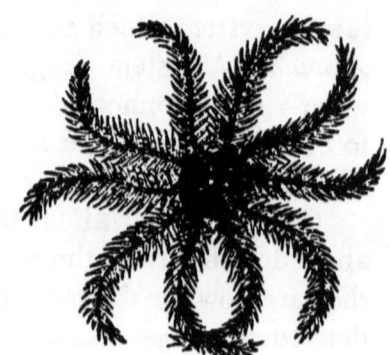

Embryo of the Feather Star, showing its stalked, encrinite-like stage.

Rosy Feather Star (*Antedon rosaceus*), adult or free condition.

becomes free in its adult stage, and has a singular history. Beginning its life as a free-swimming embryo, it soon becomes fixed, and appears as a stalked organism (fig. 28), but, after existing in this state for a short period it loses its attachment, becomes free, and forms the exquisitely tinted rosy feather star, with ten to forty arms, found in our seas.

CLASS II. **Starfishes (Stellerida)**, (fig. 3, p. 7).— The form of the animals of this class is expressed by

Starfishes. 51

the name. They all possess a central disc from which five to twenty arms radiate. The surface is generally roughened with stiff ridges and spiny points, and under this layer is a layer of calcareous plates; each arm has on its under surface a groove in which lie the ambulacral vessels, and the nerve-cord; and many starfishes have imperfect red eyes at the end of this ambulacral groove.

On our sea-shores there are two kinds of starfishes to be found, the first kind or Brittle-stars have a rounded, or five-sided flat disk at the centre, and slender, jointed, snake-like arms, which, as they do not contain processes of the viscera, the animal can break off when irritated. These brittle-stars chiefly are found on seaweeds. The other and commoner kinds of starfishes have thick, flattened triangular arms which are continuous with, and not jointed to, the disk. These have a mouth in the middle of the under surface of the body, and around it on the skin are curious little spines whose extremities are movable, and two- or three-bladed, like little pincers. To these little grasping organs, which assist in seizing the prey, the name

FIG. 30.

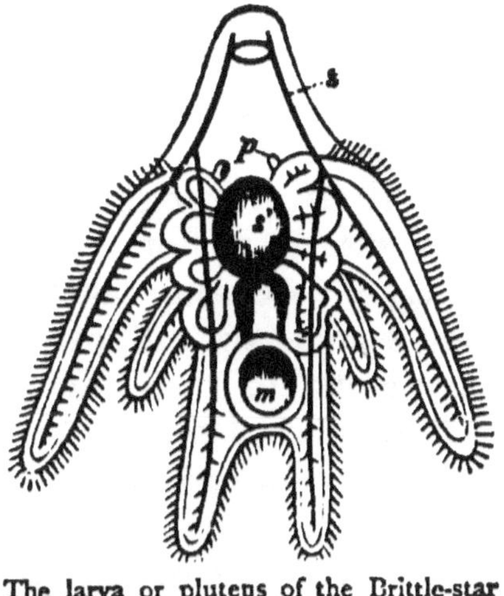

The larva or pluteus of the Brittle-star (*Ophiolepis*). *m*, mouth; *s*, stomach; *s*, calcareous skeleton.

pedicellariæ ('little feet') is given. From the central stomach, which communicates directly with the mouth, long blind pouches extend into the arms (usually two pouches into each arm) thus increasing the size of the digestive sac. There is an ambulacral ring around the mouth, and radial vessels extend from it into the arms to supply the little feet; and to convey sea water into the central ring there is a canal, usually filled with sand, which starts on the dorsal surface of the disk from a spot where there is a wart-like, finely perforated plate, which from its likeness to a piece of coral is called the *madreporiform plate*. Through it, as through a sieve, the sea-water filters into the sand-canal, and thence into the ring around the mouth.

Besides the ambulacral vessels, there exist in starfishes fine vessels on the surface of the digestive cavity, which unite to form a second vascular ring around the mouth; this second system is one of blood-vessels directly concerned in the nutrition of the body. The larvæ of starfishes, on leaving the egg, appear very dissimilar from the adults, looking like little easels, and are hence called *plutei* (fig. 30); those of the brittle-stars have a delicate calcareous skeleton, which is wanting in those of the common five-fingered starfishes, which in many respects seem to resemble the comb-bearing Hydrozoa. In their adult states these starfishes move mouth-downwards and are extremely voracious, attacking molluscs, dead fishes, and other kinds of animal matter in the sea.

CHAPTER X.

SEA URCHINS AND SEA CUCUMBERS.

CLASS III. **Sea Urchins (Echinoidea).**—The globular or heart-shaped sea-eggs, found along our sea coasts, are representatives of the next group of Echinoderms. In these the surface is covered with movably jointed spines, each of which shows on section a beautifully reticulated structure which varies in each species and the attached end of each spine is hollowed to fit on a tubercle (fig. 27, p. 48) on the hard shell beneath, with which it thus forms a ball-and-socket joint. On removing the spines there is found under them a shell composed of numerous flat angular plates, arranged in meridional rows. This shell has the mouth at one pole, which in the living animal is undermost and the excretory orifice at the opposite extremity; and from mouth to apex the shell is divided into ten meridional segments, five of which consist of plates pierced with holes for the ambulacral feet, and five of unperforated plates; these are placed alternately, and each segment, perforated or unperforated, consists of two rows of plates (fig. 31, *a*, *b*).

FIG. 31.

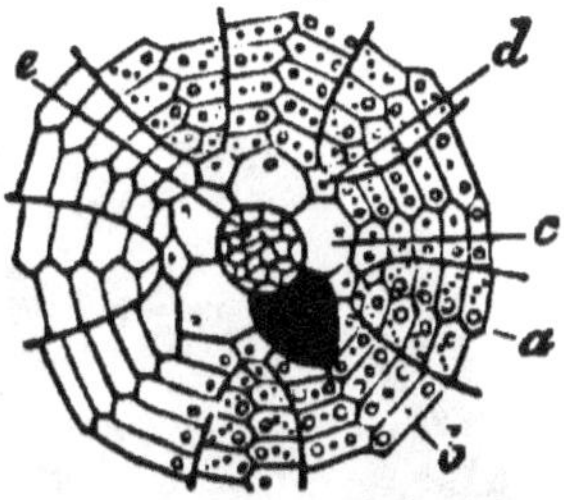

The apical end of the shell of *Echinus esculentus*. *e* anal opening, *c* ocular plates, *d* ovarian plates, *b* madreporiform plate.

The mouth is surrounded by a soft area of skin bearing modified spines, modified tube-feet and pedicellariæ, somewhat like those of starfishes; the opposite or aboral pole is surrounded by five plates, each placed at the end of one of the imperforate meridians, and each pierced by the end of the duct from one of the five large egg-secreting glands which lie within the shell between the ambulacra. Between these ovarian plates and at the end of the ambulacra are five smaller plates, each pierced by the end of the radial nerve threads, and bearing a little eye-speck; these are called 'ocular plates.' One of the former set of plates is always unsymmetrical, swollen, and finely pierced with holes, being in fact the combination of an ovarian plate with the madreporiform tubercle at the end of the sand canal as in starfishes.

Sea Urchins have ambulacral vessels just like those of starfishes, with a tubular ring around the mouth and five branches, one along the inner surface of each set of perforated plates, through the holes in which the tube feet project.

FIG. 32.

Tooth apparatus of the Sea Urchin, showing the arrangement of the muscles.

Most Sea Urchins have the mouth armed with a complex system of teeth, five of which are placed around the orifice with their points directed towards it, each being situated in the centre of a wedge-shaped jaw (fig. 33), which itself consists of two symmetrical halves. Twenty-five accessory pieces are appended to these parts, and the whole apparatus is moved by thirty muscles (fig. 32). This apparatus is fixed by

FIG. 33.

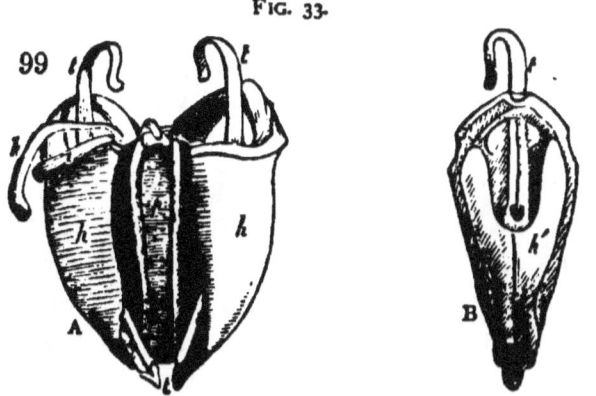

Jaws of the Sea Urchin. A, two jaws seen laterally; B, interior view of a single jaw; *h*, surface of jaw; *t*, teeth.

muscles and fibrous bands to calcareous loops which project inwards at the mouth end of the shell, and it can easily be dissected in the common sea urchin. The larvæ of sea urchins are pluteus-like, containing a calcareous skeleton.

Two types of sea urchins are found in American seas. One like the common *Strongylocentrotus dröbachiensis* is globular or slightly flattened, with ambulacral areas extending from pole to pole, and with the mouth and anus at opposite poles; the other type, represented by the heart-urchin (*Schizaster fragilis*) found in deep water, has the anus not opposite to but approximated to the mouth, and the ambulacral rows not extending from pole to pole, but in petal-like areas on one surface of the shell alone.

CLASS IV. **Sea Cucumbers (Holothuroidea).**—Singular, elongated or cylindroidal animals, closely allied to sea urchins, but without either spines or hard test, make up this class. They are found among the tangles or in moderately deep water along our shores. The body-wall is muscular, and contains in its surface-layer calcareous spicules, resembling anchors, wheels, &c. The mouth is surrounded by plumose tentacles, and, on the surface of the body are rows of tube-feet, more irregularly disposed than in sea urchins. The intestine is often of great length, and ends in a small aboral sac or cloaca, into which also open (in most species) two very remarkable tree-like organs which lie in the body cavity, and which are adjuncts to the water-vascular system for purposes of breathing. In organisation they resemble sea urchins, and often reach very large sizes. In tropical seas some of these Holothurians are inhabited by little parasitic fishes, and even in temperate regions small shelled mollusks are found in or on their bodies as parasites. One species, the Trepang, is imported in large quantities from NE. Australia into China, where it is regarded as a luxury of diet.

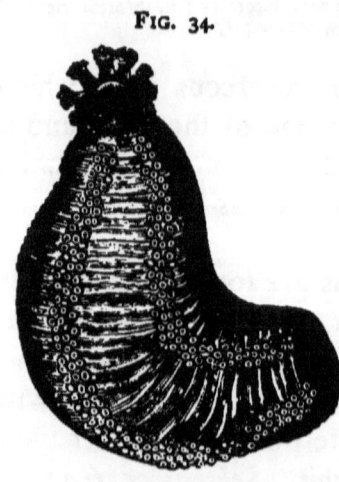

FIG. 34.

Cucumaria doliolum. One of the Sea Cucumbers.

Recapitulation.—Echinoderms are characterised by the presence of highly differentiated tissues, a distinct nervous system, a digestive canal which in the adult is separate from the body cavity (though in the embryo, the body cavity arises as an outgrowth from the primary intestine), a radiating symmetry tending to become bilateral, and a water-vascular system whose little tubular feet or offsets act as locomotory feet.

The chief sub-types may be tabulated thus—

A. Body stalked at some period of life, ambulacral feet not locomotory = Class I. Crinoidea (mostly fossil).
B. Never stalked, star-like, with ambulacra as organs of locomotion. = Class II. Stellerida.
    a. Arms jointed to the disk, not containing viscera = Order I. Ophiuroidea (Brittle Stars).
    b. Arms not jointed, containing viscera = Order II. Asteroidea (common Starfishes).
C. Never stalked, globular, disk-like or heart-shaped, with a continuous test = Class III. Echinoidea.
D. Never stalked, elongated, with a soft integument containing spicules = Class IV. Holothuroidea.

The Echinodermata are all marine, and are never united together into colonies.

CHAPTER XI.

SUB-KINGDOM V. : VERMES.

WORMS, though often mean and uninteresting in external appearance, are yet in many respects among the most curious forms in the animal kingdom. They are elongated, soft-bodied creatures, which have their organs arranged in a bilaterally symmetrical manner. In many of them the body consists of successive segments, arranged in a chain, each intermediate segment being like its preceding and succeeding neighbours. There is a nervous system in most forms, consisting of two or more nerve knots above the pharynx and a cord prolonged backwards along the under side of the body, beneath the digestive canal. A water-vascular system exists in some form or other in all worms, but it has never any connexion with the function of locomotion. It usually consists of a system of tubes, one in each of the successive segments of the body, opening by one extremity on the surface and by its other end communicating with the body cavity. These sets of tubes are commonly known among the higher worms by the name of *segmental organs*. Blood-vessels often exist, and sometimes contain coloured blood, but there is no heart, and the colour does not depend on the existence of minute floating coloured corpuscles in a colourless fluid, as is the case with the blood of vertebrates. The common earth-worm and leech may be taken as well-marked examples of the sub-kingdom.

Many worms are parasitic and live within the bodies of higher animals; among these the circulatory, water-vascular, and digestive systems become rudimental, the nervous system remains undeveloped, the body cavity often vanishes, and the reproductive organs alone are fully represented. This sub-kingdom includes the following classes :

Planarians. 59

CLASS I. **Turbellaria.**—The simplest worms with which we are acquainted are found on the seashore, under or adherent to stones, or else in fresh water pools, as small ciliated, flattened soft bodies, which glide with a slug-like motion over wet surfaces, or swim by the vibrations of their cilia. These *Turbellarians* (so called from the commotion produced by their cilia in the water around them) have a mouth placed generally *beneath*, not *at* the anterior extremity, and the part of the digestive canal immediately within the mouth is protrusible as a kind of proboscis. This contains, in some of the larger forms, a spine or dart, which is used as a weapon of offence, and being supplied with poison from a little poison-gland at its base, acts as a formidable weapon against the minute creatures upon which these animals feed. The digestive canal

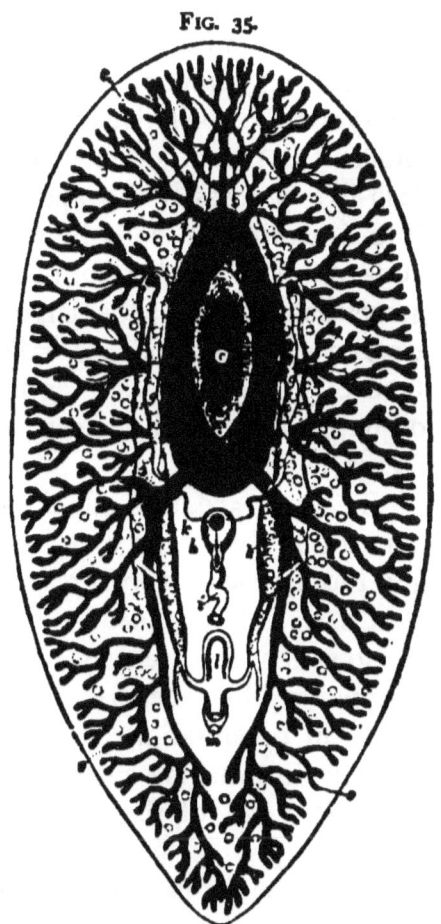

FIG. 35.

Polycelis lævigatus, a common Turbellarian.

in the smaller flatter forms is often tree-like, branched (fig. 35). In others it is a simple pouch with no excretory orifice, but in the larger forms it is elongated. The water-vessels appear as two lateral tubes, and the egg-producing organs are usually complex. The young Turbellarians on leaving the egg are usually unlike the parent, often helmet-shaped, with a whip-lash-like process at the apex, but this larva develops into a worm-like body by moulting or shedding its surface. The smaller forms are generally flattened, somewhat elliptical; the largest are worm-like, sometimes very long, and are called Nemertean worms. One of these, Borlasia, found not very uncommonly on our own shores, has been taken measuring twelve feet in length.

The 2nd, 3rd, and 4th classes of worms are mostly parasitic in their habit and are called suctorial, round, and thorn-headed worms respectively.

CLASS II. **Cotylidea.**—The sucker-bearing worms are so called because they are armed with rounded or irregular cup-like suckers. These worms are generally simple in organisation; and their body cavities and digestive organs are either abortive or rudimentary. The two types of these worms are *Tapeworms* and *Flukes*.

The tapeworms are so called from their great length and flatness. They exist principally in the digestive canals of higher animals, especially in fishes. The human race is not exempt from occasionally harbouring at least three species of these parasites. One of these, the common tapeworm, or *Tænia solium*, is common in Britain and Western Europe, and may be taken as the type of the order. On examination, it presents to us a very small roundish head armed with twenty-six little hooks arranged in two rows, and four round suckers, followed by a long slender neck, at first undivided but soon exhibiting traces of transverse segmentation, which, as we trace the worm from the head, become more and more clearly marked until we reach a part consisting of distinct joints, each of which joints contains a complete egg-producing apparatus.

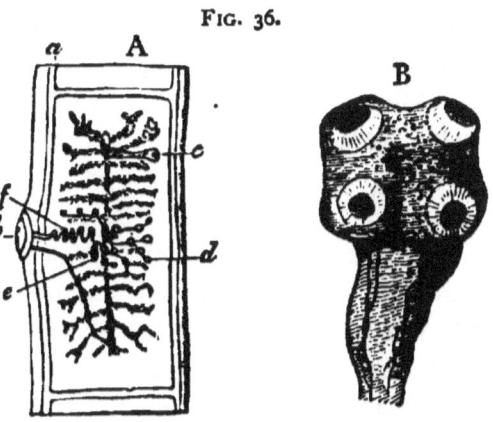

FIG. 36.

A, Proglottis, or perfect joint of Tapeworm (*Tænia solium*); *a*, water-vascular tube; *c*, egg-producing organ. B, Head of *Tænia mediocanellata.*

When we remember that these worms may attain the length of 25 feet, and that there are at least twenty perfect joints in a foot, and that each joint can produce many scores if not hundreds of ova, we can form some idea of the amazing fecundity of these parasites. The growth of the individual takes place from the head, so that the oldest segments are those which are most remote from it and the newest are the fine joints close thereto.

The life history of the tapeworm is curious. The eggs are protected by a very firm horny capsule and thus they can maintain their vitality for long periods of time, and can resist maceration and even short exposures to high temperature. On entering the digestive organs of some animal with its food or drink, the embryo is set free and travels through the tissues of its new host as a little oval body armed in front with weak hook-like or boring spines. On reaching a suitable site it anchors, and the body dilates into a sac full of water. In this cystic condition the animal may remain stationary for a length of time, and by budding the number of cysts is capable of a rapid increase. When the flesh of an animal containing such cysts is eaten by another, the liberated saccular worm has its outer wall dissolved away, and its inner portion lengthens and in a short time becomes a true tapeworm. In most cases it requires two animals as hosts for the proper perfection of the worm. Thus the human tapeworm has its cystic stage in the flesh of the pig, the condition of pork called 'measly' being due to these little cysts in the muscles of the pig. Similarly, the tapeworm of the dog develops from cysts found in the hare; that of the cat from cystic worms in the mouse, that of the fox from cysts in the field-mouse, &c.

In Ireland, the commonest human tapeworm has four suckers but no hooks on its head (fig. 36 B), and is known as *Tænia mediocanellata*; its larva inhabits the ox.

In Russia and Switzerland, the human tapeworm is quite a distinct species, with very flat body, no hooks, and two long grooves on its head in place of suckers; its larvæ live in the waters of certain lakes, and it has been supposed that it is through these waters being used for drinking purposes that they gain entrance into the human body.

Flukes. 63

Trematodes or Flukes.—The second order of sucker-bearing parasitic worms consists of the 'flukes,'

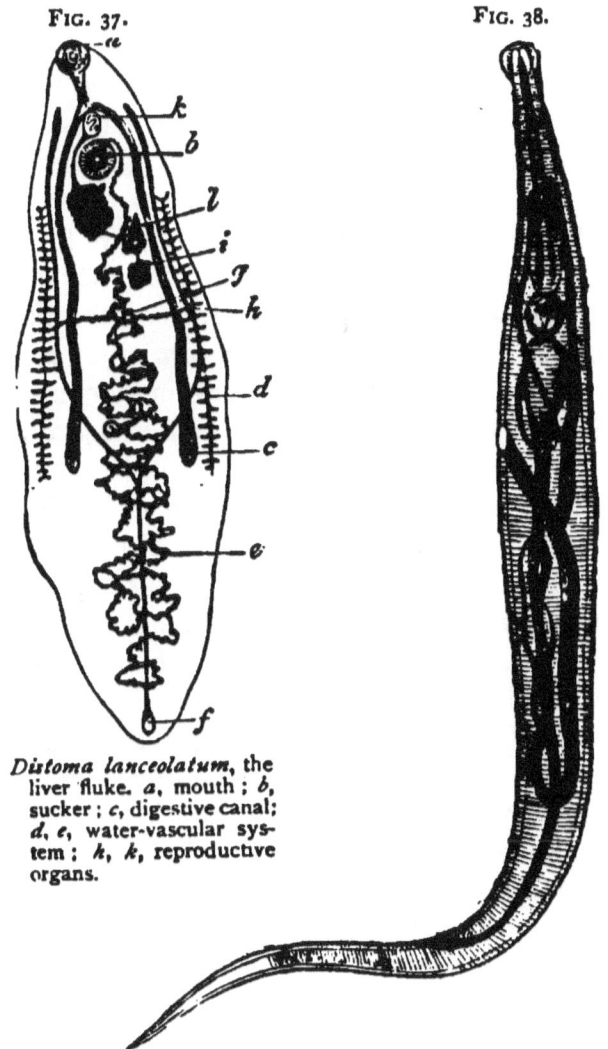

Fig. 37.

Distoma lanceolatum, the liver fluke. *a*, mouth ; *b*, sucker ; *c*, digestive canal; *d*, *e*, water-vascular system ; *h*, *k*, reproductive organs.

Fig. 38.

Oxyuris vermicularis, the common threadworm of children.

met with in the liver of the sheep, and of allied forms (fig. 37); these are not united in chains as in the tapeworms, but each consists of a single segment bearing one or two suckers (*a, b*). In many respects they resemble the Turbellarian worms, but are not ciliated and often present formidable armatures of recurved hooks. They are like tapeworms in the development and complexity of their ovaries, and many of them show in their history alternations of generations as curious as those of their relatives the tapeworms; for example, the larvæ of some liver flukes live for a time free, in water; and develop within their bodies little cylindrical worms, which are set free on the bursting of the wall of the parent, and in turn enjoy an independent life. Within these worms again there may form another brood of internal buds, which also grow, burst their envelope, and become for a time free, but soon attach themselves to some soft aquatic animal in whose body they become encysted, to develop finally into the mature forms when their first host is eaten by some larger animal. Thus the flukes found in water-fowl have their larvæ in water molluscs, &c. To these flat sucker-bearing parasites the name *Trematoda* is given.

CLASS III. **Nematelmia.**—These, the commonest forms of parasitic worms, are cylindrical, tapering to each end, and possessing a body cavity (fig. 38.) They are never divided into successive joints, although their surface may be finely ringed, and there is always a digestive canal with an outlet, as well as a mouth.

The round worm, often found in the small intestines of children, is a good example of the order. It is about seven or eight inches long, ringed on its surface, with the mouth at its anterior end, surrounded by three little lobes; from this, a tube, the *œsophagus*, passes

Thread-worms.

to the stomach, which is a small suctorial muscular cavity, communicating by a straight intestine with an outlet which is not terminal. Beside the common round *Ascaris lumbricoides*, the human digestive canal is the occasional dwelling-place of two other worms, one of which, *Oxyuris vermicularis*, is a small thread-like worm (fig. 38), the other *Trichocephalus dispar*, much more common, has a very slender neck and a thicker body. A species closely allied to the last named is the *Trichina spiralis*, a minute worm found in the flesh of pigs, calves, &c., which when introduced into the human body, often multiplies rapidly in the voluntary muscles of the system, causing dangerous and even fatal symptoms.

These worms are as prolific as their fellow parasites, and the early stages of many live for a time in water, from whence they enter into the bodies of their hosts, and in those whose life-history we know, the free and parasitic conditions appear very dissimilar. It has been supposed and with reason that most of the free Nematelmians found in stagnant pools are early stages of parasitic species.

Gordiaceæ. — The horsehair-like thread-worm which is found in rainwater pools is an example of a second order of round worms. This remarkable animal begins life as a little larva living in mud or in water pools; it is armed with boring spines, whereby it pierces into the body of a beetle or other aquatic or terrestrial insect; here it becomes encysted, and, having grown in this condition to a considerable length, often ten times as long as its host, it becomes free and aquatic and produces its eggs. So rapidly do some of these multiply, as, for example, the common *Mermis albicans*, that they have given rise to the belief that they have fallen as 'worm-rains.' These worms are called Gordiaceæ and are distinguished from the other round-worms by the rudimentary condition of their digestive canal. They are also remarkable for their extreme tenacity of life, as they can be dried into hard brittle threads and yet appear lively and active on being moistened.

CLASS IV. **Acanthocephala.**—The 'thorn-headed' worms are rounded, or cylindrical, each with a protrusible proboscis armed with many recurved hooks. They are remarkable for the total absence of the mouth and intestine in their adult condition. The commonest species are found in the intestines of swine, &c., with their heads buried in the substance of the wall of the digestive tube.

CHAPTER XII.

NON-PARASITIC WORMS.

CLASS V. **Wheel-Animals, Rotatoria.**—On tracing the development of the more complex free worms we find that the larva, after emerging from the egg, appears as a free-moving creature, with circlets of vibrating cilia around its extremities, these ciliary lobes being in some forms large and rounded (fig. 47, A).

In rain pools and ditches, small creatures are frequently met with which resemble the larvæ of worms,

Spoon-worms and Leeches. 67

but which remain permanently in this ciliated condition. In these, the ciliary lobes are prominent and rounded, acting as locomotory organs, and from the rapid vibration of the cilia which clothe them they seem like rotating wheels, hence these little creatures are called *Rotatoria*. They are microscopic in size varying from $\frac{1}{500}$th to $\frac{1}{9}$th of an inch in length, but from the exquisite transparency of their bodies the details of their organisation can be seen by the aid of the microscope. The male rotifers are few and small and have no digestive canal; the females have a complex nutritive system, and many species are provided with an organ of mastication like an anvil acted on by two hammers. These animals can bear much ill usage, and are capable of reviving again on being moistened, after having been almost completely dried up.

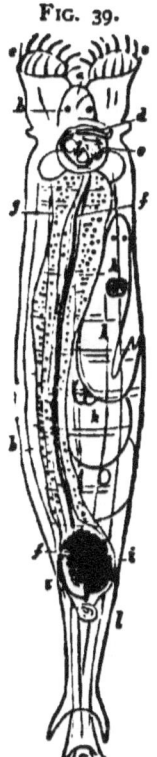

FIG. 39.

Rotifer vulgaris.

On irritation the trochal disks (fig. 39, *c*) can be retracted into the cavity of the body, from which they are gradually protruded again on the cessation of the stimulus. Some rotifers are rooted; others possess a forceps posteriorly, whereby they can hold on to foreign bodies; others again are contained in a vase-like sheath, into which they can retract themselves, on being irritated.

CLASS VI. **Spoon-worms** or **Squirt-worms, Gephyrea.**—These are interesting marine worms whose

68 Invertebrata.

elongated or sac-like bodies contain a long tortuous intestine, ciliated inside and outside. They rarely exhibit a division into segments, nor have they locomotory processes of any kind, and they never have any calcareous

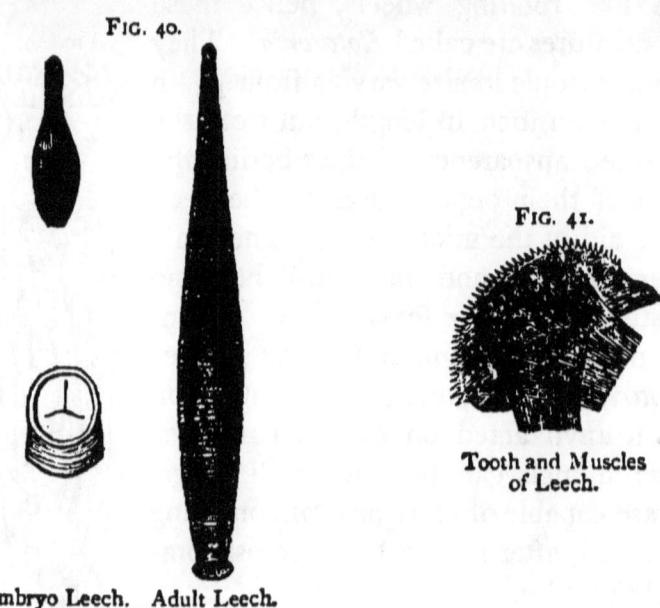

Fig. 40.

Fig. 41.

Tooth and Muscles of Leech.

Embryo Leech.   Adult Leech.
   Mouth of Leech.

or siliceous spicules in their skin, although sometimes there are a few bristles scattered on the surface. The mouth is at the anterior end, and it is provided with a protrusible proboscis, sometimes of great length.

CLASS VII. **Leeches.**—The next group of worms is exemplified by the common horse-leech or by the medicinal leech. They are soft-bodied annulated worms which live parasitically on the outside of vertebrated animals, from which they draw their nourishment. Their bodies are composed of segments, which are indistinctly or not at all marked from each other

Leeches.

on the surface, but can easily be distinguished within, as the organs of the body are arranged in successive groups. Leeches have at their front end a sucker, and some have a second suctorial disk at the hinder extremity, and several species are even provided with lateral suckers. The mouth is generally situated in the front sucker, and it is armed with three horny jaws or plates (fig. 41) with serrated edges. These plates act as teeth, enabling the leech to make incisions in the skin of its host through which to suck the blood. The digestive canal is straight and consists of a central tube with a row of blind pouches along each side (fig. 42, B) which can become distended, hence the body can take in a great quantity of blood.

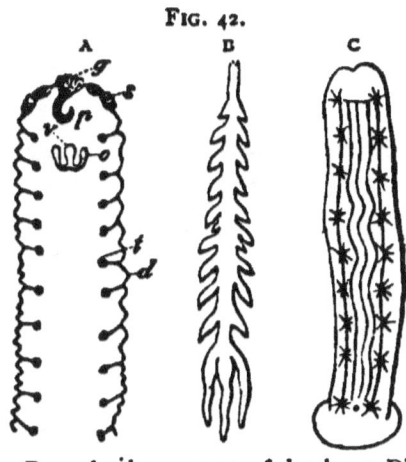

FIG. 42.

A Reproductive organs of leech. B Digestive canal of leech. C Nervous system of Malacobdella.

There is a nerve-ganglion in each segment of the body, the first (fig. 42, C) of these is comparatively large and made up of several smaller ganglia grouped together; the successive ganglia are united into a chain by fine filaments and they lie on the ventral or under side of the digestive organs.

Leeches possess proper blood-vessels in which their own nutritive fluid circulates. Their water-vascular system takes the form of a series of *segmental organs* or tubes opening laterally, one on each segment. The egg-producing organs are very complex.

Locomotion takes place by the suckers: the hinder one being fixed, the animal elongates itself and, fixing its front sucker, sets free the hinder one, then shortening its body it proceeds in a similar manner. Leeches can also swim, and when so progressing the body becomes flattened by the contraction of vertical muscular fibres which run from the dorsal to the ventral surface, and then by undulating movements it advances like a wavy ribbon.

Medicinal leeches are principally imported from Hungary and Sardinia.

CHAPTER XIII.

NON-PARASITIC WORMS.

CLASS VIII. **Bristle-footed Worms (Chætopoda).**—We can scarcely turn over a stone on the sea shore

FIG. 43.

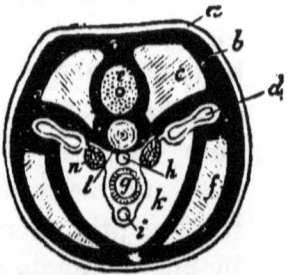

Transverse section of a Worm, of Amphioxus, and of a Vertebrate contrasted. *a*, outer or skin layer; *b*, dermal connective layer; *c*, muscle plates; *d*, segmental organ; *h*, arterial, and *i*, venous blood-vessel; *g*, intestine; *l*, notochord.

without finding under it some species of the group of

Worms. 71

bristle-bearing worms, a class of which the lug-bait or the hairy-bait of fishermen may be taken as representatives. These worms have bodies made up of a succession of similar joints, and their locomotion, either creeping or swimming, is accomplished by means of little stumpy bristle-bearing eminences, with which their bodies are provided. Each joint of the body exhibits two pairs of these processes, two of which are on the upper or dorsal surface, and two are on the ventral or under surface, one on each side of each surface; these are known as dorsal and ventral oars. The mouth is on the second segment, and is often armed with sharp teeth. The intestine is usually straight and very often has lateral pouches appended to it like those in the leeches. There is a vascular system consisting of long tubes, dorsal, ventral and lateral, and the blood contained in these is often red, green, or white. The gills are usually arranged along the dorsal surface of the body springing close to the root of the dorsal oar, and in these the blood is purified by being exposed to the oxygen held in solution in the sea-water.

FIG. 44.

Arenicola piscatorum.
Lug-bait worm.

There are also segmental tubes opening one on each side of each segment, and sometimes the eggs, which are produced within the body, escape through these canals. The chain of nervous ganglia is also well-developed. Some worms secrete a glutinous material from their surface, which cements together sand-grains and other foreign bodies into a tube wherein the animal lives. Other worms secrete from their surface calcareous matter which makes up a tube as a dwelling-house, in which the animal is permanently contained. Such forms have the gills developed only on the foremost segments of the body, and have the dorsal and ventral oars of all the other joints rudimentary; but they possess tentacle-like, branching processes about the head. Of these the common Serpula, whose white calcareous snake-like concretions are so common on the stones and shells on the sea shore, and the Spirorbis, whose minute white whorled shells dot the surface of the shore-tangles, are examples.

A few worms are phosphorescent; many others, ike the sea-mouse, are clad with iridescent scales and bristles.

The common earthworm has much smaller and fewer bristles, which are in the form of recurved hooks, not elevated on stumpy processes of the surface. The body is closely ringed and tapers from the middle forwards to an acute point in front. Each ring bears its armature of hooks, which can easily be felt by drawing the body of a worm between the fingers from tail to head, although they are scarcely to be detected when we feel the body in the reverse direction. In beginning to burrow, the worm lengthens its body and pushes its sharply pointed head into the mass of soil which it is about to perforate, then having insinuated the few foremost rings of its body into the mould, the whole animal contracts in length, thus swelling the front of the body in thickness and forcibly dilating the opening made by its fore part, the worm being prevented by its hooks from slipping out of the opening; then it again lengthens its body in front, its hooks giving it a fixed point from which to act, and by a succession of such elongations and thickenings it can 'worm' its way through even a hard gravel walk.

The mouth of an earthworm is placed on the second segment, near the apex of the body, and from it the digestive canal extends as a straight tube through the body. This tube is very wide and is always found full of earth, as these animals devour large quantities of the soil for the sake of the organic particles contained in it, the remaining part being passed out, and heaped by the worms at the outlet of their burrows, as 'worm casts.' For the better division of the material swallowed, the digestive canal is provided with a muscular gizzard about fifteen rings behind its mouth.

The eggs in earthworms are produced in the body cavity beginning at a point about seven rings rom the mouth, and they usually fill the body for tbout seven segments. distending it and producing a thick white band or ring which we often notice in the body of worms during early autumn. Worms are propagated exclusively by eggs, the common belief that, when cut in pieces, each part is capable of independent life not being strictly true. If we divide an earthworm about its middle, the hinder segment dies after a short time; the fore segment will probably live and its wound heal. Similarly, if we cut the anterior four or five segments away the small fore fragment will soon die, while the large hind mass will recover.

CHAPTER XIV.

MOSS POLYPS AND TUNICARIES.

CLASS IX. **Moss Polyps (Bryozoa).**—The broad leathery fronds of the tangles along our shores are often encrusted with beautiful lace-like patches of regular and minute patterns. If we put a fresh, living piece of this into a vessel of sea-water, we find that each of the cell-like spots is the home of an elegant little organism which may be seen to protrude through the mouth of its cell a delicate little crown of tentacles. Each colony of these animals consists of a common stock, bearing numerous little cells, and each cell contains its delicately organised inhabitant. Some of the little creatures become modified into bird's-beak-like graspers with two horny jaws, for the protection of the colony (fig. 45, B); others become altered into globular pouches for the reception of the eggs after their extrusion. Each of the dwellers in these little cells consists of a saccular body containing a looped digestive canal, in the bend of which a nerve ganglion is placed, and it is provided with a crown of hollow tentacles guarding the mouth. Most of these moss-polyps are marine and have

Tunicata.

a circular protrusible basis, supporting the tentacles; some few are inhabitants of fresh water, and these have the tentacles on a horse-shoe-shaped basis; these also have a little valve to shut the mouth, which is present in only two of the marine forms. Each of the little constituent animals of one of these colonies has its own digestive canal, its own nervous system,

FIG. 45.

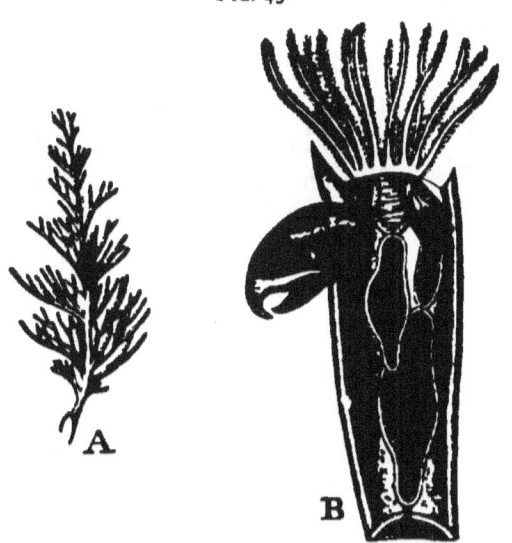

A. Natural size of *Acamarchis avicularia*, one of the Moss Polyps; B. Magnified view of one Polype, showing its 'bird's head.'

and its own egg-producing apparatus, and these are essentially like the corresponding organs in worms.

CLASS X. **Tunicata.**—These also are marine soft-bodied animals, met with in abundance attached to shells and stones among the tangles on our sea shores. They are often called sea-squirts, on account of their ejecting little jets of water from their terminal openings when irritated. They appear as irregular or oval

Invertebrata.

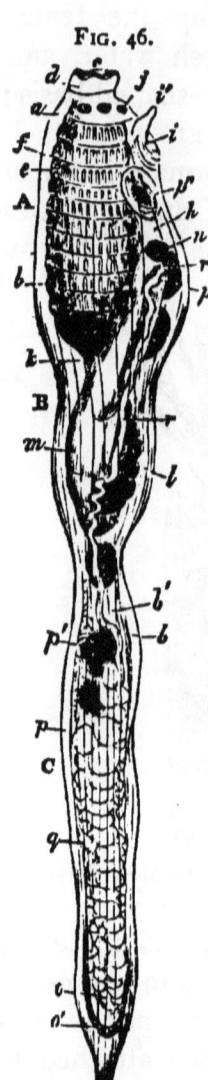

Fig. 46.

Amouroucium, a tunicated worm.
A, Pharynx, or respiratory portion of the body; B, stomach; C, egg-producing organ.

masses of semi-transparent, often gristly material, and of a whitish, pink, or brownish colour. They vary in length from 1 to 6 inches.

In each tunicary there are two apertures on the surface; one of these (c, fig. 46) opens into a large chamber whose wall (e) is a vascular membrane, and at the bottom of which is the mouth (k). The digestive canal ends at the bottom of a second chamber (p''), of which the lower or hinder opening is the outlet. Between these two chambers, which thus lie over the digestive canal, there is a partition wall which is pierced by many small holes whereby the water which enters into one can pass into the other, thus bathing the surface of the lining membrane, and enabling the blood contained in the spaces in its texture to become aerated. The first chamber (fig. 46) is called the branchial chamber, the second is called the atrial.

Between the opening of the branchial chamber and the atrial orifice there is a nerve ganglion sending a fine loop of branches around the mouth. The heart lies at the lowest part of the body and from it the vessels pass into the wall of the branchial chamber. In the action of this heart a curious appearance is observed; the blood is driven by this vessel first from one end to the other, for a second the action stops, then it is resumed in the opposite direction, again another cessation, and another reversal, &c.

The 'tunic,' or outer wall (f) contains a starch-like compound which is interesting as it is almost the only instance of the occurrence of a starch-like compound in the Animal Kingdom.

Young tunicates as they emerge from the egg appear as small, tailed larvæ, with bodies consisting of two cavities. The axis of the tail consists of a cartilaginous or gristly rod; in one cavity of the body the nerve ganglion is developed, in the other space the viscera are formed. Thus they foreshadow the structure of vertebrate animals.

Tunicaries are sometimes solitary, but many species are found united into social assemblages, and this union may go as far as the perfect union of the blood-vessel systems, a single vascular apparatus supplying the whole colony. In one group, the Salpæ, there is an alternation of generations, solitary and colonial forms succeeding each other in a cycle.

Many of the tunicates are phosphorescent, Pyrosoma, a compound form inhabiting the Atlantic ocean, being the most vividly luminous animal met with in the seas.

Summary.—The chief types of worms may be tabulated thus:
1. Unjointed, ciliated, non-parasitic forms without ciliated head-lobes = Class Turbellaria.

78   *Invertebrata.*

2. Unjointed or obscurely segmented minute forms, with ciliated head-lobes = Class Rotatoria.
3. Parasitic, flat-bodied forms, with no body cavity, and provided with suckers = Class Cotylidea.
4. Parasitic forms with no suckers nor digestive canal, and with a hook-bearing proboscis = Class Acanthocephala.
5. Cylindrical, unjointed, non-ciliated forms, with digestive canal and body cavity, mostly parasitic = Class Nematelmia.
6. Segmented forms with a proboscis, and convoluted intestine, non-parasitic = Class Gephyrea.
7. Segmented, bristle-clad worms with no suckers, moderate intestine, non-parasitic = Class Chætopoda.
8. Segmented, unbristled, sucker-armed, external parasites = Class Hirudinea.
9. Sessile, one-jointed, colony-building worms living in cells and with a crown of protrusible tentacles = Class Bryozoa.
10. Sessile or free, one-jointed worms, with one nerve ganglion but no protrusible crown of tentacles = Class Tunicata.

CHAPTER XV.

SUB-KINGDOM VI. MOLLUSCA, SOFT-BODIED ANIMALS.

THIS division includes all such forms as oysters, whelks, snails, and cuttlefishes. Most of these are aquatic and in none is there an inner skeleton (except some small gristly organs in cuttlefishes) nor are there

Molluscs. 79

any limbs, properly so called, in the whole group
The outer tunic of the body is generally thick and
extended to form a leathery envelope or mantle, the
outer surface of which secretes a shell of carbonate of
lime for the protection of the animal.

The earliest condition of existence of a mollusc,
after it has left the egg-stage, is as a small ciliated,
worm-like body having at its head an expanded lobe,
richly clothed with cilia and resembling the trochal

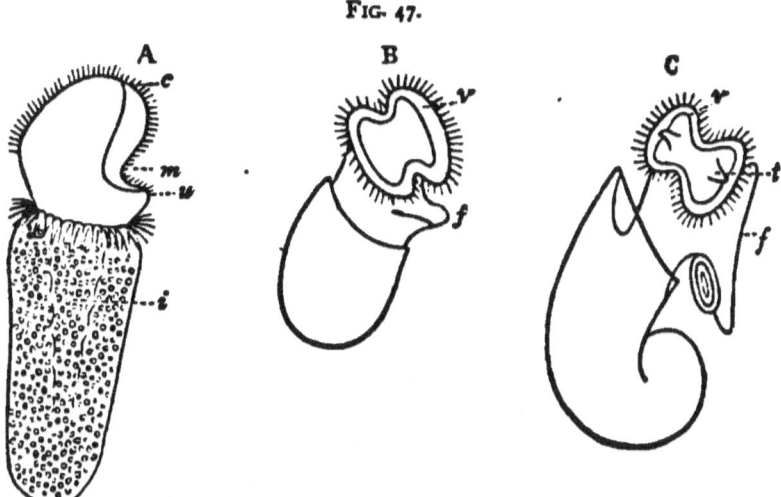

FIG. 47.

Larval forms of Worms and Molluscs. A, Larva of a Gephyrean Worm ;
B, C, Larvae of Molluscs, showing the ciliated velum v, and the rudimental foot, f.

discs of a rotifer, or the tentacle-bearing basis of the
moss-polyps (fig. 47, B). This process is lost in the adult
in general, but is interesting as one of the many evidences of the relationship between worms and molluscs.

The shells secreted by molluscs consist of one,
two, or several valves, or pieces, and are very various

in shape, and often brightly coloured. All molluscs have a digestive canal, and sometimes a complex arrangement of teeth. They have likewise a nervous system consisting of a ring around the fore-end of the digestive canal, on which are formed ganglia over and under the tube; besides this there are often other nerve masses and organs of sense. There is a heart which propels the blood, but there are few or no blood-vessels, the circulation being chiefly carried on in the interspaces of the tissues. There is rarely much of the body-cavity to be found free, with the exception of a small space around the heart, which is called the pericardium, and from this two short tubes pass out representing the segmental organs of worms. Four classes are included in this sub-kingdom.

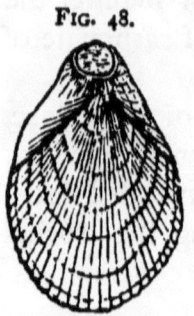

FIG. 48.

Lamp-shell or Terebratula, one of the Brachiopods, dorsal surface.

CLASS I. **Brachiopoda.**—Of this class comparatively few representatives are now living, and these in few places, usually at considerable depths in the sea; but at an earlier period of the world's history they were very abundant. They possess shells of two valves, one of which is large, placed ventrally or downwards, and having a beak pierced with a hole, through which a foot-stalk projects whereby the animal is anchored. The other valve is smaller and placed dorsally; it bears on its inner surface a delicate shelly loop for the attachment of the peculiar arms from which the name of the class is derived. The valves are joined, either by horny matter as in the duck-bill shells (*Lingula*) of Australia, or by tooth-like hinges, as in the lamp-shells (*Terebratula*), and there are several muscles for opening and others for closing the valves. The mantle in Brachiopoda is full of blood-spaces, which are the only breathing organs in these animals, and there is said to be a heart lying on the stomach for driving on the blood. Some anatomists dispute the presence of a heart, and claim that the blood is impelled through the body by ciliary action alone.

The larvæ of Brachiopoda are freely locomotive and possess eyes and ear-sacs, but the eyes disappear in the fixed adult in which the ciliated head lobe of the embryo becomes converted into the basis of the arms. These arms are long and hollow, usually spiral and clothed with tentacles, and their to-and-fro motions cause currents which bring the food within the reach of the mouth of the stationary animals.

CLASS II. **Lamellibranchiata.**—More familiar to us are the representatives of the second great group of molluscs, oysters, mussels, cockles, &c. These are easily recognised by their bivalve shells, and by the two-lobed mantle under whose folds are the gills or breathing organs arranged in layers or lamellæ.

The freshwater mussel, or the large Mya or clam, easily found along our coasts buried in the sand, out of which the tips of their long siphonal tubes project, are good examples. The shell of one of these exhibits to us a beak or point on each valve, and is marked by numerous lines parallel to its margin ; the inner surface also differs in texture from the outer, being whiter and often exhibiting a mother-of-pearl lustre. The cause of the difference in appearance is seen on making a microscopic section through a shell, as the outer surface is composed of long, nearly vertical, prisms, while the inner surface consists of fine layers whose edges overlap each other. These edges

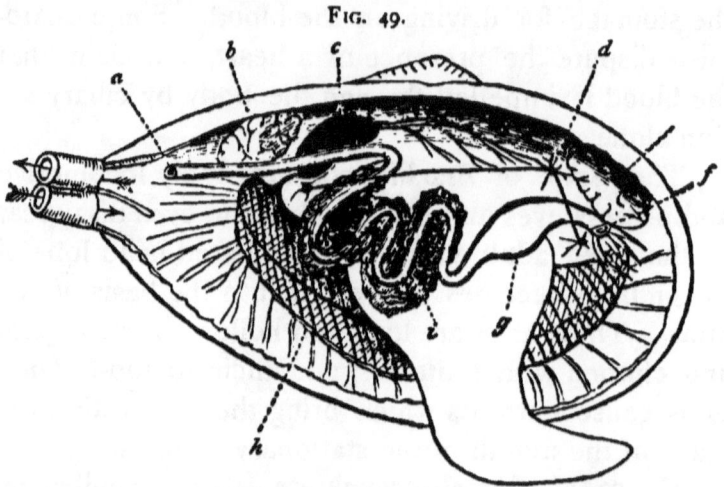

FIG. 49.

Diagram of the anatomy of a Lamellibranch, or Bivalve Mollusc. *g*, stomach; *i* intestine surrounded by the liver, the two tubes on the left marked by arrows are the canals of the siphon. *a*, the anus; *b*, hinder adductor muscle; *c*, heart; *d*, nerve ganglia; *e*, fore adductor muscle *f*, mouth; *h*, gills.

are often finely waved, and so decompose the rays of light which fall on them, thus producing the iridescent appearance seen in so many shells. The nacreous or mother-of-pearl layers are secreted by the surface of the mantle, while the prismatic material is formed by the margin of that structure. Thus the shell is constantly increasing in size by the formation of new prismatic matter, the lines of growth being the concentric curves before noticed. The edge of the mantle

Structure of Bivalve Molluscs. 83

is sometimes fringed, and the irregularities secrete corresponding processes on the shell in the forms of ridges, spines, &c. On the inside of the shell a line of demarcation shows where the nacre-secreting surface ends, and the prism-secreting portion begins, this is called the pallial line (fig. 50).

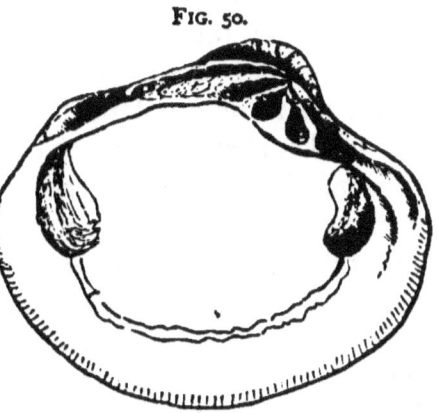

Fig. 50.

Shell of Galathea, showing the hinge, mantle line and the two adductor scars.

Hinge.—The two valves of the shell in Lamellibranchs are usually similar to each other; they are disposed laterally, one on the right and one on the left, and are united by a hinge of interlocking teeth at the dorsal margin. A highly elastic ligament unites the valves outside to the hinge, and is so arranged that it keeps the valves slightly open. On the inside of a bivalve shell there are to be seen one or two oblong scars in each valve to which are attached muscles running from valve to valve for the purpose of closing the shell, and hence called adductor muscles.

Soft Parts of Bivalves.—The lobes of the mantle are usually more or less united along the under border, and are often prolonged backwards into a long tube or siphon which projects at the hinder end of the body; when this tube exists, the pallial line is indented posteriorly into a sinuosity called the pallial sinus.

Many bivalves are fixed in the adult state; in the oyster, scallop, &c., the animal lies on one side, the under shell adhering to the surface on which it rests. The common mussel is fixed by means of an anchorage of strong fibres (called *byssus*) secreted by a gland on its foot. Under each lobe of the mantle lie the lamellar gills, between which is a fleshy protrusion, the foot or organ of locomotion. At the front is the mouth (fig. 49, *f*) from which the digestive tube is continued backward, to open above the posterior adductor muscle as seen in the sketch. The last portion of this digestive tube passes right through the cavity of the heart. The siphon, when it exists, is a double tube, consisting of an upper and a lower passage; through the latter the food and water for breathing purposes enter into the mantle cavity and bathe the gills; through the upper tube the excreted matter and the water returning from the gills are ejected. There is a nerve ganglion above and below the digestive canal at the base of the little lobes around the mouth ('labial tentacles,' seen in fig. 49 as lancet-like processes), and another exists in the foot below the digestive tube; a fourth is placed posteriorly beneath the hinder adductor muscle. These animals have no recognisable head, but some of them have eyes on the siphon, as in the razor-shell (Solen); others have eyes along the edge of the mantle lobes, as in the common scallop. The larvæ of all bivalves have eyes, but these are lost in the course of development, and when such organs appear in the adult they are of secondary formation.

Gasteropod Molluscs.

Bivalves are wonderfully prolific; the freshwater mussel has been estimated to lay between two and three millions of eggs in a season, and the oyster, it is computed, will produce over half a million of eggs in a year.

Classification.—Bivalves are subdivided according to the number of the adductors, according to the equality or inequality of the two adductors when both are present and (when there are two equal adductors) according to the presence or absence of a pallial sinus (page 82). The oyster is an example of the group which has one adductor. The mussel, of the group with two unequal adductors. The freshwater mussel and the cockle are examples of the group with two equal adductors and no pallial sinus, and the gapers, stone borers, and razor-shells, belong to the section with equal adductors and a pallial sinus.

CHAPTER XVI.

HEAD-BEARING MOLLUSCS.

CLASS III. **Cephalophora.**—The snail, whelk and limpet are examples of a class of molluscs, each of which has a distinct head furnished with sensory organs, such as eyes, ear-sacs and feelers. These possess a mouth armed with teeth, arranged on a ribbon placed at the bottom of the mouth cavity; this band can be drawn backwards and forwards by a set of muscles, and thus can act like a chain saw. This band can be easily found in the common limpet or whelk, where it exceeds an inch in length.

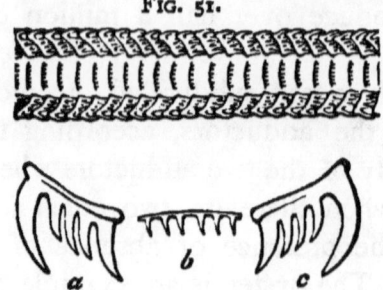

Tooth ribbon or radula of the Whelk or Buccinum; *a, c*, lateral teeth of one row; *b*, medial teeth.

In all but the little elephant's tooth shell, the mantle lobes do not entirely include the body, and the shell consists only of one valve. It varies in shape, sometimes being conical as in the limpet, but usually it is spirally coiled, the curvature being due to the mode of growth, as one side of the animal grows rapidly, the other slowly, or not at all; hence the body becomes coiled towards the aborted side, and the gills and other organs are generally developed only on one side. In most coiled shells, curvature is towards the left side, throwing the mouth round to the right side; in a few rare cases, or as an anomaly of growth, the coil may be reversed, winding to the right, and with the mouth at the left side. The bodies of these molluscs usually project, but they can be retracted into their shells. Progression takes place with a gliding motion, produced by the undulatory movement of the under side of the foot, as may be seen by placing a snail on the outside of a window pane, and watching it from within. The foot sometimes bears at its hinder part a little shelly lid which, when the animal is retracted into the shell, acts as a door to shut up the cavity;

Sense Organs of Molluscs. 87

this lid (or *operculum*) can be seen in the whelk and it is in shape similar to the outline of a section across the opening of the last whorl of the shell.

The mouths of some shells are channeled at their front end (the end farthest from the coiled part), and

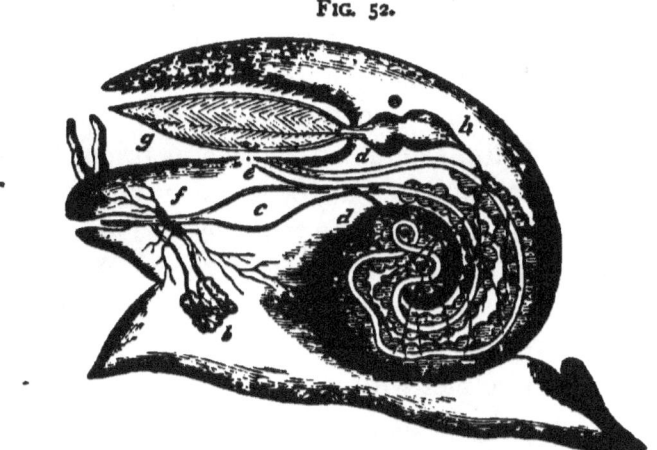

FIG. 52.

Diagram of the Anatomy of a Whelk, the shell being removed. *c*, stomach; *e*, end of the intestine; *g*, gills; *d*, auricle; *h*, ventricle of the heart; *f*, nerve-ganglia of the mouth; *b*, salivary gland.

sometimes at their posterior end; these channels are for siphon-like tubes, and as a general rule such molluscs as possess these siphons are carnivorous, while those with unchanneled or entire edges are herbivorous.

Some univalves, like the common snail and slug, live on dry land; in such forms gills would be useless, and hence they are absent, and a part of the mantle cavity is set apart for air-breathing, and the lining of this region is full of dilated blood-vessels. The mouth of this air-chamber is small, and can be seen opening and closing periodically in the common black slug on the left side of the body, under the edge of the little saddle-like rudimental shell, which in this mollusc is enclosed in the mantle.

The heads of univalve molluscs bear several organs of sense, tentacles, eyes and ear sacs, the tentacles are long soft feelers, the 'horns' of the snail, which can be retracted by being involuted, or turned out-side in by muscles. In the common snail the eyes are placed on the extremities of the upper or longest pair of horns, and can be seen as bright black spots. In other molluscs the eyes are either stalked or placed at the bases of the tentacles. The organs of hearing are small sacs placed near the foot, filled with fluid and containing small concretions. Most univalve molluscs lay their eggs inside little cases often to be met with under stones on the seashore. The little ciliated larva has a shell even at its earliest stage, and in some molluscs this shell is lost in development; in others it is retained and can be seen at the tip of the adult shell as the 'nucleus.'

Classification.—The head-bearing molluscs are very numerous, and are divided into several subclasses. The first of these includes the little elephant's-tooth shells, or Dentalium. This animal has no heart, and is completely enclosed in its mantle, which in the embryo forms at first a minute two-valved shell. Eventually, however, this shell becomes tubular, open at both ends. The second sub-class consists of small molluscs found swimming in the ocean, by means of two large wing-like processes on the upper part of their foot, and hence are named

Sense Organs of Molluscs.

Pteropoda. The third sub-class includes all the remaining forms, a few of which are free, swimming with the foot flattened into a screw-propeller. Most of them crawl on the under surface of their body, and hence are called *Gasteropoda.* Among these, a large number are branchiate, or gill-breathing; these make up one order; the others are pulmonate or air-breathing, and make up a second order. The branchiate forms have the gills either in front of the heart or else behind the heart, as in the great group of shell-less naked-gilled molluscs like the Doris or Æolis, so common on the shore. Some of the former sub-order have shells of eight valves, like the common Chiton; others have the gills all round the body, under the mantle, and equal on both sides, as in the limpets, or they may be unsymmetrical as in the ear-shells, cones, shoulder-of-mutton shells, etc.

Snails.—The air-breathing order are the land shells or snails; they have their breathing chamber placed behind the heart, and the larva has in general a very rudimental ciliary lobe. A curious difference has been noted between the gill-bearing and lung-bearing molluscs, namely, that the intestinal tube is bent towards the hæmal side of the body, that is, towards the heart, in the former, while it is turned towards the nerve-ganglion in the latter.

CHAPTER XVII.

CUTTLEFISHES.

CLASS IV. **Cephalopoda.**—The highest class of molluscs is that which consists of Nautili, Cuttlefishes and Squids. These are all highly organised marine animals with a central mouth, around which there are processes of the foot, disposed in the form of a circlet of arms or tentacles; each of these arms is provided with one or more rows of large suckers, and thus they form a powerful grasping organ, which they use in taking the prey whereupon they feed.

Shells.—Very few of these are enveloped in shells, and most of them progress, when creeping, with the head down, and with the large mantle cavity at the hinder side. There are three kinds of shells found clothing, or contained in, some animals of this class. These are 1st. The chambered shell, such as that of the pearly nautilus (fig. 54, p. 92), a coiled spiral divided by numerous partitions into successive chambers (*b*), each of which, however, communicates with the neighbouring chambers by means of a tube or siphuncle (*c*). 2. The enclosed shell, a horny or calcareous plate or oval mass, embedded in the integument, or lying in a closed cavity along the front wall of the animal's body; such a shell is found in the cuttlefish and squid. 3. In one species there is a singular shell secreted by two of the arms which lie beside the mouth, and which are flattened organs, and the shell so secreted is a slightly spiral

Cuttlefishes. 91

FIG. 53.

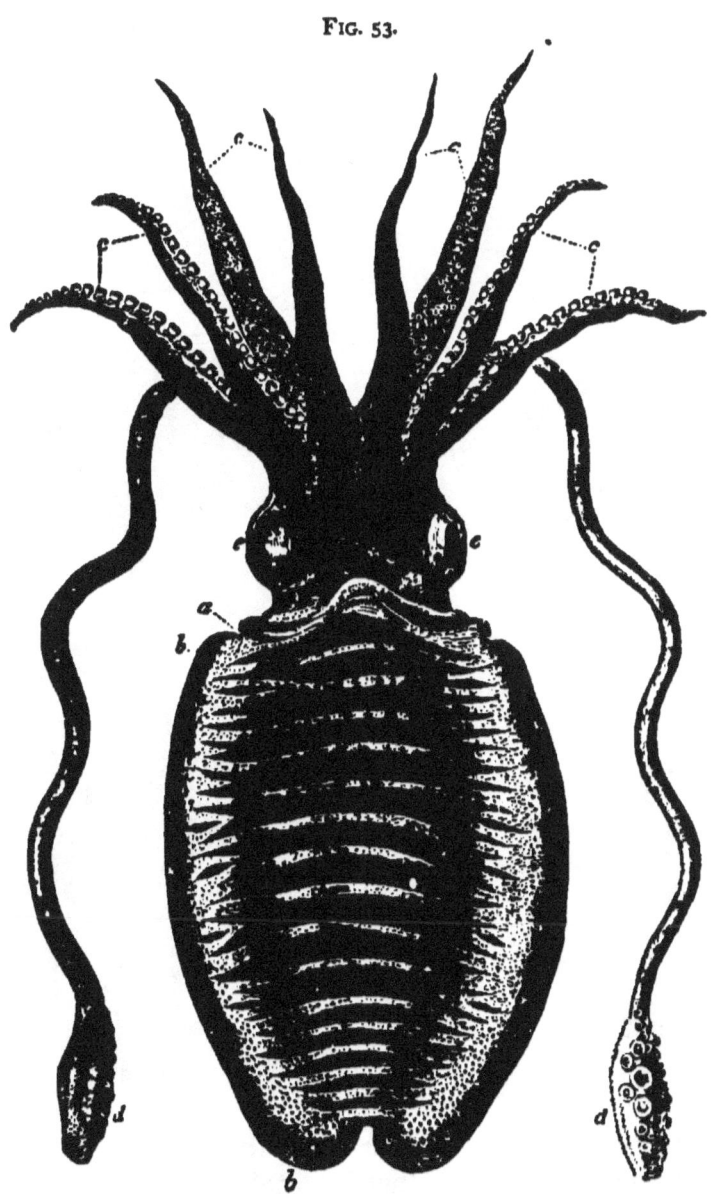

Cuttlefish or Sepia. *c*, Arms bearing the suckers; *d*, long tentacle-like arms; *a*, mantle; *b*, lateral fins; *e*, eyes.

rapidly expanding shell of a delicate paper-like texture to which the name 'paper nautilus' or Argonaut has

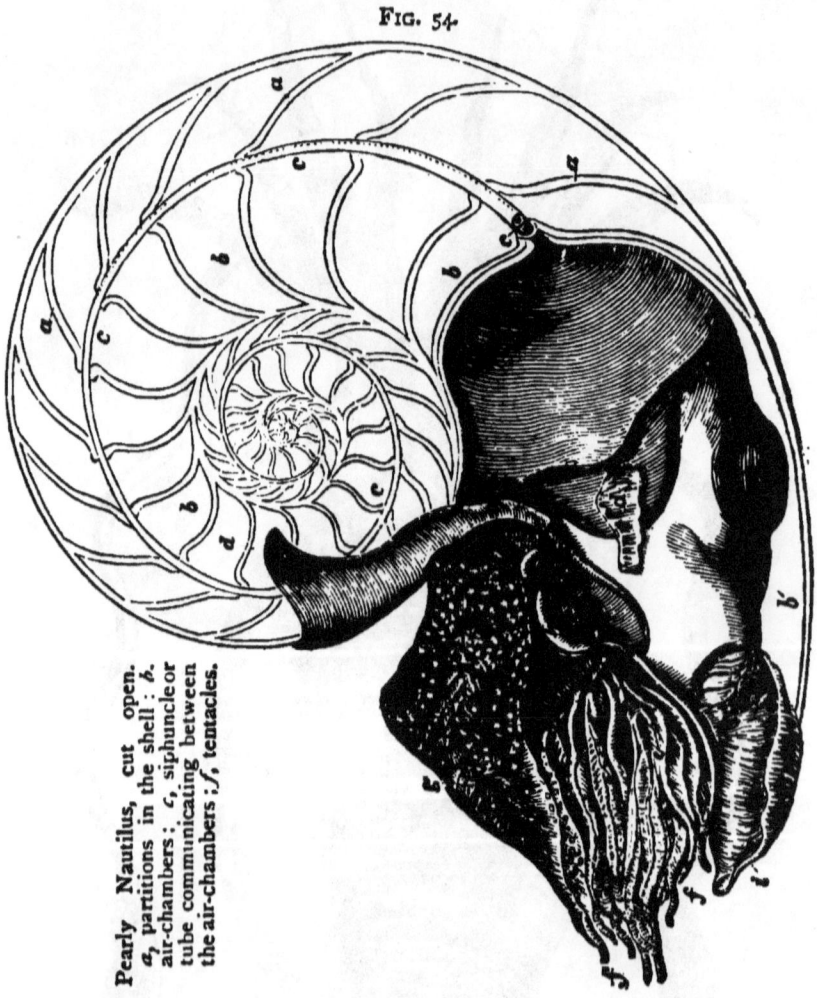

Fig. 54.

Pearly Nautilus, cut open. *a*, partitions in the shell; *b*, air-chambers; *c*, siphuncle or tube communicating between the air-chambers; *f*, tentacles.

been given. Other species, like the Octopus or seaspider, have no shell either internal or external.

Anatomy.—On account of the fore-shortening of

the body the mouth is brought into the middle of the foot in the adult, and hence the name 'head-footed' (*Cephalopoda*) given to this class. The lobes into which the foot is divided are usually eight or ten in number and are long tapering muscular processes which in the common species in our own seas vary from a few inches to two feet in length, but in one rare form they attain very much greater size. During the year 1873, a specimen was captured on the Newfoundland coast, with arms forty-two feet long.

The mouth is furnished with a strong beak, like that of a parrot, with two formidable horny jaws. By reason of the numerous suckers on the arms (a common octopus possessing about 60 on each arm), which seize hold of their prey with a cupping-glass-like tenacity, these cuttlefishes are among the most terrible of marine monsters, and those of large size would probably prove to be more than a match even for man himself.

Each of the sucking disks is singularly perfect in its structure. There is a muscular adhesive disk of a circular shape, around whose edge is a hard crown of horny consistence, and in the centre there is a muscular retractile piston, whose contraction produces a vacuum, and thus causes a close adhesion of the sucker.

There is a large mantle cavity with a strong muscular wall. When the animal is swimming it moves with its arms directed backwards and the upper or pointed end of the body forwards; in this position the opening of the mantle cavity or funnel is directed backwards, and the propulsive force which drives the body forwards is the sudden and often repeated contraction of the wall of this cavity, which by driving a column of water in the opposite direction with great force, propels the creature by rhythmical jerks, and at a rapid rate.

On slitting open the mantle two large gills are seen, one on each side, above and between which is the heart-ventricle. The blood enters the gills by large veins which form dilatations at the base of these breathing organs, then after being aerated, it is collected in two cavities called *systemic auricles*, from whence it passes into the muscular ventricle which drives it through the arteries into the lacunæ (or tissue interspaces of the body).

Along the hinder edge of the long digestive canal there is a slender tube, whose opening is also at or near the mouth of the funnel, and whose upper end expands into a large spongy-walled sac lying close beside the liver. This sac secretes a brown or black inky material which is poured out in enormous quantities when the animal is pursued, and which by rendering the water opaque covers the flight of the cuttlefish.

At the mouth of the mantle-cavity but not actually connected with it there is a funnel, which when the margin of the mantle contracts forms a narrow tubular outlet for the fluid of the cavity.

Cuttlefishes possess a brain, made up of large confluent ganglia around the pharynx, and over this there is a cartilaginous cover, interesting as being one of the first signs of an internal skeleton, like that of vertebrates in the animal kingdom. There is also a large and complex eye, more like that of a vertebrate animal than is the eye of any other group of invertebrates.

Cephalopods were abundant in former ages, but there are now about 230 species living; of these the Nautili possess a chambered shell, four gills, and many tentacles, while all others have only two gills, and eight or ten sucker-bearing arms.

Recapitulation.—Having thus very briefly reviewed the sub-kingdom Mollusca, we may, by way of recapitulation, place in a tabular form the distinctive characters of the group and its divisions. They are all soft-bodied, never distinctly divided into segments nor provided with jointed limbs; enveloped more or less in a dermal mantle, which often secretes a shell, and their larval stage is usually ciliated, worm-like.

The divisions are:

A. Having no distinct head, bivalve shells with the valves dorsal and ventral; no separate gills = Class I. Brachiopoda.
B. Having no distinct head, bivalve shells with the valves right and left, gills lamellar = Class II. Lamellibranchiata or Acephala.
C. Having a distinct head, univalve shells (at some period of existence) = Class III. Cephalophora.

   a. Entirely enclosed in a mantle, secreting a tubular shell = Sub-class I. Scaphopoda (Dentalium).

   b. Not entirely enclosed in a mantle, swimming by finlike processes on the upper side of the foot = Sub-class II. Pteropoda.

c. Creeping by the foot or swimming, but not by finlike processes = Sub-class III. Gasteropoda.

d. Having the foot around the head, and modified either into tentacles or sucker-bearing arms = Class IV. Cephalopoda.

CHAPTER XVIII.

SUB-KINGDOM VII. ARTHROPODA (JOINTED ANIMALS).

General Characters.—This sub-kingdom includes those animals whose bodies are furnished with an external hard protective layer, and which bear jointed limbs appended to each segment of the body (fig. 55). The armour-plating of the body is known by the name *exoskeleton*, to distinguish it from the bones, which form the axis of support for vertebrate animals, to which the name *endoskeleton* is given. The exo-skeleton consists of *chitin*, a horny substance, which is capable of resisting all reagents except the most powerful corrosives. This layer is usually coloured, laminated, and to the microscope shows very little structure except the numerous fine canals which pierce it from within, to which the name *pore-canals* is given.

The body of an arthropod consists of a chain of segments, all built on a common pattern, and each

FIG. 55.

Sandhopper, or Talitrus.

Jointed Animals.

one strengthened by the possession of a ring of exoskeleton consisting of two parts, a dorsal, and a ventral half arch. The limbs are articulated on each side, between the half arches, each segment possessing one pair. These generally remain distinct, even when the segments, as often happens, fuse together, so that the number of constituent segments can be very often detected from the limbs, even when the body rings are united into a continuous shield.

The bodies of arthropods are bilaterally symmetrical. They are also remarkable for the absence of cilia at all periods of life.

Each limb consists of several joints, each having an external chitinous exoskeleton, containing the muscles which move it. In the simplest arthropods, the limb consists of a basal segment bearing two appendages, an outer and an inner. In the higher forms the limbs are divided into five, seven, or more joints. These limbs are used for various purposes, becoming modified into feelers, water-bailers, jaws, swimmers, pincers, or walking feet.

All arthropods have a circulatory system and most of them possess a heart which is a dorsal tube, divided by valves into successive chambers, but there are rarely fine blood vessels. There is a distinct respiratory system, and a complex digestive canal, except in parasitic forms, and they have all a symmetrical nervous system, consisting of two ganglia, one above, the other below the throat, followed by a chain of ganglia in the ventral portion of the body. They are divided into four great classes, 1. *Crustacea*, including all those that breathe by gills, as crabs, lobsters, &c.;

H

2. *Arachnoidea*, spiders, mites, and scorpions; 3. *Myriopoda*, centipedes, &c., 4. *Insecta*.

Many arthropods are parasitic, and these are at first not unlike allied non-parasitic species, but shortly after hatching they retrogress, such parts as are not necessary disappear and hence the adult parasites are in their organisation much simpler even than they themselves were in their embryonic states; but as has been already noticed, the egg-producing organs are much increased in development.

From two to six of the foremost segments of the body in arthropods become united to make up a head, which carries sentient organs, such as the eyes, ears, and antennæ or feelers, with the mouth. In the head likewise is the large supracesophageal nerve-ganglion or brain, which sometimes is large and complex, as in ants.

CHAPTER XIX.

CRABS AND LOBSTERS.

CLASS I. **Crustacea.**—The animals of this class are all water-breathers, either provided with gills, or else with a thin integument through which the blood becomes directly aerated. The structure of a crustacean can be easily understood by examining a lobster or freshwater crayfish. In either of these we notice that the body is divided into two regions, an anterior, covered by a dorsal shield of two pieces, and a posterior, consisting of a series of rings, ending in the fan-like tail. In the body of the lobster we notice

Segments of a Lobster.

three openings,—the mouth, the terminal opening of the digestive canal in the middle line of the last joint of the tail on the under surface, and the opening of the egg-producing organs at the base of the third pair of walking limbs. Through this last the eggs are extruded, and are carried in clusters under and around the bases of the hind series of feet.

In the large anterior mass of the body, sheltered by the dorsal shield, there are fourteen segments united, comprising the head, thorax, and abdomen. The head segments bear their six pairs of appended limbs, the first pair of which are modified into stalks for the eyes, which are remarkable organs, each consisting of a large number of rods of a crystalline appearance, each placed at the end of a nerve fibril or thread, and surrounded by a mass of pigment. The numerous united fibrils of the optic nerve pass in the centre of the stalk, and each fibril ends in its crystal rod, the mass of rods being arranged in a cluster, slightly divergent so as to exhibit a rounded outer surface, over which the chitinous skin extends as a fine, perfectly transparent covering.

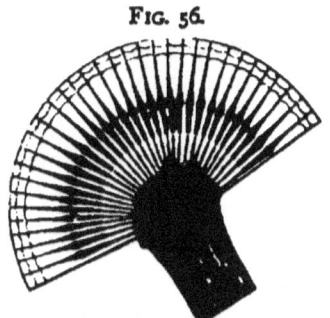

FIG. 56.

Vertical section through the eye of an Insect, showing the stalk or optic nerve, the white radiating lines or secondary optic nerves and the crystal cones.

The second pair of limbs are feelers called the antennules or lesser antennæ, consisting of three basal joints, terminated by a pair of slender processes each made up of many little rings; these are followed by the third pair of limbs, or the large antennæ, consisting of five basal joints succeeded by a long feeler. The bases of the fourth pair of limbs are modified into biting-jaws or *mandibles*, and they bear an internal appendage named the mandibular palp. The fifth and sixth pairs of limbs are also jaws, and are called maxillæ; they also bear rudimental appendages. The three segments that follow the head segments, and are united thereto, make up the thorax, and their limbs are also in the lobster modified into organs of mastication, and hence are known by the name of foot-jaws; each of these except the first bears outer and inner appendages, but the third pair is of very little use as a chewing organ, but bears a gill as does also its anterior neighbour, the second pair of foot jaws.

Following the limbs of the cephalo-thorax, for so the united head and thorax is often called, we come to five pairs of walking legs, each pair being the limbs borne by a segment of the abdomen. These five abdominal segments are also in the lobster covered over dorsally by the dorsal shell, but on the under or ventral surface, their separateness can be very well recognised. The first pair of limbs consist of the pincers or *chelæ*. These formidable organs in the lobster are made up of seven joints, the last but one of these is very large, and its outer angle is prolonged into a finger-like process capable of being opposed to the last joint, thus making a grasping organ of great power. In the lobster the two pincers are not quite symmetrical; one is armed along the edges of the blades of the pincers with rough tubercles, the other with small serratures; the former claw is probably used as an anchoring apparatus, the latter for seizing articles of food.

The two succeeding pairs of abdominal limbs are also pincer-like at the extremity; the two following are simply pointed, but still exhibit seven joints. All the abdominal limbs, except the last, carry gills appended to the basal joint, and placed under cover of the dorsal shell.

The six movable rings which form the 'tail' of the lobster, bear laterally limbs adapted for swimming, each made up of a basal part, and two flattened appendages external and internal; the last of these segments not only carries the widely expanded swimmer or tail fins, but bears at its hinder extremity also a single median flap or 'telson,' sometimes regarded as a separate segment. These movable rings make up the post-abdomen.

The ear in the lobster is a sac at the base of the antennule; the gills lie under the hinder and lateral parts of the dorsal shield. The stomach is a gizzard-like cavity with calcareous masses lining its walls, followed by a narrow soft-walled digestive stomach and intestine, below which lies the nerve-cord, and above it is the heart.

The crab differs from the lobster not only in shape but in the comparative immobility and small size of its abdomen, which is turned in and sunk into a groove. While the young lobster only differs from the adult in the possession of small outer appendages on the walking limbs, and the smaller size of the tail, the crab emerges from the egg in a form utterly unlike the adult, as a little swimming creature with a dorsal shield armed with a strong median spine (fig. 57, A) and followed by a jointed abdomen which bears no appended limbs.

A closely allied animal common on our shores is the hermit crab, which protects its soft, almost limbless abdomen by inserting it into the deserted shell of a whelk, or other univalve mollusc. In these

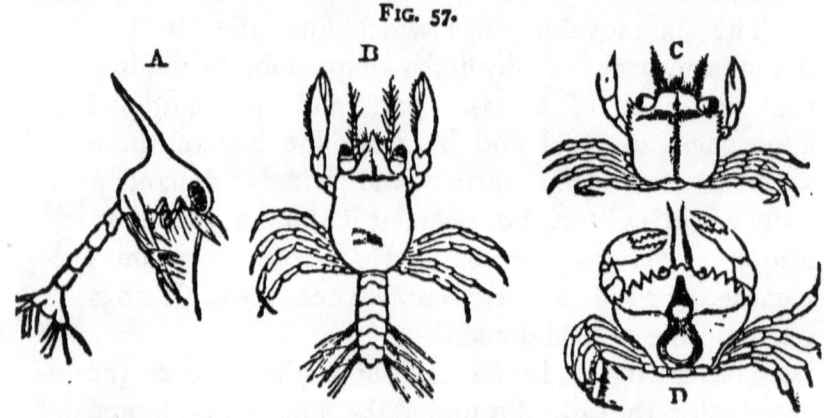

Fig. 57.

Stages in the development of the common Shore Crab (*Carcinus mænas*). A, First or zoea stage; B, early stage with tail; C, D, advanced stages of growth.

the pincers are usually unequal, so that on the animal being molested, one can be retracted while the larger one blocks up the passage. The soft abdomen acts as a sucker, whereby the hermit crab retains its hold on its habitation.

There are many varieties of form among crustacea, and those above described are among the most highly organised, all having stalked eyes and ten walking feet. The mantis shrimps have their thoracic limbs fitted for walking, as well as the abdominal legs, so that instead of ten, there are fourteen or sixteen legs.

Small Crustaceans.

All these forms make up a sub-class of crustacea named *Podophthalmia* on account of their stalked eyes.

The sand-hoppers (fig. 55), wood-lice, and freshwater shrimps, make up a second sub-class, characterised by possessing sessile eyes. These also have bodies made up of twenty segments, each of which, except those of the head and thorax, has its own independent chitinous ring, and the two hinder pairs of foot-jaws are used for locomotion. Some of these, like the sand-hoppers and freshwater shrimps, have the three hindmost pairs of abdominal feet arranged so that their joints bend forwards while all the other limbs bend with their joints concave backwards. These are called *Amphipoda*, to distinguish them from those like the wood-lice, and slaters, whose legs are all directed one way, which are called *Isopoda*.

The king crabs of the Mollucca Islands and of North America form the types of a third sub-class. They resemble the lobster in having the head, thorax, and abdomen covered by a great dorsal buckler, but differ in that there are six walking limbs around the mouth, whose bases are spiny, and compressed, acting as jaws. The eyes are not stalked, and there is a long bayonet-shaped tail, behind the abdomen, corresponding to the telson of the lobster. The segments of the abdomen are faintly marked in the adult king crab.

In the past ages of the world, larger allied forms existed abundantly; other allied fossil forms had three-lobed bodies, and hence are known as *Trilobites*, and they are only found in palæozoic rocks. In stagnant pools of fresh water little creatures called water fleas can be seen, by the aid of the microscope, actively darting about; these are representatives of a fourth sub-class. They are all minute at the present day. Certain forms bear gill processes appended to their feet, and hence are known as 'gill-footed' or Branchiopods. Many closely allied species have the dorsal wall extended in the form of an enveloping shell, just like the gill-covering laminæ in the lobster.

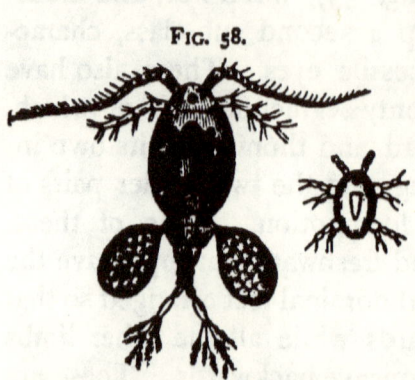

Fig. 58.

Cyclops quadricornis carrying its egg sacs. The small figure is the Nauplius or larva.

Those crustaceans which are parasitic are closely related to the water fleas, and undergo retrogression until they become reduced to little sacs with bristles for jaws, with sucker-like fore feet, and often with no trace of segmentation (fig. 59, A). Some live on the bodies of larger crustaceans such as lobsters, others on tunicates, but they are mostly found attached about the gills of fishes. The early stages of these are little, free, marine larvæ with developed jaws and a moderate post-abdomen (fig. 58). Many non-parasitic species remain for their whole life in a state like that of the larvæ of these parasites.

In all these lower crustaceans the earliest stage of existence after emission from the egg is in the form of a minute oval body with three pairs of limbs and one central eye. This is known as a Nauplius, and it assumes its adult form by the growth of new segments and new limbs. The nauplius stage of

Metamorphoses of Crustaceans. 105

higher crustaceans is transitory, and sometimes is passed over before the embryo leaves the egg, and in crabs the form assumed by the newly hatched young is that of a small shield-covered body with two eyes and long jointed abdomen (fig. 57, A); this curious larva is called Zoëa, and by the shortening of its

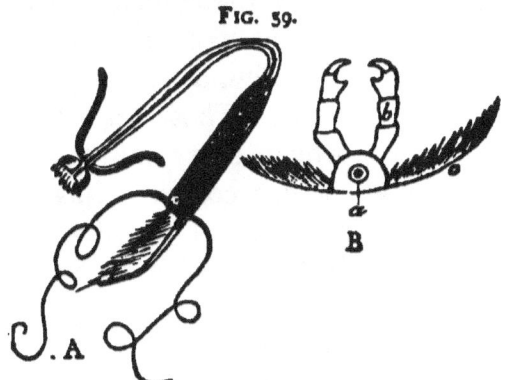

FIG. 59.

Pennella, parasitic on the Sunfish. A, Entire animal, half real size; B, head.

tail and the vanishing of its dorsal spine, it becomes changed into its adult form.

All crustaceans undergo successive moultings or changings of shell, and during these changes lost parts become restored and the several changes in metamorphosis can be seen at these periods. Crustaceans part with their limbs easily under circumstances of fright or seizure; thus if a limb be taken hold of forcibly the animal will probably break it off between the first and second joints in its efforts after freedom. At the next moult, there appears a new limb budding on the soft uncovered body, and when the new shell forms and hardens, a small limb is seen in place of the lost one.

Some of the metamorphoses of crustaceans are strange; in none more so than in the barnacles and acorn-shells (figs. 4 and 5, pp. 9 and 10), the lowest subclass of the series. Acorn-shells or Balani, are the little limpet-like shells which encrust the rocks along all our coasts and which can be at once recognised by the opening at the top of the conical shell, which is closed by the lateral valve-like or beak-like plates. Barnacles are commonly found adhering to logs of wood or to ships' bottoms. These begin life as active nauplius-like larvæ, which every autumn are to be found swimming along our coasts. This larva at its early moults develops a lateral mantle-fold. At its fourth change in shell, the front of its head becomes fixed by the flattening of one of the joints of the antennæ and by the secretion poured out by a gland which, though placed in the body, has its duct opening in the altered joint of the antennæ. At the fifth moult the eyes and antennæ vanish, the head becomes fixed by a broad base of attachment, the mantle-like fold of integument surrounds the body and becomes calcified into a shell of many valves, within which the hinder parts of the body are enclosed together with their six pairs of limbs. These limbs remain free and capable of slight protusion, while the mouth with its mandibles lies at the bottom of the mantle cavity.

Some Balani select curious places of residence. Coronula lives on the skin of the whale; Anelasma often is adherent to fishes, and many others to corals. One closely allied group of degraded forms are parasites on the abdomen of crabs. To the sub-class

Classes of Crustaceans.

comprising all these forms the name Cirripedia, or tentacle-footed, has been given.

Recapitulation.—We have thus seen that the seven classes of water-breathing, many-jointed forms which make up the class Crustacea are very dissimilar in details. They may be arranged in a tabular series as follows:—

A. Sessile Crustaceans, often pseudo-parasitic, usually enclosed in a many valved shell = Sub-class I. Cirripedia.
B. Free, with a cephalo-thorax and two pairs of thoracic limbs, none of the feet bearing gills = Sub-class II. Copepoda (fig. 58).
C. Free, with the body enclosed in a bivalve shell made of the extended dorsal integument = Sub-class III. Ostracoda.
D. Free, with no enclosing shell, feet gill-bearing, segments less or more than twenty = Sub-class IV. Branchiopoda.
E. Free, with a large cephalo-thorax, small walking limbs, six pair of which are arranged around the mouth=Sub-class V. Pœcilopoda. King Crabs.
F. Free, with a cephalo-thorax, stalked eyes and a body of twenty segments = Sub-class VI. Podophthalmia.
- A. Thoracic limbs masticatory, ten abdominal limbs alone fitted for walking = Order I. Decapoda.
    - a. With a long abdomen: Lobsters = Sub-order I. Macrura.
    - b. With a soft limbless abdomen: Hermit Crabs = Sub-order II. Anomura.

c. With a short up-turned abdomen: Crabs = Sub-order III. Brachyura.
B. Some thoracic limbs ambulatory, thus making twelve, fourteen, or sixteen pairs of walking limbs = Order II. Stomapoda.
G. Free, with a cephalo-thorax, twenty segments and sessile eyes = Sub-class I. Edriophthalmia.

CHAPTER XX.

SPIDERS AND MITES.

CLASS II. **Arachnoidea.**—These are terrestrial air-breathing creatures in which the segments that compose the head and thorax are united to form a single cephalo-thorax, but their articulated limbs are to some extent represented, and of these, four pairs are usually used in walking. There is an abdomen with a variable number of rings. Whenever eyes are present they are not compound bundles of crystal rods covered by a common *cornea*, as in crustaceans, but they consist of separate transparent cones surrounded with pigment and always few in number. There are never any antennæ developed as such, but the mandibles are always present, and, in scorpions, the maxillary palps form pincers or claws like those of a crab; such claws are called *chelicerœ*. The second pair of maxillary palps form the first pair of walking limbs, while the first and second pairs of thoracic limbs, as seen in the true insects, are developed as the second and third pairs of legs, and the third pair of thoracic limbs is absent; at the base of the abdomen is a curious pair of comb-like organs in the scorpion. The parts of each limb are like those in Crustacea; the body and its organs are however much shorter than in that class. The nervous system is concentrated, the digestive canal often has blind pouches appended to it. There is an abdominal heart in all, except in a few mites, and there is usually a series of breathing tubes. Organs of touch, smell and hearing seem to be deficient.

Many of these animals are parasites, either external, or internal; but except in these, there are few in which the young undergo much metamorphosis after hatching.

The outer surface is often hard and chitinous, but never calcified. The dorsal surface layer is seldom extended over any of the neighbouring segments or appendages, or when extended it is immovable.

Mites.—The three orders in the class consist of mites, spiders and scorpions. Of these the mites are the simplest and are exemplified by the cheese-mite, found in mouldy cheese, or the sugar-mite often met with in brown sugar. In these the abdomen is unsegmented, and usually indistinctly separate from the cephalo-thorax. The breathing organs are fine tubes named tracheæ, which open on the surface, and break up within the body into branches, which admit air into the tissues. The mouth in mites is often proboscis-like or armed with a spiny beak. Most of them are parasites either upon animals or plants. One curious group inhabits the body cavities of vertebrate animals, wherein their worm-like bodies may be mistaken for tape- or thorn-

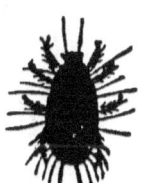

FIG. 60.

Cheese-mite (*Acarus*).

headed-worms. They are however easily distinguished by their embryos bearing true jointed limbs, although these are lost in the adults.

One form has been found in the contents of the small fat glands on the human face, and another is the cause of the disgusting skin disease known as 'itch.' Other larger forms are the 'ticks' found so commonly on sheep, dogs, bats, camels, &c. Of non-parasitic forms, the little 'red-spider' so often seen on the sea-shore under stones between tide-marks, and the 'glass-' and 'garden-mites' found in damp moss and among vegetables are examples.

Spiders.—In spiders the cephalo-thorax is joined to the sac-like abdomen by a narrow stalk, and the latter portion never bears any limb-processes. The tracheæ, instead of being bundles of branching tubes, are condensed and flattened, and included in definite spaces, in which the compressed tubes look like the leaves of a book, the whole laminated organ on account of its being circumscribed and lung-like, is called a *tracheal-lung*, and the spiders are often called pulmonary arachnoids on account of their possessing these organs.

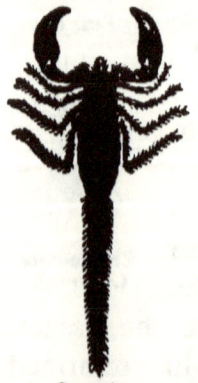

Fig. 61.

Scorpion.

Spiders have little clusters of simple eyes on their foreheads, bright small specks usually eight in number and generally arranged in two rows. The mandibles have at their inner side the duct of a poison-gland whose secretion they instil into the insects which constitute their prey. The stomach is like a hollow ring from which radiating blind pouches pass off, and the digestive tube is short.

Near the hinder end of the abdomen in spiders, there is a flattish 'spinning area' upon which open the glands which secrete the web. On this area there are usually three pairs of little wart-like spinnerets; and numerous small pores, from each of which a minute thread of web-material issues, open on the surface of each spinneret. Sometimes one pair of the little knobs consists of a palp-like process. In the common house-spider (*Tegenaria domestica*) there are 400 such holes on each wart, hence each thread of the web consists of several hundred strands; the material is at first fluid, but rapidly becomes hard and chitinoid. In commencing to spin, the spider applies the spinnerets to the surface of some fixed body, and then as it moves away, the material is drawn out. The hind feet press the several strands of the web-thread together, their comb-like claws appearing to be important instruments for this purpose.

In the web of the garden spider, whose geometrical nets are frequently seen on old fences and palings, there are three kinds of threads to be noticed. 1st. The marginal and stoutest radial threads. 2nd. The intermediate radial threads, both of which are uniform, though differing in size and in elasticity, wherein the secondary exceed the primary. 3rd. The concentric threads which are bedecked at regular intervals with little viscid globules.

Other spiders excavate cavities in the ground; these they line with a silky web, and over the mouth of them they make a trap-door lid of alternate layers of earth and web united together and hinged by a silken hinge. These trap-door spiders are found along the shores of the Mediterranean, in California and Jamaica. Some spin little cocoons or silken cases for their eggs, which they carry about with them, and in protecting which they exhibit great activity. The maxillary palps are never pincer-bearing or used for walking, although sometimes long.

Scorpions.—The scorpions and their allies are characterised by the possession of a long segmented abdomen, ending in a tail-like portion. The maxillary palps form pincers, like crabs' claws, and breathing takes place by pulmonary sacs like those of spiders. The last joint of the abdomen bears in scorpions a sharp spine at its end, perforated by the duct of a poison-gland, and thereby it inflicts painful wounds. A little creature named Chelifer, somewhat allied to scorpions, but with no tail nor sting, is often found in old books.

CHAPTER XXI.

CENTIPEDES. GALLYWORMS.

CLASS III. **Myriopoda.**—This comparatively small class includes the centipedes, whose long jointed bodies are to be seen rapidly crawling under old rotten sticks and stones and shunning the light. In this country they rarely exceed three inches in length, but in the tropics they reach from six to twelve inches or even more, and their bites are poisonous and severe. One

Centipedes.

British form is phosphorescent, and another is described as capable of giving electric shocks. The body consists of many segments which, with the exception of the head and the last joint, are similar in appearance; the head bears the eyes, which are usually simple like those of spiders, and generally in two rows. Near these there are the sensitive, slender, thread-like antennæ, consisting rarely of seven, usually of fourteen joints or more. These animals are usually carnivorous and have a strong pair of mandibles, situated on each side of the mouth, and two pairs of maxillæ, either or both of which are sometimes united together in the middle line, forming a lower lip for the mouth; the anterior of these have jointed palps. The hindermost segment of the body has often a pair of long limbs directed backwards. There is a straight digestive canal with a number of tortuous glands appended to it, and a long tubular heart made up of a chain of chambers one in each segment separated from each other by valves.

FIG. 62.

Centipede (*Lithobius*).

On each side of the body open the mouths of the tracheæ or tubes for breathing; there may be one on each segment or one on every second joint. Each opening is the beginning of an air-tube, which on entering the body branches irregularly, the fine branches freely communicating with each other. To keep these tubes open there is a spirally coiled thread of *chitin* in their lining membrane, which like a spring prevents them from collapsing, and to keep the mouth from being choked there is usually a raised margin sometimes provided with little processes. One curious group has no tracheæ.

Many of these centipedes have minute pear-shaped glands placed along the sides, which secrete a brown irritating fluid, emitting a disagreeable odour.

There are more than twenty segments in the body (except in one little species), and each bears one or two pairs of legs, all with six or seven joints like those of a spider or crustacean; each limb terminates in one or two claws.

Subdivisions.—There are three orders of these animals, millepedes, centipedes, and pauropods. Millepedes possess two pairs of limbs on most of their segments, a condition due to the union of the true segments in pairs. They have also small antennæ of seven joints and tracheal openings in front of the articulation of each leg. They are found in this country in the rotten wood of decaying trees, and when disturbed roll themselves up into balls.

Centipedes are found under stones in damp out-houses, or in rotten palings. They have but one pair of limbs on each joint of the body, and never more than one pair of stigmata. The native forms are small, but the tropical Scolopendræ are of very large size and their bites are exceedingly severe. The one species of Pauropus is a minute white creature found in decaying leaves, with no tracheæ, ten segments and five-jointed antennæ.

Structure of an Insect.

CHAPTER XXII.

INSECTS.

CLASS IV. **Insecta.**—Insects, the most numerous and the most highly organised of invertebrates are found

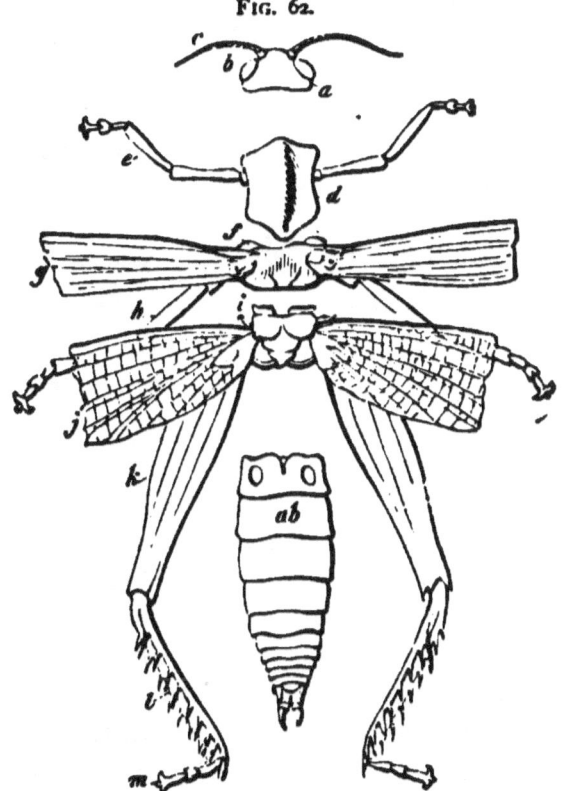

FIG. 62.

Grasshopper, showing the structure and composition of an insect's body. *a*, head; *b*, eye; *c*, antenna; *d*, thorax, foremost segment; *e*, foremost pair of legs; *f*, middle segment of thorax; *g*, foremost pair of wings; *h*, second pair of legs; *i*, hindmost segment of thorax; *j*, posterior pair of wings; *k*, femur of third pair of legs; *l*, tibia; *m*, tarsus; *ab*, abdomen.

in almost every conceivable locality on the earth's

surface. Scarcely a plant exists but it harbours some one of the tribe, and many animals, living or dead, supply food for other species. Insects are usually of small size and have the six foremost segments united to form a head. The three succeeding segments form a *thorax*, which alone bears the legs, one pair on each of its rings, and when wings are present they are borne by the middle and hindmost of these thoracic rings. The abdomen consists of seven segments not bearing any limbs, and followed by one, two or three abdominal rings, to which are appended the sting or its equivalent, the ovipositor. A black beetle, a bluebottle fly, and a butterfly may be taken as types of the class.

Organs of Sense.—The head of an insect bears a pair of compound eyes, and often several simple eyes in a cluster. The former have a cornea or transparent surface divided into many facets, each of the nerve rods having its own pigment mass and its own cornea. In the common house-fly there are 2000 such facets in each eye, and in the dragon-fly there are 28,000.

The head of an insect also bears one pair of *antennæ* or feelers, jointed organs which vary much in shape and structure, being sometimes simple, filiform, comb-like, or lamellar. These are organs of touch and hearing, possibly of smell and taste, and also of communication between one insect and its fellow.

Mouth.—The mouth is on the fore and under part of the head and varies in shape according to the method whereby the insect obtains its food. In beetles, dragon-flies, &c., the mouth is armed with chewing jaws. There are two lips, an upper or labrum (fig.

Mouths of Insects.

65, *e*) and lower or labium. The lower (*i*) represents the second pair of maxillæ in the lobster and crayfish, which here are united together, but sometimes as in cockroaches (fig. 64) and locusts remaining separate. The labium bears a pair of feelers called labial palps (*k*). Between the labrum and the labium are two pairs of jaws placed vertically, so that

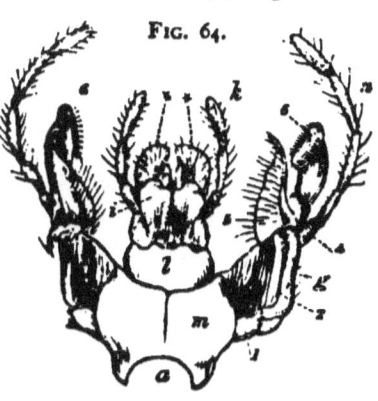

Fig. 64.

Under side of mouth of Cockroach. *h*, maxillary palp ; *i*, ligula ; * paraglossæ ; *k*, labial palp; 1, cardo of hinge ; 2. stipes ; 5, maxilla ; 6, galea, or sensitive process of maxilla.

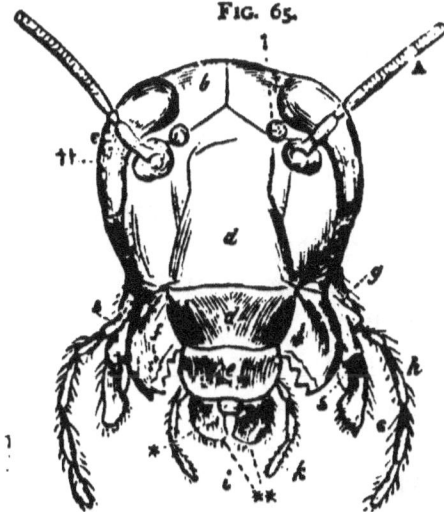

Fig. 65.

Upper side of head of Cockroach. *b*, epicranium, or top of the head ; *d*, clypeus ; *e*, labrum ; *f*, mandibles ; A, antennæ.

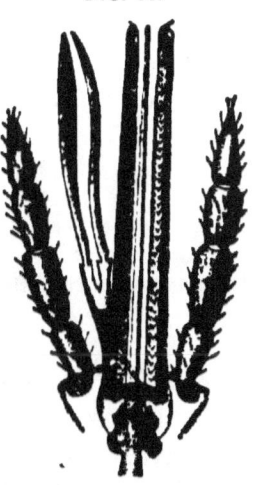

Fig. 66.

Mouth of Flea. Showing the slender stylelike labrum between the long mandibles medially, and the labial and maxillary palps laterally.

in acting they move in a horizontal plane. The upper

pair are named mandibles or biting jaws, the lower pair maxillæ or chewing jaws. The last-named have usually appended to them on each side a pair of small jointed feelers or maxillary palps. In the bluebottle and house-fly the lower lip is lengthened into an elongated gutter-like sheath in which are contained the maxillæ and mandibles, which are reduced to mere bristle-like processes.

In the bee (fig. 77, p. 132) the upper lip and mandible are strong and fitted for chewing, while the maxillæ and lower lip are long and channelled, so that when placed in apposition they make a tube through which the insect sucks in honey. In these creatures the lower lip consists of two parts, an upper or tongue and a hinder part or mentum. In the butterfly, the mouth has lost all trace of its chewing function and the maxillæ form two half tubes, and when opposed as they always are they make up a canal, and being very long and curved, this is sometimes called the proboscis. Each of these maxillæ has within it also a fine tube, and thus a transverse section through the proboscis shows three tubes, one medial between the maxillæ and one lateral on each side within each maxilla. Behind this proboscis lies the labium, which has usually large palps between which the proboscis lies when retracted; for, unlike the tube in the bee, this proboscis is freely retractile.

FIG. 67.

Head and proboscis of Butterfly, showing antennæ and eyes.

Nervous System of Insects. 119

Body.—The head is joined to the thorax by a narrow neck, and this region is generally strong, and the limbs are attached to the under part of the side of each of its three rings. Each limb is composed of five joints: hip (*coxa*), a ring segment (*trochanter*), thigh (*femur*, fig. 63, *k*), a shin (*tibia*), and a *tarsus* of several joints ending in the claws to which sucking cushions or pads may be appended. The wings are jointed to the middle and hinder rings of the thorax; these are modified lateral flaps of the body wall, such as exist in some crustaceans; the thin skin folds of which they consist are supported by chitinous ribs (*costæ*) containing branches of the tracheæ.

Internal Structure.—On the sides of each abdominal ring are the apertures of the long, finely branching tracheæ, which sink into the body and are distributed widely among the tissues. Each tube has a membranous wall strengthened by a coiled spiral chitinous thread which keeps it open for conveying air from the surface through the body. Each motion of the body by altering the tension of the vessels promotes this method of respiration. The dorsal tubular heart placed in the abdomen, consists of a chain of chambers separated the one from the other by valves. This receives the impure blood and the new blood from the intestines, and propels it by the chief bloodvessels into lacunæ or interspaces between the tissues which are thus nourished. The blood is colourless, or green, rarely red.

Insects have two large and complex nerve ganglia in the head, and ganglia in all the segments from the head backwards. The head ganglia send branches to the eyes and appendages, while the thoracic ganglia supply the limbs. Some cave-dwelling insects have no eyes, others have these organs rudimental. The digestive canal of insects consists of a stomach to which the long œsophagus or gullet leads from the mouth; to this a thin walled sac or sucking stomach may be appended as in butterflies, in others there is a gizzard with hard horny tooth-like processes, and this is followed by the glandular thin-walled true digestive stomach which ends in an intestine, whose length depends on the nature of the food, being longer in those that feed on solid than in those that feed on fluid matter, and longer in the herbivorous than in the predaceous forms. Glandular tubes opening into the end of the intestine exist in many insects, and from their first describer are known as Malpighian.

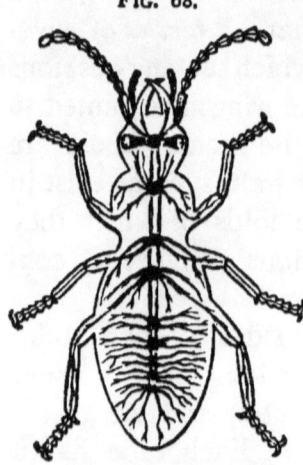

FIG. 68.
Nervous system of Beetle, showing central double nerve cord and chain of ganglia.

Some insects are luminous. In the glow-worm (*Lampyris noctiluca*) there is a large fatty body in the abdomen richly supplied with tracheæ and nerves from which a bright light is emitted. The fire-fly (*Elater noctilucus*) sends out light from two oval spots on the thorax. Grasshoppers and crickets emit sounds by rubbing one part of the

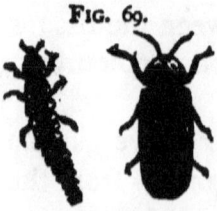

FIG. 69.
Glow-worm, female and male.

body against another, and such have usually a special hearing organ which in crickets and locusts is placed under the knee on the outside of the foremost pair of limbs.

Development and Metamorphoses.—Insects' eggs have often a sculptured shell, and are laid in such places as are suitable for the supply of food to the newly hatched larvæ. For this egg-laying the parent has often an organ formed of the modified appendages of the abdomen. These organs are in the form of bristles, pincers, or saws, and by these the insect prepares the place for and deposits its eggs; hence, the organ is called an ovipositor.

The young of most insects emerge from the eggs as worm-like animals called caterpillars or larvæ. These are little jointed creatures, having a head which bears eyes and a pair of antennæ. Its mouth is armed with strong jaws, and the surface is often covered with bristles. Each of the three anterior segments of the body of a caterpillar is usually provided with a pair of little stumpy feet, and sometimes, as in the larvæ of butterflies, flies and saw-flies, the hinder joints have also foot-like processes. Caterpillars are most voracious in their habits and grow rapidly, frequently moulting or shedding their skin. On reaching the limit of size, many caterpillars begin to spin for themselves a case or cocoon. The glands from which this proceeds are two long tubes placed behind the head, but opening on the lip, and the material of the cocoon is silk. When caterpillars are fully fed they give up eating, and their skin thickening they become fixed and rigid and are known as pupæ, or from their occasional metallic lustre, chrysalides. In this pupa stage the animal lies for a considerable time; this skin then bursts and the perfect insect emerges, at first soft and moist but soon becoming firm and fit for independent life.

Caterpillars differ much in structure from the adult insect; thus the digestive canal of the caterpillars of butterflies is fitted for the digestion of solid food, while that of the imago or perfect insect is only fitted for sucking the juices of plants. The antennæ likewise of caterpillars are attached to the front edge of the forehead shield, and outside the articulation of the mandible, whereas the antennæ of the imago or perfect insect is articulated further forward, and on a plane with the joint at the base of the mandible; thus the antennæ of the caterpillar represent the long antennæ of the crab and lobster, while those of the perfect insect represent the antennule of crustaceans. Insects display an amount of intelligence far superior to that of the lower vertebrates; ants, wasps, and bees, the most highly organised as well as the most intelligent of the class, exhibit a wonderful power in the mode of ordering and governing their communities, and the skill shown in the construction of their habitations is scarcely inferior to that of man himself.

There are at least thirteen orders of insects known to the naturalist, a few of the commoner and more interesting representatives of which are shortly described in the next two chapters.

Bugs. Springtails. Earwigs. 123

CHAPTER XXIII.

ORDERS OF INSECTS.

ORDER I. **Rhynchota.**—This group consists of those insects which either undergo no metamorphoses or a very slight change in the process of growth. They have almost all suctorial mouths (fig. 70), consisting of a long tubular labium, whose base is open or covered by the labrum like a little lid. The mandibles and maxillæ are altered into piercers or bristles which work within the tube. A few, however, like the bird-lice, have hook-like mandibles and chewing mouths. Many of the insects of this order are parasites and wingless,

FIG. 70.

Mouth of Bug.
Showing the median elongated labium, the four bristle-like mandibles and maxillæ, also, at the sides, the antennæ and eyes.

such as lice and bugs; others, the aphides, the small green insects which are so abundant on roses, geraniums, &c., are plant parasites.

These aphides are marvellously prolific, a single pair being capable in one year of producing a progeny of twenty thousand millions or even more. Some aphides have glandular tubes on the abdomen which secrete a sweet honey-like fluid. This fluid is used as food by some species of ants, especially in this country by the red and yellow ants, which can be seen to 'milk' the honey tubes with their antennæ and swallow the fluid. Several species of aphides appear to be kept as 'milch kine' by these ants, and are fed by them apparently for this secretion.

Other representatives of this order are the cochineal and lac insects, the 'water boatmen' and 'water scorpions,' as well as the numerous and often brightly coloured field bugs.

ORDER II. **Thysanura.**—Spring-tails, an unimportant group, consisting mostly of very small creatures, sugar-lice and spring-tails, which live in dark, damp cellars, or in sugar stores, and can be seen hopping or springing about and shunning the light.

They scarcely undergo metamorphoses, and their mouths are suited for chewing. The extremity of the abdomen is prolonged into a pair of bristles or a forked tail, whereby the animal is enabled to progress by leaping. The scales of the bodies of some of these Poduræ or spring-tails are marked with very minute furrows.

ORDER III. **Euplexoptera.**—This order includes the earwigs, which are remarkable for their curiously folded hind wings, that lie folded like a fan under cover of the hard-shielded forewings. They have a masticating mouth, and posteriorly there is a pincer-like long abdominal appendage in both male and female. The earwig is remarkable for sitting on her eggs to hatch them, and for the maternal protection which the female exercises over her young which resemble her except in the absence of wings.

ORDER IV.—**Thysanoptera**, or fringe-winged insects, including a not uncommon little fly, named Thrips, whose contact with the face in warm weather is often a source of considerable itching from the titillation caused by its plumose wings and bristled body. One species of this order by piercing the immature wheat grain with its bristle-like mandibles causes the seed to shrivel, and occasionally destroys even the corn stalks.

ORDER V.—**Orthoptera**, straight-winged insects, includes cockroaches, grasshoppers and locusts. These have four wings, of which the often parchment-like front pair are the smaller; the second pair are usually large, and when at rest are folded like a fan. The mouth is masticatory and both pairs of maxillæ are free. Some of the tropical forms of this order are wingless and assume extraordinary forms, the walking leaves, mantis, and walking stick (*Bacterium*) sometimes resembling dry twigs or bits of branches. In the common cockroach (*Periplaneta orientalis*) which is a native of the East, the legs are fitted for running and have spiny tibiæ, the head is overlapped by the front segments of the thorax and bears long antennæ, and the parts of the mouth are distinct (figs. 64, 65). The wings are very small, especially in the females. The Drummer Cockroach of the West Indies adds to its other disagreeable qualities that of making a knocking noise, which is sometimes sufficiently loud to keep awake the inhabitants of houses infested with these insects. Troctes pulsatorius, a minute insect found in books, old pictures, &c., also produces a sound which has earned for it the name 'death-watch' or 'death-tick.'

Locusts are terrible scourges in tropical countries, devouring all vegetation and leaving bare the regions over which they pass. Their body is long and laterally compressed and the long hind legs act as leaping organs. They produce a chirping sound by rubbing the thighs against the elevated ribs of their wings. In the grasshopper and cricket a similar sound is produced by the rubbing together of spots on the wings provided with raised ridges.

The white ants or Termites of tropical regions also belong to this order, and build ant-hills of extraordinary size and hardness. Their colonies are very complex, and consist of several kinds of inhabitants, females, males, workers and soldiers.

The dragonflies, which also belong to this order, have aquatic larvæ, breathing by means of tracheal

FIG. 71.

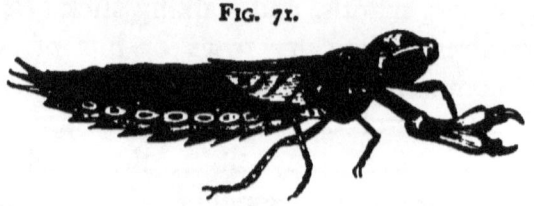

Larva of Dragonfly, showing the 'Mask.'

gills or tuft-like processes of their body-wall containing tracheæ, but with no openings. These processes are lost in the perfect insect; in one American genus, however, these appendages are retained during life. The larva of the common dragon-fly has a long and jointed under lip, which is folded over the face when at rest and is called the mask, but when the animal is feeding it becomes extended as a formidable tongs-like weapon for the grasping of prey (fig. 71).

CHAPTER XXIV.

INSECTS WHICH UNDERGO PERFECT METAMORPHOSES.

THE four orders of insects which follow are small, but contain some interesting forms which deserve a passing notice.

ORDER VI. **Neuroptera,** nerve-winged insects, including the scorpion-flies (fig. 72), snake-flies, and ant-lions. These in their perfect stage possess a mouth fitted for chewing, and four equal membranous wings, of which the hinder pair are never folded. Few of these insects are natives of this country.

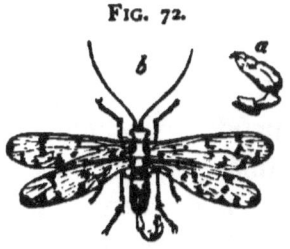

FIG. 72.

Panorpa, or Scorpion-fly.

ORDER VII.—**Trichoptera,** including the caddis-flies which have hair-clad or scaly unequal wings, the hinder of which are folded. Their larvæ agglutinate small shells, stones, straws &c. by silken threads secreted by a small spinning gland placed on the lower lip, and of these they make cases in which they live. Having attained its full size, the pupa fixes its case under water and spins a silken network or grating over each end of it, thus shutting itself in for its pupa sleep, while it does not exclude the water which it requires for breathing. After this stage of rest the pupa by its strong jaws bites through its prison, and after moulting assumes its adult form.

ORDER VIII.—**Strepsiptera** includes the curious

parasites which live on the abdomen of bees and wasps. In these the males have four wings, two in front, small and twisted, from which the order is named, two behind, large and fan-like; the females never lose their last pupa-skin, and are wingless, with a worm-like abdomen and are viviparous.

ORDER IX. **Aphaniptera.**—Includes fleas which have laterally compressed bodies and exceedingly rudimental wings, the scale-like traces of which are with difficulty noticeable. The suctorial mouth (fig. 66), without upper lip, has long slender saw-like mandibles, which are sheathed by the three-jointed labial palps at their base.

The antennæ are very small and lie in a groove, but the maxillary palps are large and prominent. The hindmost pair of limbs are long, muscular, and well-fitted for leaping. The larvæ are white footless grubs which feed on animal matter for about twelve days, spin for themselves a cocoon, and pass to the pupa stage. After about fourteen days' quiescence in this stage the perfect insect emerges. In many respects the flea is closely allied to the next order.

ORDER X.—**Diptera,** two winged flies, including flies, gnats, mosquitoes, &c. In this order the hind pair of wings is rudimental and represented by scale-like or pin-like processes under the developed pair of wings, and the mouth is a proboscis. The larvæ are footless, often headless maggots, such as are found on putrid meat. Some forms of Diptera, like the gnats and mosquitoes, are provided each with a long proboscis enclosing six long sharp bristles. The larvæ of the gnats are aquatic and breathe air by means of a tube with which they are provided which opens at the surface of the water. Some of these insects are very destructive to vegetation; the larvæ of the common daddy-longlegs for instance, feeds on the roots of grass and will thus sometimes destroy large patches of meadow. The Hessian fly is still more formidable, often destroying whole fields of wheat by attacking the young plants before they are in flower.

ORDER XI.—**Lepidoptera**, is also a large order, and includes those most beautiful of all insects, the butterflies, characterised by possessing four wings covered with fine dust-like scales. These microscopic scales overlap each other on the surface of the wings, and are of different shapes in different species. Butterflies have suctorial mouths (fig. 67), the proboscis-like sucker being rolled up when not in use. The larvæ or caterpillars consist of thirteen joints and are very unlike in mouth, structure, and general appearance to the perfect forms which emerge from them.

On the lower lip in the larvæ of some moths there is the outlet of two spinning glands, which when the larva has reached its full size secrete the material for a silken cocoon within which it is enclosed in the pupa state.

These insects vary in size; some, as the clothes moths and fur moths, are very small.

The larvæ of the leaf-rollers, a form nearly allied to the clothes-moth, roll up the leaves of plants on which they feed into tubes, within which they live and pass their pupa sleep, and whence they emerge in due time as little broad-winged moths.

Another related form often found on apple trees is

the looper or canker-worm moth, named from the peculiar looped attitude which the larva assumes in walking. The silkworm moth, a native of North China, secretes by its two glands the silk of commerce. The sphinx moths, called so from the attitude in which the cater-

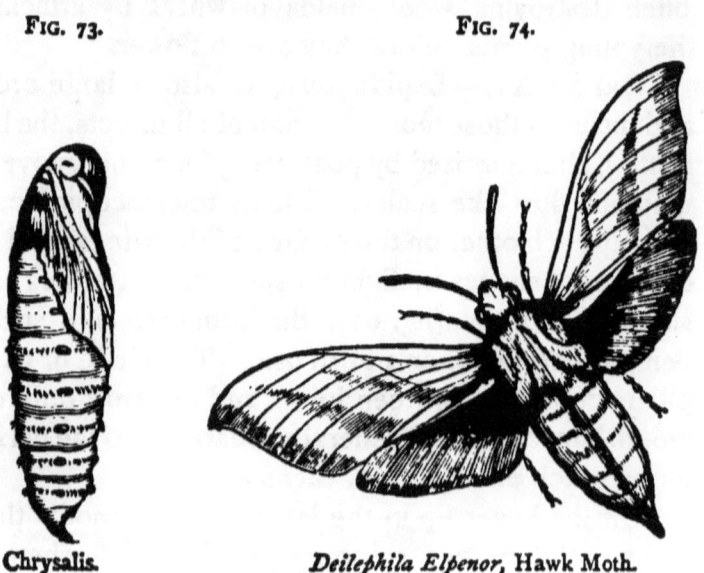

Fig. 73. Chrysalis.

Fig. 74. *Deilephila Elpenor*, Hawk Moth.

pillars are often found, with their heads and fore parts raised, are known by their prismatic antennæ and by the long horn on the tail end of the caterpillar. One of these, the tomato or tobacco sphinx moth (whose large green larva feeds on leaves of those plants) bears on each side of its abdomen five large yellow patches.

While nearly all moths are nocturnal, the true butterflies, recognised by their brighter colours and their club-shaped antennæ, are diurnal in their habits.

The best known examples are the white cabbage butterfly, the nettle tortoiseshell, and the thistle painted

Beetles.

lady butterflies. The larvæ of the true butterflies do not spin a cocoon.

ORDER XII. **Coleoptera.**—Beetles form numerically the largest sub-division of the animal kingdom, there being over seventy thousand species. In these the fore wings are converted into a hard thick pair of wing-covers or *elytræ* overlapping the hinder pair, which are membranous, folded, and usually capable of flight. Beetles are found in almost every condition and feed on almost every kind of material; cayenne pepper, cantharides, medicinal rhubarb, animal effete matter, putrid flesh and decaying vegetables are the favourite nourishment of some forms.

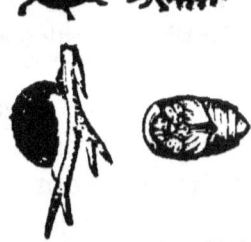

FIG. 75.

Coccinella, or Ladybird perfect insect, larva, and pupa.

There are forty-eight families included in this 'polymorphic' order; one of these contains the little ladybird or *Coccinella*, whose spotted bodies are often seen on nettles in pursuit of the aphides on which they feed. It has only three large joints in the tarsus of each foot. The destructive Colorado or potato beetle (*Doryphora*) somewhat resembles the ladybird but is ten-striped and not spotted. Many beetles are extremely destructive to vegetation, both in their larval and perfect states, the strong mandibulate mouths being able to cut even hard woods. Of these, the turnip-fly, the wire-worm (which is the larva of the beetle called *Agriotes*), the pine-beetle, the typographic beetle, Scolytus the elm-beetle, Lymexylon the oak-beetle, are illustrations.

Other beetles are found in articles of food, such as *Tenebrio*, the meal-worm often found in ships' biscuits, *Dermestes*, or the bacon grub; others are the pests of museums, like the little *Anthrenus* or *Ptinus* the herbarium beetle, and *Ptilinus*, the bookworm.

Fig. 76.
The blistering beetle (*Cantharis vesicatoria*).

A few are temporary parasites; thus the larva of Rhipidius lives in the abdomen of the cockroach. Some beetles are luminous, such as the glowworm and the firefly.

Some beetles emit an ammoniacal smell when irritated; others, like Meloë, secrete a drop of acrid oil under the same circumstances. This secretion renders the bodies of some of them useful in medicine for blistering purposes; thus the bodies of Cantharis vesicatoria (fig. 76) are the Spanish or blistering flies of commerce. Some species of beetles inhabit caves and are eyeless; others are aquatic and fitted for swimming. The sizes of beetles are also exceedingly variable; some, like the large Hercules beetle, being nearly six inches long, while others are of microscopic dimension. The antennæ are of very variable shapes and sizes, being in some much longer than the body, in others very short and inconspicuous; in some, like the common cockchafer, lamellar, in others stag-horn-shaped, &c.

ORDER XIII.—**Hymenoptera** (membrane-winged) includes bees, wasps and ants, and in these the complexity and intelligence of the class culminates. They are characterised by having four naked membranous

Bees. Wasps.

wings, with few veins, and a mouth with strong mandibles but with suctorial labium and maxillæ. The abdomen is often joined to the thorax by a narrow foot-stalk and the abdominal tip is modified into a sting which consists of two poison glands opening

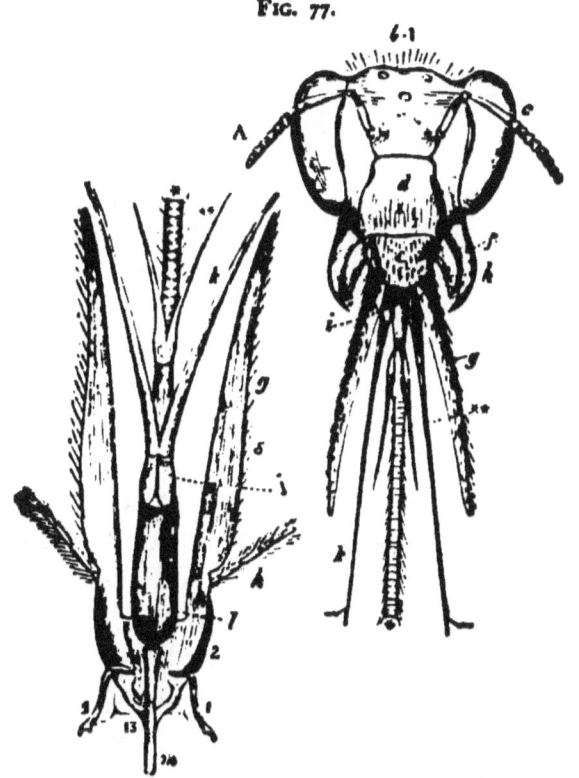

FIG. 77.

1. Mouth of the Bee. *d*, clypeus ; *e*, labrum ; *f*, mandible ; *g*, *h*, maxilla and its palp ; *¹*, lingua ; *¹¹*, paraglossæ. 2. Tongue, more highly magnified.

into a common vesicle whose duct is elongated into a tube provided with a piercer barbed at the point.

In bees the wings are not folded and the basal joint of the hindermost tarsus is flattened and often bristle-clad to collect the pollen for the food of larvæ;

hereby many of them lay the vegetable kingdom under great obligation, as they convey the pollen from flower to flower and thereby fertilise the seeds of many plants. Many bees secrete wax by means of a wax gland placed in the abdomen, and with this material they build their hexagonal cells for the shelter of their eggs and larvæ.

The common humble bee makes a nest of moss; others use clay or wood; and some, like cuckoos, lay their eggs in the nests of other species.

In the hives of the common honey bee the inhabitants are of three kinds, the queen or perfect female, the drones or males, and the workers or imperfect females.

Wasps have no special organ for the collection of the pollen, and have their wings longitudinally folded; they also have a more slender petiole or stalk joining the abdomen and thorax. Many of these also live in colonies, making nests of paper formed of vegetable matter chewed by their jaws into a pulp and moulded into hexagonal cells with rounded bases. Other examples are the saw-flies which have a saw-like organ for the deposition of their eggs, and the Ichneumons, which have the singular instinct of laying their eggs in the bodies of the larvæ of other insects, so that the young are hatched in the midst of abundant food, for they feast upon the tissues of their host and barely leave him enough of organ to prolong existence until they are ready for emergence.

Other Hymenopterous insects lay their eggs under the cuticle of plants; and thereby form small tumours or galls. One such species infests the oak and produces the nut-galls so important in the manufacture of ink. Another species attacks the rose, and a singular gall-fly has a cuckoo-like habit of laying its eggs in the galls formed by other insects.

The ants are probably the most intelligent of insects, having the most complex social organisation and possessing the most complex nervous system in proportion to their size of any invertebrate. The males and females are winged, the workers are wingless, and their sting gland secretes formic acid, the material whereby they irritate or sting. No group of animals are better worthy of study, and their house-building and polity, slave-holding, aphis-cow-keeping, and other habits have long been favourite subjects of observation with entomologists.

The ants form a fitting termination to the Invertebrata, as in intelligence and in interest they may be looked on as bearing to the other invertebrates something of the relation which man has to his neighbouring vertebrates.

Recapitulation.—The sub-divisions of insects are by some looked upon as deserving of a higher than ordinal rank, but as the nature of a group depends on the nature of the range of organic structure in the forms comprehended therein, and not on the number of included individuals, we cannot but see that, in each order of insects, the component species are constructed so much on one type as to forbid us from making of them more than ordinal groups.

The orders of insects which we have briefly noticed may be summarised as follows :

A. Insects with imperfect or no metamorphoses.

  a. With suctorial mouths, wings absent, or when present having the fore pair thickened. Order Rhynchota.
  Wings four equal, membranous. Order Thysanoptera.
  b. With masticatory mouths, abdomen with a terminal appendix of bristles or a bifid tail. No wings. Order Thysanura.
  Abdomen with a terminal two-bladed forceps. Order Euplexoptera.
  Abdomen with no appendages, wings with reticulated costæ. Order Orthoptera.
B. Insects which pass through a quiescent pupa stage.
  a. Mouth masticatory, wings membranous, equal. Order Neuroptera.
  Wings hair-clad or scaly, unequal. Order Trichoptera.
  Fore-wings converted into hard wing-covers. Order Coleoptera.
  b. Mouth suctorial, with rudimental wings and compressed bodies. Order Aphaniptera.
  With two wings. Order Diptera.
  With four wings, the anterior short, twisted. Order Strepsiptera.
  Wings large and scale-covered. Order Lepidoptera.
  Wings naked, membranous, few-veined. Order Hymenoptera.

INDEX AND GLOSSARY.

ABD

ABDOMEN, the group of segments of the body which contains the digestive organs.
Aboral, the extremity opposite to the mouth.
Acamarchis, a moss-polype, 75
Acanthocephala, 66
Acarus, a mite, 109
Acephala, headless molluscs, 95
Acineta, 27
Actinia, a sea anemone, 42
Adaptive characters, 10
Adductor muscles, 83
Agrites 131
Alcyonaria, 46
Alcyonium, 46
Alternation of generations, 40
Ambulacra, the tube-feet on which sea-urchins move, 49
Amœba, 22
Amœbiform, composed of protoplasm like amœbæ.
Amphipoda, 103
Analogy, similarity in function, 12
Anelasma, a barnacle which lives on living fishes, 106
Anemone, sea, 42
Animalcule, a minute animal,
Anomura, 107
Antennæ, jointed feelers, as in insects.
Antennules, 99
Anthrenus, 132
Ant-lion, 127
Ants, 127, 135
Aphaniptera, fleas, 128
Aphides, 123
Arachnoidea, 98, 108

CAL

Arenicola, the lug bait, 71
Arthropoda, 14, 96
Ascaris, round worms, 65
Assimilation, the process whereby food is converted into blood.
Auricles, 94

BACTERIUM, the walking-stick insect, also the most minute protoplasmic particles, 125
Balani, acorn shells, 106
Barnacles, 106
Bees, 134
Beetles, 131
Bilateral symmetry, equality and proportion of the two corresponding sides of an animal.
Bivalves, 80
Blood, 2
Borlasia, a large sea worm, 60
Brachiopoda, 80
Brachyura, 108
Branchiæ, gills.
Branchiopoda, 104
Breathing, the process whereby oxygen is taken in to aerate the blood.
Bryozoa, 74
Bugs, 123
Butterflies, 129
Byssus, a fibrous material whereby mussels and other molluscs anchor themselves, 84

CADDIS FLIES, 127
Calcareous, consisting of lime.

Calcified, being impregnated with salts of lime
Cantharis, 132
Capsule, 24
Cardo, part of the mouth of an insect, 117
Carnivorous, flesh-eating.
Caryophylla, 44
Caterpillar, 121
Cells, 2
Centipedes, 112
Cephalophora, 85
Cephalopoda, 90
Cephalothorax, 100
Chætopoda, bristle-footed worms, 90
Chalk, 21
Chamber, atrial, 76
Chelæ, the pincers or first pair of abdominal feet of a crab or lobster, 100
Cheleceræ, the pincers or mandibular palps of a scorpion, 103
Chelifer, 112
Chitin, a hard material which forms the outer layer of insects, 96
Chiton, a multivalve shell, 89
Chrysalis, 122
Chrysaora, 39
Cilia, minute vibratile hairs made of protoplasm, 3
Cirripedia, barnacles and acorn shells, 106
Classification, 10
Cliona, a boring sponge, 31
Cloaca, the excretory chamber of animals, 56
Clypeus, 117
Cnidæ, the thread cells or stinging cells of jellyfishes, 33
Coccinella, the ladybird, 131
Cochineal insect, 124
Cockle, 85
Cockroaches, 125
Cocoon, 121
Cœlenterata, 14, 32
Cœnosarc, 35, 45
Coleoptera, 131
Colonies, clusters of animals united on a common stalk.
Colorado beetle, 131
Colpoda, 28
Commensals, 17
Contractile vesicle, 26
Copepoda, 107
Corals, 44
Cornea, 108
Coronula, 106

Costæ, 119
Cotylidea, 60
Coxa, 119
Crayfish, 98
Crinoidea, 49
Crustacea, 97, 98
Ctenophora, 41
Cucumaria, 56
Cuttlefishes, 90
Cyclops, 104
Cyst, a membranous sac.
Cystic, possessing a sac-like membranous envelope.

DADDY-LONG-LEGS, 129

Daphnia, 103
Decapoda, 107
Deilephila, 130
Dentalium, 86, 88
Dermestes, 132
Differentiation, the setting apart of separate tissues for different purposes.
Diptera, 128
Distoma, 63
Distribution, 15
Dorsal, 71
Doryphora, 132
Dragonflies, 115, 126

EARWIG, 124
Echinocardium, 55
Echinodermata, 14, 47
Echinoidea, 53
Echinus, 53
Ectoderm, 32t
Edriophthalmia, an order of crustaceans, 108
Elater, the glow-worm, 120
Embryo, the immature condition of an animal, as developing from the egg, 8
Encrinites, 49
Encystation, the condition of being enclosed in a cyst or enveloping layer, 23
Endoderm, the inner layer of jellyfishes, sea anemones, &c., 32
Endoskeleton, an internal firm framework of bones or gristles for the support of the organism, 96
Epeira, the garden or geometrical spider, 111
Epicranium, part of an insect's head, 117

Index and Glossary.

EUP

Euplectella, a sponge called Venus, flower-basket, 31
Euplexoptera, an order of insects, including earwigs, 124
Euplotes, a minute animalcule, 28
Exoskeleton, an external firm framework for the purpose of protection or support, 96

FAMILY, a group of genera, 11
Fauna, the collective name for all the animals of a country, 15
Feather stars, 50
Femur, the thigh bone in vertebrates, or the third joint of an insect's leg, 119
Fission, the process of multiplication in animals by splitting, 5
Flagellata, a group of microscopic animals, 28
Flagellum, a minute vibratile hair-like filament which is the chief organ of locomotion of the Flagellata.
Fleas, 128
Flies, 128
Flukes, parasitic worms, 63
Food, 1.
Foraminifera, a group of microscopic shells, 19
Function, the office performed by any organ or part of the body, 3
Fungia, a mushroom-like coral, 46

GALATHEA, a genus of bivalve shells, 83
Galea, part of an insect's head, 117 (fig.)
Gall-flies, the flies which produce nut-galls on oaks, &c.
Gallyworms, 112
Ganglion, a swelling on a nerve which acts as a centre for the evolution of nerve-force.
Gasteropoda, a class of molluscs, 89
Gemmation, multiplication by the production of buds, 5
Genus, a group of closely allied species united under a common name, 11
Gephyrea, a group of marine worms, 67
Gills, vascular organs which are fitted for aerating the blood which

KOI

they contain, by means of the air dissolved in the water which bathes them.
Gizzard, a stomach with thick muscular walls.
Globigerina, a minute shell, 18
Gordiaceæ, threadworms, 68
Gorgonia, a horny coral, 46
Grantia, a sponge, 32
Gregarinæ, microscopic parasites, 22

HAIRY-BAIT, 71
Halichondria, a sponge, 32
Heliophrys, 22
Heliozoa, minute animals found in bog pools, 22
Hessian fly, 129
Hinges of shells, 83
Hirudinea, leeches, 68
Holothuroidea, sea cucumbers, 56
Host, an animal inhabited by a parasite.
Hyalonema, a sponge, 31
Hydra, a minute fresh water polype, 32
Hydroida, animals like the hydra, 34
Hymenoptera, an order of insects, including ants and bees, 132

ICHNEUMON, a group of flies, 134
Imago, the perfect or adult state of an insect, 122
Infusoria, animals found in stagnant waters, 25
Insecta, 98
Integument, the skin of an animal.
Iridescent, producing a play of colours by decomposing incident rays of light
Isis, a genus of corals, 46
Isopoda, an order of crustaceans, including woodlice and their allies, 103

JELLY-FISHES, 3

KOINOSITES, animals which live on, and feed with, their hosts, 17

140   *Index and Glossary.*

LAB

LABIUM, the lower lip of an insect's mouth, 116
Labrum, the upper lip of an insect's mouth, 116
Lac insect, 124
Lacunæ, interspaces between tissues.
Ladybird, 131
Lamellibranchs, bivalve molluscs, such as the oyster, 81
Lampyris, the firefly, 120
Larva, the first active stage of an animal while as yet immature, 121
Leaf-roller moths, 129
Leeches, 68
Lepidoptera, 129
Life, 1
Ligament, a fibrous band uniting two parts.
Ligula, part of the so-called tongue of an insect, 117
Limulus, the king crab, 103
Lingula, the duck-bill shell, 81
Lithobius, the common centipede, 113
Locusts, 125
Lug-bait, 71
Lymexylon, a wood-boring beetle, 131

MACRURA, lobsters, 107
Madrepores, reef-building corals, 45
Madreporiform plate, a rough plate on the surface of star-fishes, 52
Magosphæra, 21
Malacobdella, a leech, 69
Malpighian glands, glands in insects, named after their first describer, Malpighi, 120
Mandibles, the second pair of jaws in insects, 100
Mantle, the leathery outer layer in molluscs, 14, 79
Mason spiders, 111
Maxilla, 100
Meandrina, brain coral, 46
Medusa, a jelly-fish, 40
Medusoids, detached portions of hydroids which resemble medusæ, 35
Meloë, 132
Mentum, part of an insect's mouth, 118
Mermis, 66

ORT

Mesenteries, folds of membrane suspending the digestive sac, 43
Metamorphoses, changes undergone by an animal in its development from its larval to its perfect state.
Metazoa, animals with an internal cavity, 28
Millepedes, 114
Mimicry in animals, 12
Mites, 109
Mollusca, 14, 78
Monads, small flagellate animals, 28
Monera, the simplest known animals, 21
Monocystis, a gregarine, 23
Morphology, the science which treats of the forms of animal organisms, 7
Moss polypes, 74
Moths, 130
Muscles, 4
Mussels, 85
Myriopoda, 98, 112

NAUPLIUS, the larval stage of crustaceans, 104
Nautilus, the most complex of molluscs, 92
Nematelmia, 64
Nemerteans, marine worms, 60
Nerve, 4
Neuromuscular cells, 33
Neuroptera, an order of insects, 127
Noctiluca, a luminous marine animalcule, 27
Nucleolus, 26
Nucleus, 21
Nutrition, 4

OCULAR plates, plates bearing eyes, 54
Oculina, a coral, 45
Œsophagus, the tube which conveys food to the stomach, 65
Oikosites, parasites which live with, but do not feed on, their host, 120
Operculum, the lid which closes the mouth of an univalve shell, 87
Ophiolepis, a star-fish, 51
Ophiuroidea, star-fishes, 75
Ophrydium, 27
Optic nerve, the nerve which connects the eye and the brain, 99
Organism, an animal made up of separate organs or parts, 13
Orthoptera, an order of insects, 125

Index and Glossary. 141

Osculum, the mouths in sponges, 30
Ostracoda, minute crustaceans, 107
Ovipositor, the organ whereby insects deposit their eggs, 121
Ovulation, the mode of reproduction by the development of eggs, 5
Oxytricha, 25
Oxyuris, a worm, 63
Oyster, 85

PALÆOZOIC, the age of the world in which the oldest fossil-bearing rocks were formed,
Pallial line, the line on a shell indicating the margin of the mantle, 83
Palp, a feeler or jointed appendage on the jaw of an arthropod.
Paraglossæ, part of an insect's mouth, 117, 133
Paramœcium, a common infusory animalcule, 26
Parasites, 17
Pauropods, 114
Pedicellariæ, jointed pincer-like appendages to the mouth in Echinodermata, 51
Pedicelli, small sucking feet in starfishes, 49
Pennatula, a sea-pen, 46
Pennella, a parasitic crustacean, 105
Pentastoma, a parasitic mite, 10
Pericardium, the space of the body cavity around the heart,
Periplaneta, the cockroach, 125
Pharynx, the upper part of the digestive tube near the mouth.
Physalia, 37
Physiology, the science which treats of the functions of organs, 7
Pixinia, a gregarine, 23
Planula, the ciliated embryo of a jelly-fish, 33
Pluteus, the larval stage of a starfish, 51
Podophthalmia, crabs, &c., whose eyes are on stalks, 107
Poduræ, 124
Pœcilopoda, king-crabs, 103
Polycelis, a turbellarian worm, 59
Polypites, hydra-like animals when in colonies, 35
Polystomata, 28

Pores, the fine openings in sponges, 30
Postabdomen, that part of the abdomen behind the openings of the reproductive organs, 101
Proglottis, one of the mature joints of a tape-worm, 61
Protamœba, one of the simplest known animals, 21
Protoplasm, 2
Protoplasta, amœbæ, 22
Protozoa, 14, 18
Provisional organs, those organs that fulfil a temporary function, and then disappear or waste, 8
Pseudonavicellæ, 23
Pseudopodia, 3, 19
Pteropoda, 89
Ptinus, 132
Pupa, the quiescent stage in the life of a butterfly before the perfect imago condition is reached, 121
Pyrosoma, a luminous marine mollusc, 77

RADIOLARIA, 24
Raphiophora, Neptune's Cup, a sponge, 31
Reproduction, 5
Rhizopods, 18
Rhizostoma, a jelly-fish, 39
Rhynchota, an order of insects, including bugs, 123
Rotatoria, wheel animalcules, 66
Rotifer, a common wheel animalcule, 67
Rudimental organ, an imperfect, functionless structure, 9

SALPA, a pelagic mollusc, 77
Sandhoppers, small crustaceans, 105
Scallops, 84
Scaphopoda an order of molluscs, 95
Scolopendra a centipede, 114
Scolytus, a wood-boring insect, 131
Scorpion-flies, 127
Scorpions, 112
Sea-cucumbers, 56
Sea-glue, 25
Sea-urchins, 47, 53
Segment, one of the successional

Index and Glossary.

SEG

morphological units of the body of a jointed animal, 13
Segmental organs, excretory tubes in the segments of worms, 58
Serpula, 72
Sertularia, 34
Shell, 90
Silica, flint.
Silkworms, 130
Siphon, 84
Siphonophora, 38
Siphuncle, 90
Snail, 87
Solen, the razor-shell, 84
Specialisation, setting apart of an organ for a special function, and for it alone, 13
Species, a group of identical individuals under a common name, 11
Spicules, siliceous or calcareous masses embedded in animal tissues, 31
Spiders, 110
Spinnerets, 111
Spirorbis, 72
Sponges, 29
Spongilla, a freshwater sponge, 31
Spoon-worms, 67
Star-fishes, 7, 47
Stellerida, 50
Stipes, part of an insect's head, 117
Stock, the common stem of a colony.
Strepsiptera, a small order of insects, 127
Strongylocentrotus, a common sea-urchin, 32 (fig.)
Symmetry, 8

TÆNIA, the tapeworm, 60
Tarsus, the last joints of an insect's leg, 115
Teeth of sea urchin, 54
Tegenaria, the house spider, 111
Telson, the middle flap of a lobster's tail, 101
Tenebrio, the meal-worm, 132
Tentacles, feelers, 32, 33
Terebratula, 80
Termites, 126
Test, a shell or exoskeleton,
Thalassicolla, sea-glue, a group of marine protozoa, 25
Thorax, the chest, or the region of the body of an insect which bears the legs, 116

VOR

Thread-cells, stinging cells of jelly-fishes, 33
Thrips, 125
Thysanoptera, an order of insects, 125
Thysanura, 124
Tibia, part of an insect's leg, 115
Ticks, 110
Tracheæ, air-tubes for breathing, 109, 113
Tracheal lungs, groups of tracheæ compressed together, 110
Trematoda, an order of parasitic worms, 63
Trepang, an edible sea-cucumber, 56
Trichina, a parasitic worm, 65
Trichocephalus, 65
Trichoptera, an order of insects, 127
Trilobites, 104
Trochal disks, the ciliated lobes on the heads of some minute worms, 79
Trochanter, the second joint in the leg of an insect, 119
Troctes, the death-tick insect, 125
Tubipora, the organ-pipe coral, 46
Tunicates, 75
Tunic, 75
Turbellaria, 59
Types, 11

UNDIFFERENTIATED, not separated into specialised parts.

VACUOLES, clear spaces in masses of protoplasm, 20
Valves of shells, 80
Ventral, the under side of the body.
Ventricle, the cavity of the heart which by its contraction drives on the blood in the circulation, 94
Venus' Flower Basket, a sponge, 31
Vermes, worms, 14, 57
Vertebrata, 14
Viscera, the digestive and other internal organs of the body of an animal.
Vorticella, 25, 27

WAS

WASPS, 134
Water-boatmen, 127
Water-fleas, 103
Water-scorpions, 124
Wax-glands, 134
Whelk, 87
White ants, 126

ZOE

Wire worms, 131
Woodlice, 103

ZOEA, the larval stage of the common crab, 102

HANDBOOKS for Students and General Readers.

ZOOLOGY

OF THE

VERTEBRATE ANIMALS

BY

ALEX. MACALISTER, M.D.

*Professor of Zoology and Comparative Anatomy in the
University of Dublin.*

Specially Revised for American Students

BY

A. S. PACKARD, JR., M.D.

*Professor of Natural History in
Brown University*

NEW YORK
HENRY HOLT AND COMPANY
1878

COPYRIGHT, 1878,
BY
HENRY HOLT & CO.

PRINTED BY TROW'S PRINTING AND BOOKBINDING CO., NEW YORK.

EXPLANATORY.

THIS Series is intended to meet the requirement of brief text-books both for schools and for adult readers who wish to review or expand their knowledge.

The grade of the books is intermediate between the so-called "primers" and the larger works professing to present quite detailed views of the respective subjects.

Such a notion as a person beyond childhood requires of some subjects, it is difficult and perhaps impossible to convey in one such volume. Therefore, occasionally a volume is given to each of the main departments into which a subject naturally falls—for instance, a volume to the Zoölogy of the vertebrates, and one to that of the invertebrates. While this arrangement supplies a compendious treatment for those who wish, it will also sometimes enable the reader interested in only a portion of the field covered by a science, to study the part he is interested in, without getting a book covering the whole.

Care is taken to bring out whatever educational value may be extracted from each subject without impeding the exposition of it. In the books on the sciences, not only are acquired results stated, but as full explanation as possible is given of the methods of inquiry and reasoning by which these results have been obtained. Consequently, although the treatment of each subject is strictly elementary, the fundamental facts are stated and discussed with the fulness needed to place their scientific significance in a clear light, and to show the relation in which they stand to the general conclusions of science.

Care is also taken that each book admitted to the series shall either be the work of a recognized authority, or bear the unqualified approval of such. As far as practicable, authors are selected who combine knowledge of their subjects with experience in teaching them.

PREFACE

IT has been the Author's design in this volume to present in as simple a form as possible the leading characters of Vertebrate Animals. All unnecessary technicalities have been dispensed with, and explanations have been given, either in the text or in the glossary, of such terms as have been unavoidably used.

In a practical science such as Zoölogy, it is only by the examination of specimens that any knowledge of the science worth acquiring can be obtained, and the function of a book is to assist in practical study. This has been borne in mind in compiling these pages. Great care has, moreover, been taken to select only such facts for discussion as are of fundamental importance. As types of the different classes of vertebrated animals are easily obtainable, the pupil is recommended to verify these facts for himself.

ALEXANDER MACALISTER.

ANATOMICAL MUSEUM,
    UNIVERSITY OF DUBLIN,
        Oct. 2, 1877.

CONTENTS.

CHAPTER I.
CHARACTERS OF VERTEBRATE ANIMALS. ACRANIA.

PAGE

The Vertebrate Body—Notochord—Skeleton—Amphioxus . 1

CHAPTER II.
CRANIOTA.

The Brain and Skull—Visceral Arches—Limbs—Ribs—Liver—Heart—Segmentation 6

CHAPTER III.
CLASS I. PISCES (FISHES).

General Characters—Scales—Fins—Lateral Line—Skeleton—Brain—Gills and Breathing—Swimming Bladder—Eggs . 11

CHAPTER IV.
ORDER 1. LAMPREYS. ORDER 2. SHARKS.

Lampreys or Marsipobranchs—Selachia or Sharks—Placoid Scales—Egg Capsules—Sawfishes—Skates . . . 22

Contents.

CHAPTER V.

ORDER 3. GANOID FISHES. ORDER 4. BONY FISHES. ORDER 5. DIPNOI.

Ganoids — Scales — Isinglass — Teleostei — Sub-order, Physostomi — Sub-order, Anacanthini — Sub-order, Acanthopteri — Sub-order, Pharyngognathi — Sub-order, Lophobranchii — Sub-order, Plectognathi — Dipnoi . . . 26

CHAPTER VI.

CLASS 2. AMPHIBIA.

General Characters—Respiration—Skeleton 34

CHAPTER VII.

CLASSIFICATION OF AMPHIBIA.

Order 1, Gymnophiona—Labyrinthodonts—Order 2, Urodela—Caducous and Perennial Gills—Order 3, Anura . . 37

CHAPTER VIII.

CLASS 3. REPTILES.

General Characters 40

CHAPTER IX.

LIZARDS AND SNAKES.

Order 1, Lacertilia—Chamæleons—Order 2, Ophidia or Snakes —Venomous Snakes and their Poison-Apparatus . . 42

CHAPTER X.

TORTOISES AND CROCODILES.

Order 3, Chelonia or Tortoises—Order 4, Crocodilia . . 49

Contents.

CHAPTER XI.

CLASS 4. AVES (BIRDS).

General Characters—Feathers and Feather Tracts—Skeleton—Muscles—Digestive Organs—Heart and Lungs—Eye—Eggs 52

CHAPTER XII.

CLASSIFICATION OF BIRDS.

Sub-class 1, Ratidæ—Sub-class 2, Carinatæ—Order 1, Psittaci or Parrots—Order 2, Coccygomorphæ or Cuckoos—Order 3, Pici or Woodpeckers—Order 4, Macrochires or Swifts and Humming-Birds—Order 5, Passeres or Perching Birds—Order 6, Raptores or Birds of Prey 62

CHAPTER XIII.

CLASSIFICATION OF BIRDS (*continued*).

Order 7, Gyrantes or Pigeons—Order 8, Rasores or Scraping Birds—Order 9, Grallæ or Snipes and Cranes—Order 10, Ciconiæ or Storks—Order 11, Lamellirostres or Ducks and Geese—Order 12, Longipennes or Gulls—Order 13, Steganopodes or Pelicans—Order 14, Pygopodes or Penguins and Auks 69

CHAPTER XIV.

CLASS 5. MAMMALIA.

General Characters—Laws—Skeleton—Teeth—Dental Formulæ 74

CHAPTER XV.

CLASSIFICATION OF MAMMALS.

Order 1, Monotremata—Order 2, Marsupialia or Kangaroos . 79

CHAPTER XVI.

PLACENTAL MAMMALS.

General Characters—Order 3, Edentata or Ant-eaters and Armadillos—Order 4, Bradypoda or Sloths—Order 5, Sirenia or Manatees—Order 6, Ungulata or Hoofed Animals — Unsymmetrically-toed Ungulates — Even-toed Ungulates—Bunodonts—Ruminants. 85

CHAPTER XVII.

PLACENTAL MAMMALS (*continued*).

Order 7, Cetacea or Whales—Order 8, Pinnipedia or Seals—Order 9, Carnivora or Flesh-Eaters—Dogs—Cats—Bears—Order 10, Hyracoidea—Order 11, Rodentia—Order 12, Proboscidea or Elephants 99

CHAPTER XVIII.

Order 13, Prosimii or Lemurs—Order 14, Insectivora, Moles, Hedgehogs, etc.—Order 15, Chiroptera or Bats . . 113

CHAPTER XIX.

Order 16, Primates—Marmosets—American Monkeys—Old-World Monkeys—Man—Races of Man 118

INDEX and GLOSSARY 125

VERTEBRATA.

CHAPTER I.

CHARACTERS OF VERTEBRATE ANIMALS. ACRANIA.

1. **Introductory.**—The animals which make up the sub-kingdom Vertebrata are the fishes, reptiles, birds, and quadrupeds; and as they present to us a greater number of interesting points in structure, function, and habits than all the other sub-kingdoms put together, and as they are for the most part of large size and of complex organisation, they require a more careful and detailed study than do the animals which make up the other sub-kingdoms. On this account, Vertebrata, though in reality constituting only a subdivision equivalent to any of the other sub-kingdoms, such as Mollusca, Polystomata, or Vermes, are yet often treated, and naturally so, as if they equalled all the other sub-kingdoms collectively.

2. **General characters of vertebrate animals.**—Every vertebrate animal possesses in the centre of its body an axis or rod of cartilage, which forms a

skeleton or support; below [1] is a longitudinal body-cavity, containing the organs of digestion, circulation, respiration, &c.; above is a second, smaller, longitudinal cavity or canal, in which lie the brain and spinal marrow, the central organs of the nervous system; these send out laterally along their whole extent numerous pairs of nerve-cords to supply the different parts of the body. Thus on cross-section the body of a vertebrate animal appears like two tubes, the smaller being above the larger, and the cartilaginous axis appears in the middle of the horizontal partition which divides them from each other.

In the young conditions of the tunicated worms there is an approach to this arrangement, but in these the gristly rod does not extend sufficiently far forward to separate the *neural* (or nervous system-holding) and *visceral cavities*.

To the central axis of cartilage the name *notochord* is given, and it is enveloped in a sheath of several layers. In the majority of vertebrates the notochord is present only as a temporary and transitory structure, for, in the process of growth, parts of its sheath enlarge and encroach on the axis itself, so as to obliterate it eventually in whole or in part. These enlargements begin in the form of a succession of paired lateral thickenings along the whole length of the sheath, which extend above and below the notochord, and become converted into rings around it, and ultimately by extension inwards they become discs.

[1] The animal is supposed to be placed with its length horizontal and its mouth forwards.

General Characters of Vertebrates. 3

The chain of these rings or disks, around or replacing the notochord, which forms the axis in the adult stage of all but the lowest of the vertebrates, is called the *vertebral column*, and each disk, with the parts immediately joined to it, is called a *vertebra* (fig. 2).

Each vertebra has attached to it behind a ring or arch (made up of two lateral projections or *processes*) which surrounds the spinal marrow, and forms the wall of the *neural cavity*. This arch is called the *neural arch*.

The mouth opens at the foremost end of the body in all vertebrates, and communicates internally with a cavity called the *pharynx*, on whose walls, directly or indirectly, the blood-vessels are arranged for the purposes of respiration. This part of the digestive canal [1] is pierced by slits at some period in the life of each vertebrate.

Below the pharynx is a narrow part of the digestive canal, called the *œsophagus*, which passes between the spinal column above and the heart below, and leads into the stomach, from whence the intestinal canal is continued, to open at the posterior end of the body; directly below the stomach the duct of the liver opens in all vertebrates, and this organ is peculiar in this sub-kingdom, in that the vein which conveys the impure blood back from the digestive organs enters this gland and breaks up within it into a network of fine vessels, which, reuniting, pass back from hence to the heart. The vessel which thus

---

[1] The digestive or alimentary canal is a tube traversing the whole length of the body, in which the food is digested, and its nourishing part taken into the blood.

Vertebrata.

conveys the blood from the alimentary canal to the liver is called the *vena portæ*.

3. **Primary divisions of vertebrates** (*headless form*).—There are two primary divisions of vertebrate animals; the first of these includes only one form, and that the smallest and simplest in the sub-kingdom, remarkable principally for its extremely simple organisation. This little creature is named the lancelet, or technically the *Amphioxus lanceolatus*, and is so called on account of its lancet-like shape, and from its being pointed at both ends. It is a small, flattened, fish-like animal, about an inch and a half long, about a quarter of an inch in depth and an eighth in thickness, found in sandbanks in our own seas. It has been taken in abundance off the coasts of North Carolina and Florida, off the S.W. coast of Ireland, in the Mediterranean, and in the Indian and Pacific Oceans.

This animal has no head, and the notochord stretches from the front to the hinder point; the neural canal and its enclosed spinal marrow likewise extend for the whole length. The mouth is a longitudinal slit, bordered with stiff, bristle-like filaments;

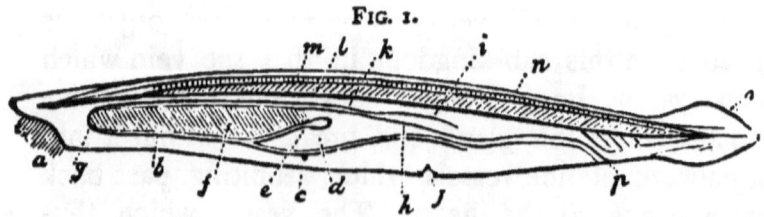

FIG. 1.

Diagram of *Amphioxus*.
a, mouth; *b*, *f*, *g*, respiratory region; *c*, body cavity; *d*, liver; *e*, heart; *h–p*, digestive canal; *l*, notochord; *m*, spinal marrow.

and the pharynx has many lateral slits in its wall,

through which the water which enters the mouth escapes into the space between the wall of the body and that of the pharynx. To this space the name 'atrium' is given, and it opens externally by a median pore or outlet placed on the under edge, and in front of the end of the intestine (fig. 1, *j*).

The liver is a simple sac, and the heart is a single dilated tube (*e*), like that of some worms; it sends branches backwards to the pharyngeal wall, one along each slit, and these join dorsally below the notochord, making a dorsal aorta or large blood-vessel, which gives off branches to the different parts of the body.

Though there is no brain, yet two of the foremost of the many nerves emitted from the spinal marrow supply structures which may be regarded as rudimentary sense-organs. Thus there is in the middle of the foremost end of the animal a small pit, possibly an organ of smell, and two or more lateral pigment-spots in front of and above the mouth, which may be organs of sight. There is a narrow membranous fringe or fin around the tail, but there are no limbs, and the blood is colourless.

The division of Vertebrata which contains this singularly aberrant form is named *Acrania* (headless), to distinguish it from that which includes the entire remaining series, which is called *Craniota* (head-bearing).

CHAPTER II.

CRANIOTA.

4. General characters of head-bearing vertebrates.
The head-bearing vertebrates are characterised by
the enlargement of the anterior end of the central
axis of the nervous system into a series of swellings
which collectively make up the *brain*. To contain
this brain the fore part of the neural canal is enormously dilated, and its walls are converted into a
gristly, membranous, or bony case, called the skull,
and in this part of the body the organs of sense are
chiefly seated. The brain in its simplest form consists of three thick-walled cavities in a series from
before backwards, the walls of the three being named
respectively the fore, mid, and hind brain. The rest
of the neural canal behind the skull remains as a
narrow tube enclosed in the canal, which is bounded
by the neural arches of the vertebræ. In the sides
of the wall of the cranial or skull cavity the organs of
the special senses are placed in a series from before
backwards; foremost of them is the organ of smell;
secondly, that of sight; thirdly, that of hearing. Each
of these organs consists primarily of a pouch of skin
bulging towards the inside of the body, and receiving
a nerve from the brain. Passing out from the brain
there are also other nerves, which are distributed to the
parts of the foremost end of the body. Around these
organs and nerves the cartilage which forms the primitive skull becomes disposed so as to protect them; and

when, as is often the case, the cartilage becomes converted into bone, the several pieces of which the osseous skull consists are so grouped around these nerves and sense organs that the bony cranium appears as if its bones were arranged in a succession of segments. These have been mistaken for true vertebral divisions, but are really due to a secondary grouping of parts in the course of growth, and are not primary morphological elements. Appended to the under or mouth side of the cranium, and to the fore part of the vertebral column, we find a series of lateral arches, which unite below in the medial line, and thus close in the sub-vertebral cavity in front. To these arches the name 'visceral arches,' is given; and very often between these arches there are slits opening inwards; these are called visceral slits. The number of these arches varies in many vertebrates, but there may be as many as ten or twelve. The foremost is in front of the part of the skull which begins at the front end of the notochord (for this structure does not in craniotes extend beyond the region of the mid-brain), and its two elements pass forwards in the middle line to unite in front; to these the name *cornua trabeculæ* is given. The second arch lies behind, below, and a little outside the cornua trabeculæ, and forms part of the deeper or palatine portion of the upper jaw in most vertebrates (or the whole upper jaw in sharks); its lower end forms the lower jaw, or parts thereof. The third or hyoid arch is that bony system on which the tongue is based; and the succeeding ones can be easily distinguished in fishes as the arches of bones which bear the gills, but, except the foremost of this set, the others are rudimental in the higher animals. The visceral slit between the first and second of these arches is the mouth; the other visceral slits remain either as the gill fissures in fishes, or else become closed at an extremely early period of embryonic life. The remnant of the first pair of visceral slits behind the mouth we find in the form of the ear passages in higher vertebrates. These visceral arches never extend backwards behind the heart.

5. **Limbs and ribs.**—Vertebrate animals have never more than four limbs, which are placed two in front and two behind. The fore limbs are usually placed a short way behind the head; the hind limbs at or immediately behind the posterior end of the visceral cavity. Each limb has a bony or gristly axis or skeleton, and this consists of two parts—first, a girdle or half-zone of bone, which is embedded in the lateral muscles, and is often attached to the vertebral column; secondly, a limb ray or projecting part made up of several sets of cartilages in a series. Some vertebrates, like whales and some lizards, have only two fore limbs and no hind limbs; others, like boas and pythons, have rudimentary hind limbs and no fore limbs; others, like most of the snakes, have no limbs at all. These limbs are always turned towards the hæmal or ventral side of the body.

In the wall of the visceral cavity, following the visceral arches, but quite separate from them, there are usually long slender bones, jointed at the back to the vertebral column, and forming supports for the wall of this space. These bones are named ribs, and the part of the body surrounded by them is called the thorax; the region between the thorax and the head is called the neck—a very short space in fishes and whales, long in many birds. The part of the vertebral column which projects behind the visceral cavity is named the caudal or tail region, and in it there are usually V-like bony arches, suspended to the lower surface of the vertebral bodies, within which a caudal blood-vessel is protected.

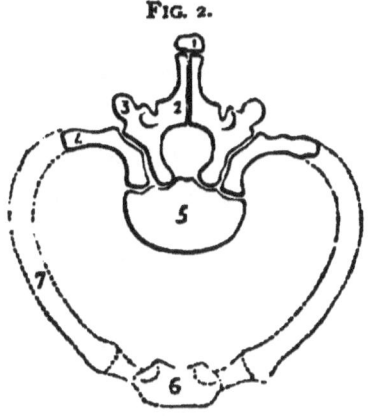

Fig. 2.

Diagram of a vertebra, with its body (5., rib (7), and breast bone (6).

6. Secreting organs.—All vertebrate animals of this division have a solid glandular liver for secreting the bile, an important fluid used in the process of digestion. They have all red blood, the colour depending on the presence of certain minute coloured corpuscles. The circulation of the blood is maintained by a muscular heart, which never possesses fewer than two chambers, one of which is for the collection and reception of the blood from the veins, and is called the *auricle*; the other, which is named the *ventricle*, propels the blood into the large blood-vessels or aortic arches, of which there are usually (in some period of life at least) more than three pairs.

In vertebrates the lining membrane of the mouth (which is named the *mucous membrane*), clothing the upper and lower jaws, and sometimes the similar membrane over other bones, developes processes or papillæ, which become converted into a very hard kind of bones for the purpose of seizing and dividing their food; these are known as teeth. In higher forms these become rooted in the subjacent bones, but in all cases they arise as papillæ of the mucous membrane.

The products of waste (which is constantly taking place) are got rid of by means of certain purifying organs. The skin, by means of its glands, removes some of these effete matters; so do certain areas of the pharynx, richly supplied with blood-vessels from the aortic arches, and which are called the respiratory organs. There are also developed certain glandular tubes in the hinder portion of the visceral cavity, of the same nature, and built on the same plan, as the segmental tubes of worms, which eliminate from the blood the nitrogenised waste products; these organs are called kidneys.

7. **Primary and secondary segments.**—In the body of a vertebrate animal there is to be seen the remains of a primary segmentation into a chain of successional divisions; thus many organs or parts are repeated in a series, such as the vertebræ, the nervous system, the muscle masses (as can be seen in fishes), and the tubes which constitute the kidney. At the same time there is such a tendency to concentration noticeable that this segmental symmetry is only to be seen in the lower forms, or in the embryonic stages of the higher, secondary modes of aggregation of parts masking completely the original systems of segments. For example, while in the embryo the primitive vertebræ can be distinguished clearly from

Cephalization. 11

each other, in the adult what appear to be the vertebral segments are really due to a secondary cleaving occurring in a later stage, after the originally separate primary segments have become fused.

As we ascend in the scale of complexity among vertebrates, we find as a rule that the head becomes more and more highly organised, and that there is a tendency towards the concentration of its elements, and that the fore parts of the body become more and more subservient to it. This reaches its climax in man, where we find the anterior pair of limbs entirely set apart to wait on the head.

There are five classes of vertebrate animals—fishes, amphibians, reptiles, birds, and mammals.

CHAPTER III.

CLASS I, PISCES (FISHES).

8. General characters of fishes.—Fishes constitute the first and simplest class of the head-bearing vertebrates, and, like the simplest forms of all the other sub-kingdoms, they are aquatic in habit, and all their organs are adapted for a watery home. Thus in shape they are for the most part of an elongated flattened outline, pointed in front, tapering behind, so as to afford as little resistance as possible in traversing the water; the fore part of the body, or head, is joined to the trunk directly, without the intervention of a narrow neck, and to the hinder extremity of the vertebral column is appended a flattened tail, which, by moving like a scull or screw-propeller, can drive the body forward. The limbs are also, in fishes, developed into fanlike bars, the fins.

9. **Scales.**—The surface of the body in fishes has only a scanty *epidermis*, or outer layer of skin, which is generally of a mucous or slimy consistence; beneath this is the *dermis*, or inner skin, whose surface consists of numerous thin, flattened scales. These structures, so characteristic of fishes, are composed of bony plates, which are ossifications of flat dermal processes, often containing or bearing little tooth-like points, composed of the same material as true teeth. In some fishes, like sharks, the entire scale consists of this *dentine* or tooth

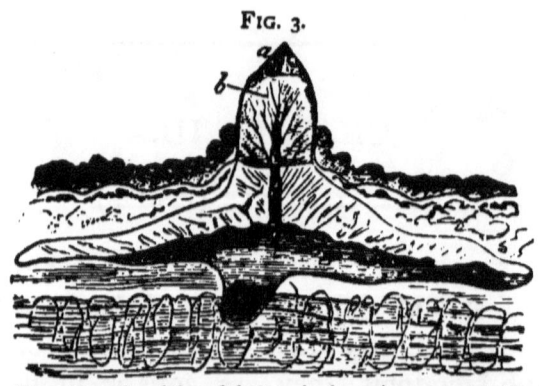

FIG. 3.

Placoid scale of dog-fish (vertical section magnified).
a, enamel layer ; *b*, dentine of spine on scale.

structure (fig. 3) ; in others the bony element, which forms around the tooth, covers or entirely supersedes the dentinal, but in its essential nature the coating of scales or dermal exoskeleton of fishes may be regarded as consisting of or containing ossified papillæ, which in their structure are identical with the tissue of ordi-

Scales and Fins. 13

nary teeth.[1] Many scales are of beautiful forms, and they vary very much in outline and surface, some-

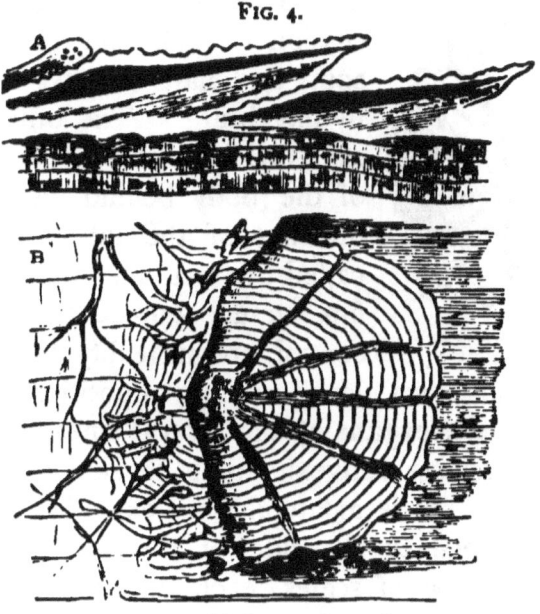

FIG. 4.

Cycloid scale of roach magnified; seen in section A, and on surface B.

times being flat and smooth-edged (fig. 4), or else spinose, ridged, or comblike (fig. 5). These structures can be examined and their varieties observed with the aid of a pocket-lens. The scales of the pike, sole, and perch are especially characteristic forms.

10. **Fins.**—Along the middle line of the body of a fish there are usually developed extensions of the dermal

---

[1] It would perhaps be more correct to say that *teeth* are really in nature a special set of dermal papillæ of the same nature as those which cover the surface of the skin in some fishes, and which, covering the jaw arches, are set apart for grasping and dividing food; but the relationship is put conversely, as the tooth form is the more familiar.

exoskeleton in the form of median fins. Of these one extends along the upper or dorsal edge, and is named the dorsal fin, consisting of a succession of soft and branched or spiny and hard fin-rays connected by membrane. The other is present on the under or ventral side of the body behind the terminal opening of the intestine; this is called the anal fin. These median fins, though apparently single and central, are in reality composed of two lateral layers placed in close apposition.

FIG. 5.
Ctenoid scale.

11. **Sense-organs of the lateral line.**—Along the line of greatest convexity of each side of the body of a fish there is a lateral line, extending from behind the eye to the side of the tail. This consists of a row of scales, each pierced by a minute tube leading into a small simple or branched sac filled with a gelatinous material, in which the extremity of a nerve is embedded. These are organs of sense, and are probably capable of being impressed by several forms of vibration.

12. **Backbone and tail.**—The vertebral column of fishes usually consists of a chain of biconcave vertebral bodies, bearing on their upper surfaces neural arches which are surmounted by long neural spines. On the under side the vertebræ bear ribs towards the front, and V-shaped bones towards the hinder part of the body. The hindmost of the tail vertebræ may either gradually diminish to a point, as in the African mudfish (fig. 14), or they may undergo modification, being replaced by a rodlike bone which turns sharply upwards,

The Sole. 15

as in the tails of most of the bony fishes. The median fin is continued around the tail end of the vertebral

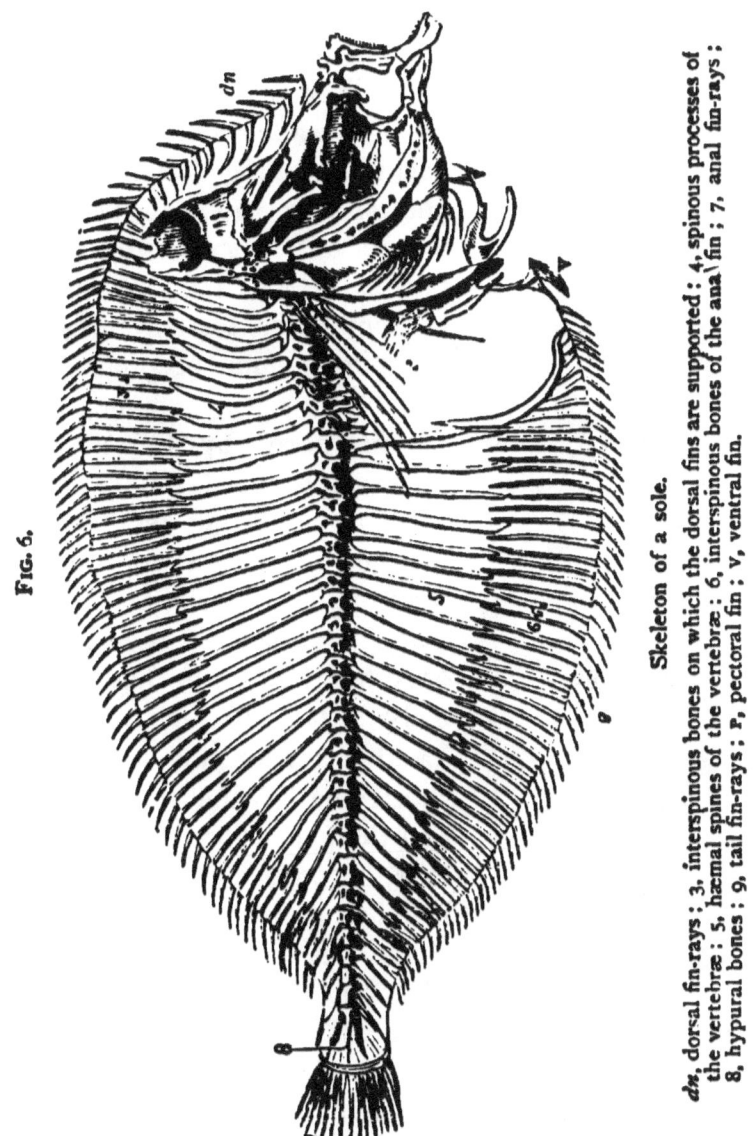

FIG. 6. Skeleton of a sole.

dn, dorsal fin-rays; 3, interspinous bones on which the dorsal fins are supported; 4, spinous processes of the vertebræ; 5, hæmal spines of the vertebræ; 6, interspinous bones of the anal fin; 7, anal fin-rays; 8, hypural bones; 9, tail fin-rays; P, pectoral fin; V, ventral fin.

column, and sometimes appears as a simple uniform fringe evenly distributed around the pointed vertebral axis, or else the whole caudal area of the vertebral column becomes upturned and the tail fin forms a large lobe on the under surface of the axis while simply margining the end of the caudal vertebræ; such a tail is spoken of as an unequally lobed tail. When, as in bony fishes, the extremity of the spinal column becomes converted into a single bone, then the fin borne by it is usually an evenly bilobed tail, such as that of a herring or salmon or sole. It is, however, an interesting fact in relation to this that the young fry of the salmon or other bony fish has originally a tail of the unevenly lobed character, which by the shortening of the upper part, and the expansion of the lower lobe, becomes even, as we find it in the adult.

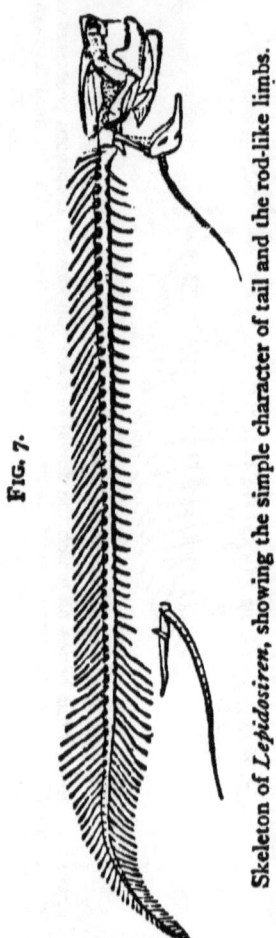

FIG. 7.—Skeleton of *Lepidosiren*, showing the simple character of tail and the rod-like limbs.

In the simplest fishes the notochord persists through life, and such fishes have generally a uniformly fringed tail, as in the lampreys.

The structure of the skull differs in the various subdivisions of the class: in some it is a simple cartilaginous box, as in lampreys and sharks; in others this cartilaginous box is covered and protected by a series of bony dermal plates, as in the sturgeon, or the whole skull may be made up of a number of closely articulated and perfectly united bony pieces as in the cod (fig. 8). In this case it must be remembered that these bones are of a twofold nature—first, the ossified pieces of the cartilage of which the primitive skull consists, and which surrounds the different apertures and nerves, forming principally the lateral walls of the skull; secondly, the ossified plates of membrane which are the equivalents of the dermal bony plates of the sturgeon, and which chiefly make up the roof and floor bones.

Besides the skull or brain-case proper, the head of a fish consists of four other series of bones, as can be seen in fig. 8. These are, first, those of the upper jaw arch, sometimes seven in number on each side; secondly, those of the lower jaw arch, sometimes four or five pairs; thirdly, those of the gill arches, four, five, or six pairs of arches on each side, each consisting of about four pairs of bones, and bearing the gills. These three series are chiefly ossifications in the system of visceral arches before referred to. Besides these, there is a fourth group of bones, those of the *operculum* or gill cover, which overlap and cover the gill arches; of these there are four or more, making up the gill cover on each side. It is thus not to be wondered at that the skeleton of the head of a fish presents an appearance of great complexity.

The limbs of fishes are converted into fins, and of these there are usually two pairs. The fore limbs, or pectoral fins, are placed directly behind the head, to which indeed the shoulder girdle is in most fishes united by small dermal ossifications. The hind limbs are called the *ventral* fins, and are rarely as well de-

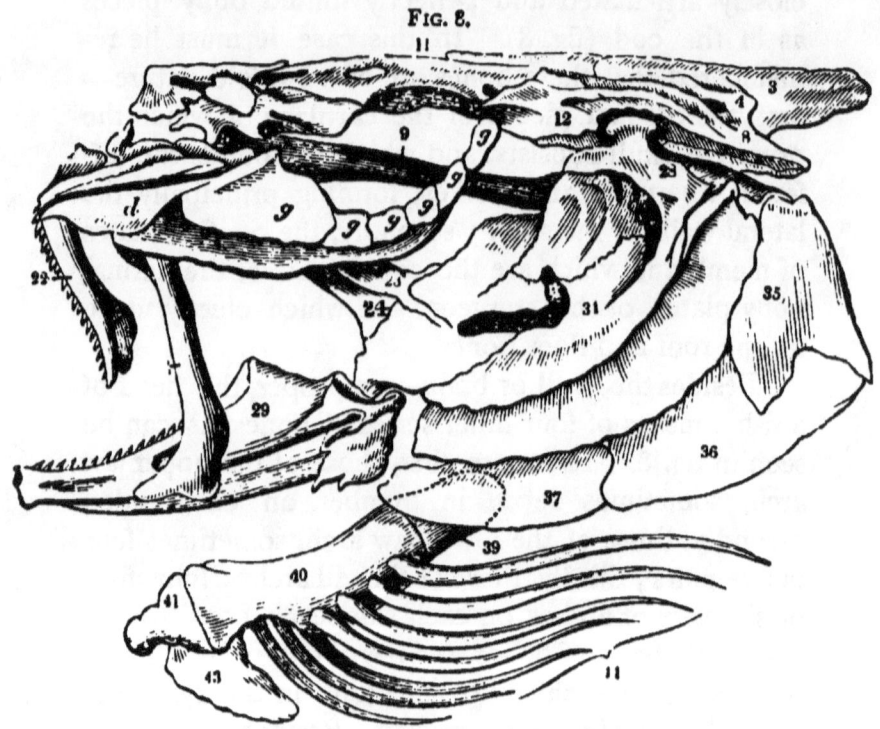

Skull of Cod.

3, supra-occipital bone; 4, opisthotic; 8, post-temporal; 11, frontal; 9, parasphenoid bone; *g, g*, sub-orbital bones; 22, premaxilla; 21, maxilla; 24, pterygoid; 28, hyomandibular; 29, articular piece of lower jaw; 23, dentary bone; 39, 40, 41, 43, hyoid arch; 44, branchio-stegal rays; 34, 35, 36, 37, opercular bones.

veloped as the fore limbs, and the pelvic girdle is seldom attached to the vertebral column. The fins are of use in directing the motion of fishes, while the tail is the principal organ of propulsion.

Brain and Heart of Fishes.

13. Internal organs of fishes.—The brain of fishes (fig. 9) is small, not filling the cranial cavity. It consists of a succession of little knobs or ganglia arranged in a chain from before backwards. Of these the foremost are connected with the sense of smell, the second consist of the fore-brain hemispheres or cerebrum, the third are the optic lobes from which the nerves of sight arise, the fourth constitute the mid-brain and the fifth the hind brain.

Beneath and behind the head lie the gills (fig. 10), which consist of numerous vascular fringes arranged in platelike layers attached to the visceral arches, and bathed by the water which enters the mouth and escapes through the visceral slits. The heart is situated in the middle of what we might call the throat, a very short distance behind the lower jaw. This organ consists of a thin-walled auricle, receiving the veins which convey to it the impure blood from the body, and a large thick-walled ventricle for propelling the blood into the gills. This latter is

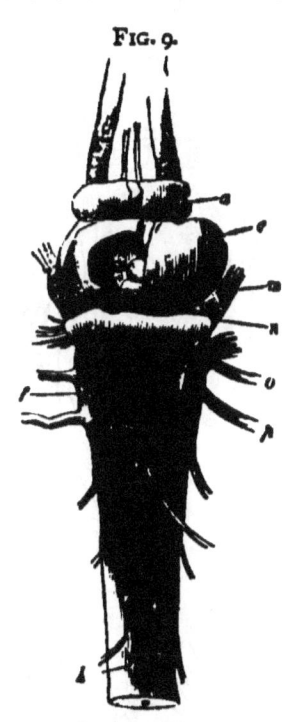

FIG. 9.

Brain of Cod.

l, nerves of sight ; *k*, nerves of smell; *a*, foremost lobe of brain ; *c*, second lobe or cerebrum ; *f*, cerebellum; *h*, hind brain or medulla oblongata ; *m*, fifth pair of nerves ; *n*, nerves of hearing ; *o*, ninth pair of nerves ; *p*, tenth or vagus nerve.

sometimes prolonged at its outlet into a conical part full of valves, called the arterial cone, which ends in the large main blood-vessel, or aorta. The arterial cone is well developed in sharks.

Sometimes, as in most of our common fishes, the aorta at its

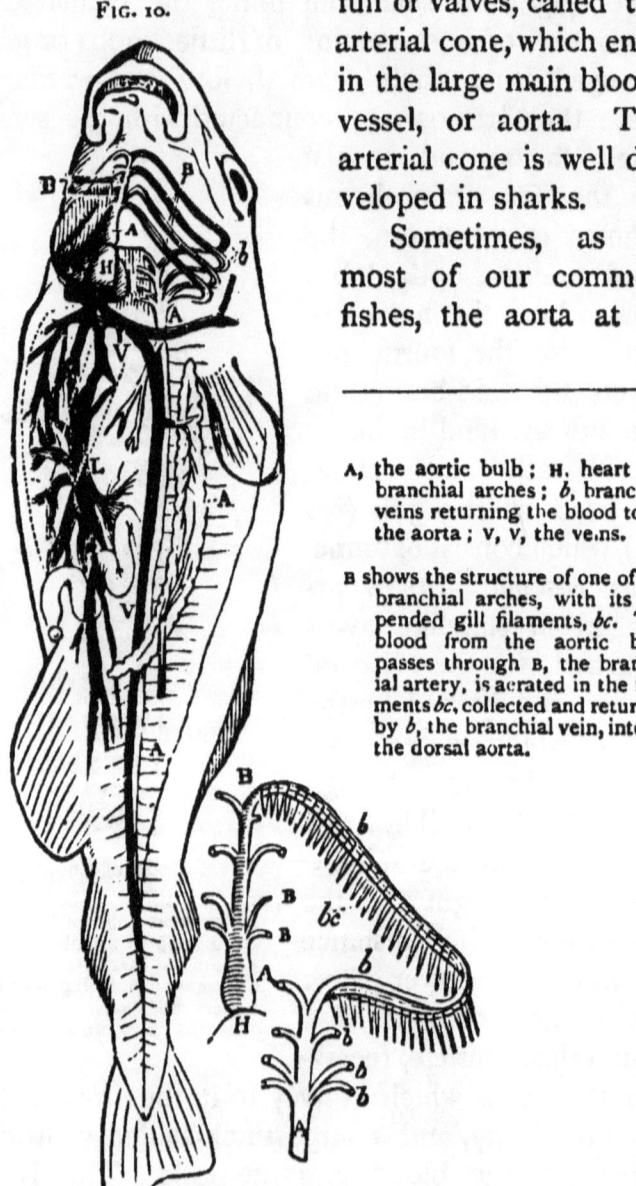

Fig. 10.

A, the aortic bulb; H, heart; B, branchial arches; *b*, branchial veins returning the blood to A, the aorta; V, V, the veins.

B shows the structure of one of the branchial arches, with its appended gill filaments, *bc*. The blood from the aortic bulb passes through B, the branchial artery, is aerated in the filaments *bc*, collected and returned by *b*, the branchial vein, into A, the dorsal aorta.

Diagram of the circulation in a fish.

Circulation in Fishes.

commencement is swollen into an aortic bulb, from which come off at least three pairs of branchial or gill arteries; these pass in the form of arches, right and left, to the gills, and there break up into fine branches in the soft, fringe-like folds. Here the blood, being exposed to the air dissolved in the water, absorbs oxygen and gives out carbonic acid, and is thus purified.

The purified blood, returning from the gills by the branchial veins, enters the dorsal vessel or aorta, which sends it to the different organs of the body to supply the viscera.

The blood of fishes is generally of the same temperature as the medium wherein they live, or only slightly warmer, and hence it usually feels cold to the touch. It contains corpuscles, or little microscopic bodies, of an oval shape and with a central nucleus.

Though the respiration of fishes is accomplished by means of the air which is dissolved in water, yet it is supplemented in some of them by direct exposure of the gills to the atmosphere, and some fishes are killed if prevented from rising to the surface.

In most fishes there is a large sac filled with air, placed beneath the vertebral column at the anterior part of the body cavity, and communicating by a duct with the digestive organs. This is called the swimming-bladder, or the air-bladder, and, by expanding or compressing it, the fish can rise or sink in the water. This sac commences its existence in the embryo as an outgrowth from the neck end of the alimentary canal.

Fishes are oviparous, that is, their young are produced from eggs, and for the most part they are enormously prolific. The egg-organ of the cod sometimes contains over a million eggs, and some other fishes are equally fruitful; the eggs are of small size, and contain very little food yolk. The majority of fishes are marine; those found in fresh water are, as a rule, simpler in organisation and retain many of the embryonic characters of the class. About 13,000 different species of fish are known, and they are divided into five orders.

CHAPTER IV.

ORDER 1, LAMPREYS; ORDER 2, SHARKS.

14. **Order 1, Marsipobranchii (Lampreys).**—This, the most lowly organised order, consists of wormlike, limbless, scaleless fishes with no lower jaw, a circular suctorial mouth, a persistent notochord, and gills in the form of lateral pouches. They are also remarkable among fishes for having circular blood corpuscles.

The most familiar examples are the little freshwater lamprey, the large sea lamprey, and that curious parasite the glutinous hag, which, by means of its large, jagged tooth, bores its way into the body of the cod, ling, or other large fish, and lives therein, feeding on the juices of its prey. In all these there is but

Lampreys and Sharks.

one median pitlike nostril, and the hag is remarkable among fishes for having a passage of communication between the bottom of this pit and the posterior part of the cavity of the mouth. No such communication exists in other fishes, in which the nose is a simple depression or cavity on the surface of the head, lined by a plaited mucous membrane and crossed over by a bridge of skin. The teeth in lampreys are horny and conical; they are shown in fig. 11.

FIG. 11.

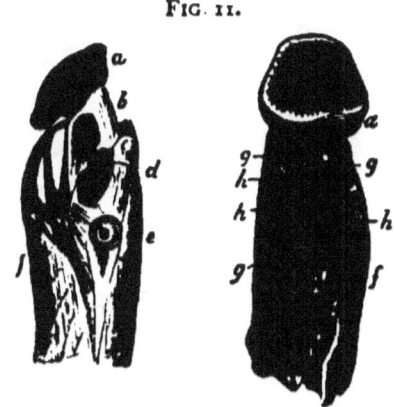

Head of lamprey dissected.

a, b, c, cartilages of the mouth ; *d, e, f, g, h*, muscles attached to the cartilages.

The name *Marsipobranchii* is given to this group on account of the pouchlike nature of the gills, which are in six or seven pairs, arranged in two lateral rows, and open by small holes on the surface.

15. **Order 2, Selachia (Sharks).**—The second order includes the sharks and rays, the largest individuals in the entire class of fishes ; but, notwithstanding their size, these exhibit in respect to many points of organisation what may be considered as

elementary characters—that is, they display in their permanent state points of structure which other more specialised fishes present only in the embryonic stages. They are for the most part marine, and the skeleton remains almost entirely cartilaginous and never becomes truly ossified. The notochord, however, rarely persists, being generally replaced by an axis of biconcave, often calcified, cartilaginous disks or vertebral bodies.

The jaws in sharks are usually placed beneath, not at the front of, the prominent snout, and they are both cartilaginous, being, in fact, two parts of a visceral arch. The gills are symmetrical lateral plates of vascular membrane, interposed between pouches which have a row of holes or slits on each side, opening superficially on the side of the neck, and internally by a row of perforations into the pharynx.

The entire surface of the dermis is covered with toothlike papillæ, composed of true tooth-tissue or dentine, and these over the jaw arches are large and developed into functional teeth, which are sometimes of formidable size and proportions. There are several rows of these, and as they are gradually worn away with use, they replace each other from within outwards. This form of dermal scales on the surface of the body is named *placoid* (fig. 3).

The vertebral axis is prolonged into the upper lobe of the tail, which thus, on account of the large size of the lower lobe, belongs to the unevenly lobed or *heterocercal* type, not like the uniform marginal fringe of the lampreys. The fins are often armed with single, strong, and sometimes serrated spines, which are used as weapons of offence.

Sharks.

The heart in sharks has a long arterial cone. The intestine, though short, is very capacious, and has the extent of its inner surface increased enormously by means of a long spiral fold of its lining mucous membrane, which stretches throughout almost its whole extent. Like the lampreys, sharks are devoid of a swimming-bladder.

Some sharks are viviparous (that is, produce their young alive); in others the young are extruded within curious horny tendril-bearing cases, which are often picked up along the sea-shore, and are commonly called 'mermaids' purses.'

The commonest examples of this order are the dog-fishes, sharks, and rays. One of the largest forms is the great basking shark of the North Atlantic; this fish is not at all uncommon on the west coast of Ireland, where it is called the sun-fish, and is often captured for its oil. It also occurs, though but rarely, on the American coast. It often exceeds thirty feet in length, and a specimen of this size will yield ninety gallons of oil from its liver. The

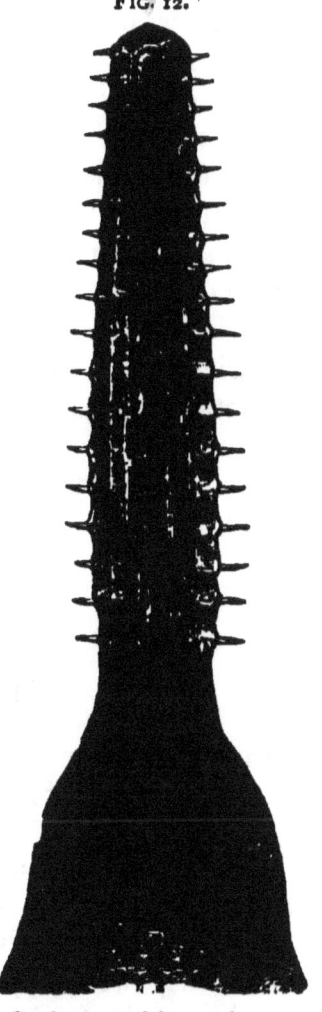

FIG. 12.

Beak of saw-fish seen from below, showing its mout nostrils, and lateral teeth.

gigantic Rhinodon of the Indian Ocean has been met with sixty feet in length. The hammer-headed shark, with its extraordinary bilobed head, and the saw-fish (fig. 12), with its long, flattened, bony snout bearing a row of strong, sharp teeth on each side, are also examples of the order.

The skates, or rays, are remarkable for their flattened form, due largely to the enormous size of the pectoral fins. One form, rarely found in British seas, though common in the Mediterranean, is the torpedo or electric ray, which has near its head two large electric batteries, whereby the fish can give severe electric shocks; these organs are joined to the brain by large nerves, and consist of closely apposed columnar elements, which morphologically are considered to consist of extremely modified muscular tissue.

CHAPTER V.

ORDER 3, GANOID FISHES; ORDER 4, BONY FISHES; ORDER 5, DIPNOI.

16. **Order 3, Ganoidei.**—The living fishes of this group are very few (about thirty), and most of them are inhabitants of rivers or of lakes but in former times they were apparently numerous and rich in species, as the fossil remains of six hundred species are already known. They are characterised by possessing ganoid scales—that is, brightly polished plates

covered with a lamina of an enamel-like substance. They have likewise unsymmetrical tails and a ventricular arterial cone. The gills are free, and are placed on bony gill-arches, under cover of *opercula* or gill-flaps, not in pouches nor on plates. Some, like the sturgeons, have a persistent notochord; others, like the Californian bony pike, have fully ossified vertebral bodies. The other forms included in this order are the Polypterus of the Nile and the reed fish of Calabar, as well as several rare and curious American species. Many of the fossil forms were of large size and of extraordinary shapes; their remains abound in some of the old red sandstone formations. All living forms have a swimming-bladder, which in the sturgeon yields the isinglass[1] of commerce.

17. **Order 4, Teleostei.**—This is by far the largest group of fishes, and includes all those which, like our common fishes, possess a bony skeleton with biconcave vertebral bodies. The tail consists of two even lobes supported on a sharply upturned and continuously ossified end of the vertebral column (fig. 6). The body has usually a uniform coating of smooth or ribbed or spinose scales, which rarely have an enamelled surface. The gills consist of free, usually comblike, filaments on bony branchial arches (fig. 10), arranged under the flaplike gill-cover or operculum. There is no arterial cone, the mouth of the ventricle having but one row of valves.

This order of fishes is divided into the following six sub-orders :—

[1] *Isinglass* is a corruption of the German *Hausenblase*, from *Hausen*, a sturgeon, and *Blase*, a bladder—i.e. sturgeon's bladder.

28   Vertebrata.

Sub-order 1, Physostomi, or those in which the swimming-bladder communicates, in the adult, with the digestive canal by means of a duct. In these also all the fin rays are soft and jointed, except perhaps the foremost ray of each fin, which may be spinose from a fusion of its separate elements. In this group are included the pike, carp, goldfish, herring, salmon, trout, and most of our fresh-water

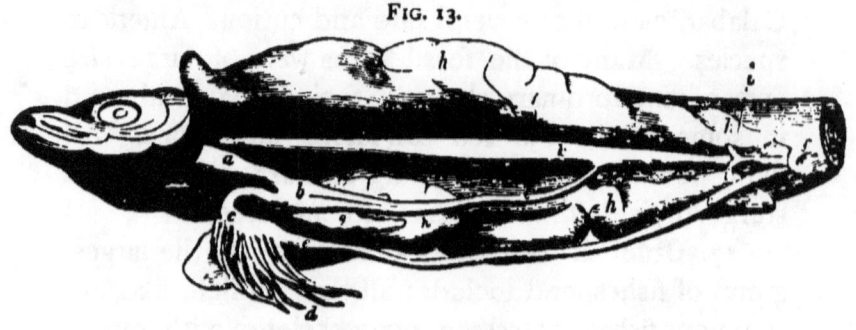

Fig. 13.

Viscera of herring.

a, œsophagus; *b, c,* stomach, with its appendages, *d* ; *e*, intestine ; *l*, duct of the swimming-bladder, *k* ; *h,* ovary.

fishes, such as the barbel, tench, roach, ide, minnow, &c. Some of these physostome fishes have no ventral fins—for example, the eels, a few of which, like the prettily marked Helen's eel of the Mediterranean, are also devoid of pectoral fins. One genus of eels, the Gymnotus, of the large rivers of South America, has a powerful electric organ, formed of some of the modified body muscles. This apparatus stretches along almost the entire body, and as the fish sometimes reaches the length of six feet, the organ is of very considerable size, and is capable of giving violent electric shocks. Two other genera of physostome fishes have also electric organs; one of these is a genus of river fishes—*Malapterurus*, from the Nile—the other—*Mormyrus*, also African—has a very small electric organ near the tail.

Some fishes belonging to a curious marine group of this sub-order—the Scopelidæ—are remarkable not only for the brilliancy of their lustre, but for the fact of their possessing several pairs of accessory eyes on the gill covers. One other species of physostome fish—*Amblyopsis* which inhabits the Mammoth Cave of Kentucky—is remarkable for the rudimentary condition of its eyes, which are covered with a layer of skin, and are hence functionless.

SUB-ORDER 2, ANACANTHINI.—This subdivision includes those soft-finned fishes which have either no swimming-bladder or have one that has no duct. In these not even the foremost fin-rays are spinous, but all are soft-jointed and branched. They are for the most part marine, and include many of the commonest of our sea fishes, such as the cod, haddock, whiting, saith, lithe, ling, &c. One interesting group —that of the flat fishes—is remarkable for the want of symmetry displayed in the body, which is extremely compressed, and the animal in progression invariably lies on one side, swimming with one side up and the other directed downwards. These fishes usually keep near or on the bottom, and the upper side is usually dark or coloured while the lower side is white. To accommodate the structures of the animal to this extraordinary habit, the eyes are twisted round both to the one side of the head—viz. that which is uppermost—so are the nostrils, and the mouth is also usually awry, so as to give the greatest amount of facility of swallowing consistent with position. As in this distorted position the dorsal and anal fins are disposed as lateral fringes, they functionally replace the paired fins as directors of motion, and hence the pectoral and ventral fins are usually small or deficient. One interesting feature in these fishes is that their embryos at a very early stage are perfectly symmetrical, and gradually develope the one-sided torsion as growth progresses, the displaced eye having been traced by observers in its curious pilgrimage around the front of the obliquely growing head from the under to the upper side. The turbot, plaice, flounder, sole, dab, and fluke are well-known examples ; the largest species inhabiting our seas is the halibut, which sometimes has been known to attain the weight of over 500 pounds. Another curious point is noteworthy—viz. that though in each genus the side to which the eyes are displaced is usually constant, yet erratic reversed examples are occasionally met with. Thus while in the flounder and plaice the eyes are usually on the right, in such *reversed* cases they are found looking to the left ; such abnormalities are easily understood by the light of the embryonic development of the group.

One genus of fish of this sub-order, named *Fierasfer*, is parasitic within the bodies of certain sea-cucumbers, or holothurians, and star-fishes, and is found in the Indian Ocean.

SUB-ORDER 3, ACANTHOPTERI. — Spiny-finned fishes with a ductless swimming-bladder, or else none. This is the most numerous and most specialised group of bony fishes. The scale-clothing of this class is usually remarkable for the comblike or spiny surface and hinder margin of each scale, whereby they are distinguished from the circular smooth scales of the physostome fishes. The most familiar examples are the perches of our streams; the bull-heads and gurnards, known by their spiny heads, found along our coasts; the sticklebacks, so interesting on account of the nests constructed by the males for the protection of the young: the mullets, which have the singular property of changing colour when they are dying; the mackerels, breams, braizes, blennies, gobies, &c.

Some of these fishes are laterally compressed, like flat fish, but without showing any distortion of the heads, such as the John d'Ory and Archer fishes; the latter are East Indian fishes, and owe their name to their habit of shooting at flies by forcibly ejecting drops of water from their long snouts. The swordfish, which sometimes attains the length of sixteen feet, is closely allied to the mackerel, and is remarkable for the long, swordlike upper jaw. The common lumpsucker, the little red or brown Lepadogaster of England, and the tropical Remora are remarkable as being provided with sucking disks, whereby they can adhere with great tenacity to foreign bodies. Fistularia (the tobacco-pipe fish) is remarkable for his long tubular snout, as is also the allied trumpet-fish. Trachinus (the weever) is said to be able to inflict poisonous wounds.

There are three aberrant groups of spiny-finned fishes, which constitute the remaining three sub-orders.

The first of these, or sub-order 4, is called *Pharyn*

gognathi, or pharynx-jaw-bearing fishes, on account of the presence of a single medial tooth-bearing bone in the pharynx, made up of the united lateral remains of one of the hindmost of the visceral arches, which does not bear gills. The flying fishes, distinguished by their long pectoral fins; the gar-pikes and parrot fishes; the cunners and tautogs, so common along our shores, are the most familiar examples of the group. They are small or moderate-sized fishes, with spiny fins, and often with strong conical teeth in the jaws.

Sub-order 5 consists of the sea horses and pipe fishes, which differ from all other fishes in having the gill filaments in symmetrical clusters or tufts on the gill arches, not in comblike plates; hence they are called *Lophobranchii*, or tufted-gilled fishes. Their bodies are clad with bony plates, and are often of eccentric angular shapes. They have no ribs, their jaws are toothless, and the males in some species are provided with pouches on the front of the abdomen, into which they collect the eggs on their being laid by the females, and within which the young are hatched.

The sixth sub-order, *Plectognathi*, or soldered jaws, consists of spiny-finned fishes in which the bones of the upper jaw are consolidated together instead of remaining separate; these are the singular globe-fishes, whose spiny bodies are capable of inflation, and whose bare, ivory-like teeth give them such a remarkable appearance. The file fishes also, with their rough, branched spines and tough skin and the angular box-fishes, which belong to this order, are likewise among

Mud Fishes.

the most singularly shaped of tropical fishes. One remarkable species—the sun fish—a large globular fish with an extraordinarily thick skin, sometimes reaches the weight of 400 pounds.

18. **Order 5, Dipnoi.**— This, the last and in some respects most interesting order, includes three living fishes, which form a transition to the next class. These fishes differ from all the foregoing in having the swimming-bladder developed as an accessory respiratory organ ; the blood returning from it being received into a small additional auricle of the heart placed to the left of the main auricle. They have a covering of horny scales, and the alimentary canal has a spiral valve. They also exhibit the peculiarity of possessing tubular nasal passages which perforate the upper lip, opening into the mouth. One of the fishes of this order is the African mud fish, or *Protopterus* of the Gambia; another is the *Lepidosiren* (fig. 14), of South America ; and the third is the

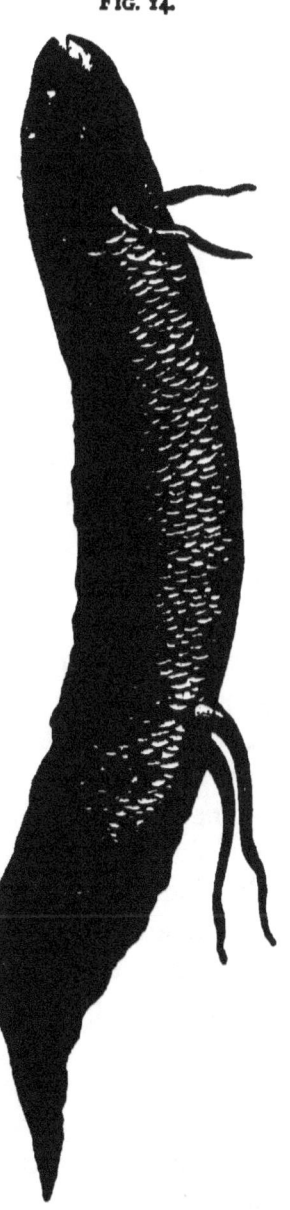

FIG. 14.

(The mud fish, *Lepidosiren*).

Ceratodus, of the rivers of Queensland. In several respects these fishes present characteristics which are identical with the embryonic conditions of many of the higher groups of animals. The characters of the skeleton can be seen in fig. 7.

CHAPTER VI.

CLASS 2, AMPHIBIA.

19. **Characters of Amphibia.**—The class *Amphibia*, to which we are structurally conducted by the last order of fishes, consists of cold-blooded animals, usually of small size. This is at present the poorest in species of all the classes of vertebrata, yet, as in the case of the ganoid fishes, at earlier periods in the world's history the animals of this class vastly exceeded their present representatives in number, size, and complexity. Like fishes, they are characterised by having a feeble development of the outer skin, or epidermis, but, unlike them, they have no dermal clothing of scales, and the surface is generally smooth, naked, and often glandular. Some of them, in the embryonic or tadpole stage of their existence, possess rudiments of the system of sense organs, like those of the lateral line in fishes, but none of them are retained in the adult state. Amphibians, moreover, have no functional fin-rays, though sometimes they have marginal membranous fringes, as in the common newt or tadpole, and even rudimentary rays, as in the

Characters of Amphibians.

toe-webs of some salamanders. They also undergo regular metamorphoses, beginning life as little fish-like creatures with large flat heads and external gills. To this stage the name tadpole is commonly given. Then, as development progresses, the air sacs (which correspond to the swimming-bladder in fishes) grow, become large, vascular, and capable of acting as

FIG. 15.

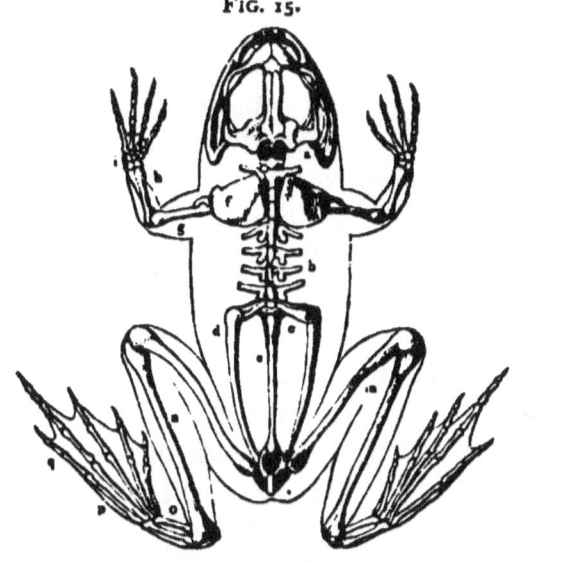

Skeleton of frog.

a, skull; *b*, vertebræ; *c*, sacrum; *d*, ilium; *e*, urostyle; *f*, suprascapula; *g*, humerus; *h*, fore-arm bones; *i*, wrist bones; *m*, thigh bone; *n*, leg bones; *o*, elongated first pair of ankle bones; *p, q*, foot bones.

breathing organs, which are then called lungs; and ultimately, in the adult state, a pulmonary or direct air-breathing system supplants the gill or branchial system of earlier life. The two-chambered larval heart at the same time becomes three-chambered, developing a special auricle in the left side for the reception of the blood which has been purified in the lungs, and is returned from hence into the heart. It may also be noted that, during this process of development in the common frog the digestive canal, which in the tadpole is long and spirally coiled, becomes shorter and straighter The blood of amphibians is remarkable for the large size of the oval red corpuscles which it contains, those in Proteus being $\frac{1}{400}$th of an inch in diameter, those in the frog being $\frac{1}{800}$th. The vertebral column in the simplest of the amphibians consists of rudimentary or biconcave vertebræ ; in frogs (fig. 15), however, it consists of a chain of a few solid disks whose surfaces fit into each other by ball and socket joints. Ribs are either very short or, as in frogs, absent. The skull articulates to the foremost vertebra by means of two lateral articular surfaces which are called *condyles*. The skull is also, as a rule, much more consolidated than the skull in fishes, but resembles the latter in having, as the most conspicuous bone in its base, a long ossification in the membrane underlying the middle of the cartilage of the base of the skull, which is known as the *parasphenoid* bone, a bone which is rudimental or absent in all higher forms. Amphibians also differ from fishes in having a middle ear, closed by a tympanic membrane, and not merely the internal ear cavity which constitutes the ear in fishes. Their nasal cavities open posteriorly into the pharynx. They have usually four limbs, which consist of parts comparable with those in higher animals, and very unlike the fins in fishes.

There are three orders of amphibians at present represented by living forms on the globe.

CHAPTER VII.

CLASSIFICATION OF AMPHIBIA.

20. **Order 1, Gymnophiona.**—A small group of worm-like forms, with no limbs, rudimental eyes (hence they are called *Cæcilia*), which are found in tropical countries burrowing in the ground. These, with one exception, have the body provided with dermal scales. They are usually marked with superficial rings like an earth-worm, and range in size from one to two feet, rarely exceeding this length. At present only a few species exist, but many fossil forms have been found which probably resembled these in structure.

A large and structurally complex order of fossil amphibians, named Labyrinthodonts, formerly inhabited the earth, which in some respects seem to have been related to the Cœcilians, but were much larger, and many of them were defended by dermal coats of bony mail something like the armour clothing of a crocodile.

21 **Order 2, Urodela.**—Limb-bearing amphibians provided with a permanent tail, which is retained during life. There are two sections in this order, in one of which the animals retain their embryonic gills through their whole existence, and are thus perennially or permanently branchiate, while in their adult condition they also possess lungs, which become developed gradually in process of growth. In the other section the gills are only transitory or caducous,

wasting and disappearing on the development of the lungs. Of the former, or *perennibranchiate* section we have interesting examples in the sirens or mud eels of Carolina, which are provided with only two limbs representing the fore limbs of other vertebrates. Another form, the proteus, inhabits the Cave of Adelsberg and other caves in Carinthia, &c., and is, like all other cave-dwellers, blind and blanched; its weak fore legs are provided with three toes, while the hind limbs possess only two. The curious axolotl (fig. 16) of Mexico is an interesting form, as it has proved to be a permanent tadpole which in certain conditions only undergoes its further metamorphosis into the salamander-like form of its adult state.

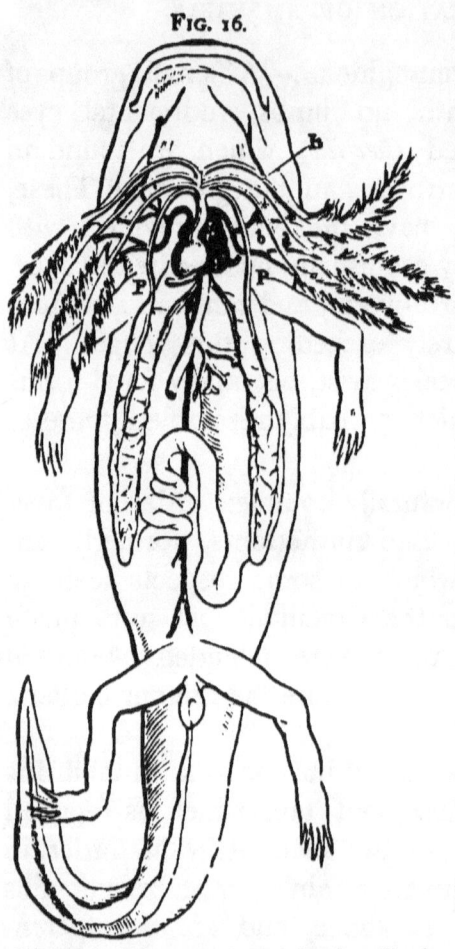

Fig. 16.

Diagram of the axolotl, showing its gills, *b*, and lungs, *p*.

In some perennibranchs the outer gills disappear,

and are replaced by an internal series, or gills of the type of those developed in fishes. This modification in the structure of these organs is of considerable interest from a morphological point of view, when we remember that in sharks there are originally in the embryo distinct external gills, which are lost as the shark attains his more perfect organisation, and are replaced by the permanent gills, which are formed directly on the aortic arches. From these conditions it seems as if external gills were a more primitive or embryonic form, and internal gills a more specialised modification of respiratory organs. The amphibians which show these internal gills are the giant *Sieboldia* of Japan, which reaches a length of four feet, and the amphiuma and menopoma of North America. The caducibranchiate tailed amphibians are the salamanders and newts, the latter of which are common in our ditches, where their metamorphoses can easily be traced. The common newt is interesting on account of the bright colours which it exhibits at certain stages, and for the remarkable dorsal crest which it also occasionally possesses.

22. **Order 3, Anura.**—The largest group of the Amphibia consist of the frogs and toads, or the tailless forms. In these, the larva or tadpole loses during its development all traces not only of its gills, but also of its tail; the hinder limbs are also in these more perfectly developed than the fore, and the two proximal bones of the ankle are elongated, so as to make what appears to be an independent third portion of the hind limb. The fore arm and the leg proper also differ from those of urodeles and of the higher verte-

brates in that there are only single bones in these regions, the separate bones, *radius* and *ulna*, which are present in these parts of other vertebrates being here united. The frogs, toads, pipas, and tree frogs are the most striking examples of this order.

CHAPTER VIII.

CLASS 3, REPTILES.

23. **Characters of Reptilia.**—Tortoises, lizards, snakes, and crocodiles are the leading forms included in this large third class of vertebrate animals, a class often confounded with the amphibians, but differing therefrom in many striking and characteristic respects. Reptiles are invariably provided with a very distinct epidermic clothing of scales which differ essentially from the dermal scales of the foregoing groups. The scales of reptiles being epidermal, and not parts of the dermis or true skin, are often shed and replaced, as in snakes, and they are sometimes hard and thick, as in the tortoise shell of commerce and in the mail clothing of the crocodile. This firm covering may be supplemented by a dermal bony layer, as in crocodiles or tortoises, but these indurations of the dermis are never superficial. The blood is cold; the aortic arches never bear gills, nor is there ever branchial respiration in any stage of existence among the animals of this group. The heart consists of three cavities, two auricles and one ventricle; but the latter is often

more or less perfectly divided by a septum, so as to act as if it were a double chamber (fig. 17). There are always at least two aortic arches, right and left, which usually unite subvertebrally to form one dorsal aorta. The notochord never persists in the adult, and in most living reptiles the vertebral bodies unite with each other by ball and socket joints, and are very rarely biconcave. The skull joins the vertebral column by a *single* median articular eminence or condyle, and there is no parasphenoid bone, the bones of the middle of the base of the skull being developed in the cartilage of the base itself, not in the membrane beneath the cartilage. The lower jaw articulates, as in the amphibians, with the end of the preceding visceral arch; and a bone at its extremity called the quadrate bone is interposed between the palatine part of that arch and the skull.

FIG. 17.

Heart of turtle.
H, ventricle; *h, h'*, auricles.

Many reptiles are ovoviviparous; others are oviparous. Like the amphibians, the reptiles at the present day, though still numerous, give us a very faint idea of their former grandeur of size and complexity. In the Mesozoic age they held the same position on the globe that the Mammalia do at the present period. Only four orders of reptiles are represented in the existing terrestrial fauna; at least five orders, and these including the giants of the class, have perished.

CHAPTER IX.

LIZARDS AND SNAKES.

24. **Order 1, Lacertilia.**—The lizards are scale-clad, and at least forelimb-bearing reptiles, with a heart possessing a single ventricle, and with a lower jaw of firmly united segments. The eyes are provided with movable and functional eyelids, and the teeth are not in sockets, but are disposed in rows either around the edge or along the side of the jaws.

The cloaca, or cavity into which the digestive canal and excreting orifices open, has usually its outlet placed transversely. Like most of the lowly organised vertebrates, lizards display a remarkable power in restoring lost parts, and in connection with this we perceive in them a facility for making their escape from capture by breaking off their extremities. Thus a lizard taken by the tail will often break off that process and escape, the fracture taking place not between two of the vertebræ which make up the organ, but actually through the middle of a vertebra, as there is a medial cartilaginous plate in the caudal vertebræ of some. In one specimen in the writer's possession a lizard whose tail was cracked, but not broken off, developed at the crack an accessory tail, while the original tail yet remained and became repaired at its injured part, thus giving a bifid extremity to the tail.

Some lizards are snakelike and ringed, like the amphisbænas, with no projecting limb-rays, but in all these traces of the limb girdles are persistent, although they may not show superficially, as in the blind worm—a pretty and innocent, though much maligned, native of Great Britain, whose scientific name *Anguis fragilis*, expresses the brittleness before referred to. The common wall-lizards are typical examples of the long fork-tongued division of the order. The monitors and teguexins, or safeguards of the tropics, are so called because they are supposed to give warning of the presence of crocodiles. They reach the length of six to eight feet, and are among the largest of living lizards, although they are but pigmies when compared with the extinct forms of which fossil remains have been found, sometimes exceeding thirty feet in length.

The American iguanas are large-sized lizards which are used as food; they usually bear tufted crests on the back, and have thick short tongues. Some lizards have large lateral flaps of skin: thus the frilled lizard of Australia bears on each side of the neck a wide fold of skin like a ruff or Queen Elizabeth collar; others, like the little flying dragon, bear on each side a winglike fold, supported on extended ribs, and these, together with the long conical chin-pouch, give this creature a very extraordinary appearance. The appropriately named *Moloch horridus* of Australia bristles most repulsively with conical spines, as do many other genera. The geckos of India are remarkable for the suckers which they bear on the ends of their fingers, whereby they can walk up perpendicular walls and along ceilings. The last group of lizards, the chameleons, are interesting for their proverbial quality of changing colour, due to the expansion and contraction of certain pigment-bearing connective tissue bodies in the skin. They also

FIG. 18.

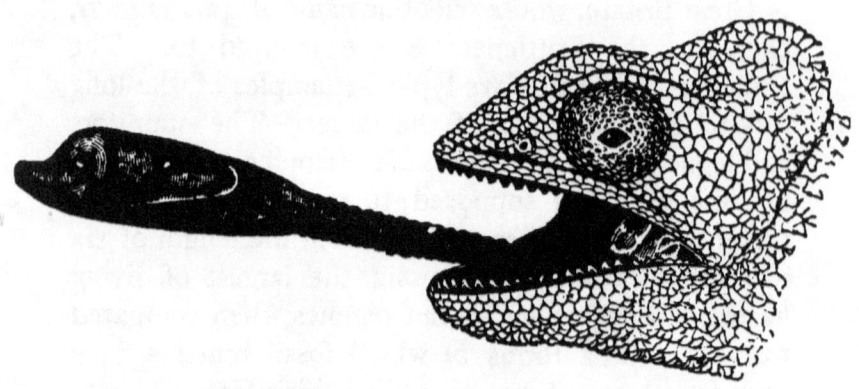

Head of chameleon, with protruded tongue.

possess circular eyelids, and a very long tongue (fig. 18) capable of being protruded with lightning-like rapidity.

25. **Order 2, Ophidia (Snakes).**—These dreaded animals may be regarded in some respects as special modifications of the lizard type. They are scale-clad and limbless, not having even a remnant of the shoulder girdle persistent. The sternum and sternal apparatus have also vanished, and the skeleton consists of a long vertebral column, often of several hundred joints or vertebræ, each of which bears two ribs, one on each side.

Serpents. 45

The vertebræ have each a concavity on the anterior side of each body, into which the ball or convexity of the hinder surface of the foregoing body fits. There are also two pairs of articular facets on the processes of each vertebra, so that the entire spine combines flexibility with amazing strength. The ribs are capable of being moved forwards and backwards, and the ventral surface of the animal's body is covered with flat, horny shields, into which muscles run from the tip of each rib. The rapid, even, gliding motion in serpents is accomplished by the successive advances of these ventral scutes, and the drawing of the body forwards towards them, while the slightly projecting hinder edges of the scutes serve as fixed points by catching the surface of the ground. The brain case is firmly built up of singularly united bones; but the bones of the upper and lower jaw-arches are loose, united together by means of fibrous tissue, and hence capable of an extreme degree of stretching during the swallowing of food, which these animals bolt in large masses.

The teeth are recurved and solidified to the jaw, not set in sockets, and they can only act as organs of prehension.

The tongue consists of a long, bifid muscular organ, capable of being rapidly protruded, or of being drawn back into a sheath when not in use. The windpipe is long and protected by complete gristly rings; only one lung is usually large and developed, the other is rudimental or simply saccular, and they are never symmetrical. The digestive canal is capacious and short, and the cloacal opening is transverse. The

Vertebrata.

eyelids are confluent and transparent, forming the clear glassy surface of the eye, and thus giving to the serpent the stony, unwinking stare peculiar to them.

The boas of the New World, and pythons of the East, are remarkable among snakes for their size and for the strength of their teeth, as well as for the possession of two rudimentary hind limbs in the form of spur-like processes placed one on each side of the cloaca. Some of these serpents, like the anaconda of

FIG. 19.

Poison fangs showing their internal hollows.

America, have been known to reach the length of forty feet, and even larger specimens are described.

The Colubrine snakes, such as the common American striped snake (*Eutæmia sertalis*), are all harmless creatures, mostly of small size, and having all the teeth solid, not grooved.

Poison Fangs of the Viper.

26. Poisonous Snakes.—The most remarkable, though not the most numerous group of serpents, are those provided with poison-fangs, the vipers and rattlesnakes. Of these the best known is the rattlesnake, in which animal the epidermal clothing of the last few tail-joints is loose, and consists of hard, horny rings loosely embracing each other; these cause the rattling noise, when the animal's tail is shaken, which has given rise to the name of this dreaded American snake. Like most other poisonous snakes, it has

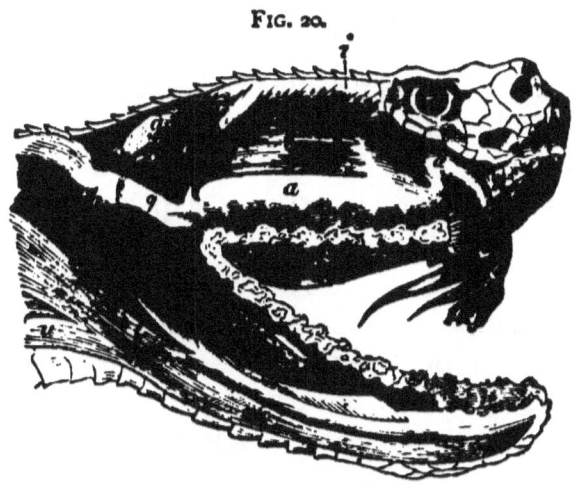

FIG. 20.

Poison apparatus of rattlesnake.
a, poison bag and duct; *e, i, g, t, u*, muscles of jaw.

a flat triangular head, and in its mouth there can be seen the two long grooved maxillary teeth in which are the channels for the poison. These are the only large teeth in the mouth, all the others being small and obscure. They are placed far forwards in the upper jaw, and are movable along with the movable maxilla, being bent upwards towards the palate in the closed position of the mouth, while in the gaping state they project, being arched downwards, ready to be inserted into the victim about to be struck. The groove in the tooth leads into a canal which traverses the base of the poison fang, and is continued by a duct into a cavity or sac, which receives the tubular ducts of the poison gland (fig. 20). In the act of striking, the muscles which close the jaws squeeze the poison sac and drive the poison through the duct into the tooth, and thence into the wound.

The poison apparatus is constructed on the same plan in the common viper (*Pelias berus*), not uncommon in Central and Southern Europe, and easily recognised by its dark green colour, and by the zigzag black line in the middle of the back. Other poisonous snakes like the asp, the cobra di capello, and the coral snake, have other solid teeth coexisting with the poison fangs, and some, like the dipsads, tree snakes, and sand snakes, have some of the hinder teeth grooved. The poison of snake-bites is rapidly fatal, death taking place within an hour in general, and it is computed that over 10,000 deaths take place annually from this cause among human beings.

The water snakes inhabit the Pacific and Indian Ocean, and have flat tails. They possess strong ungrooved teeth behind the true poison fangs. In one species, allied to the coral snake (*Callophis intestinalis*), the poison gland extends into the abdomen.

One curious group of non-poisonous snakes possess teeth on the anterior surface of the neck vertebræ in addition to feeble jaw teeth. These animals feed on eggs, and use these teeth for breaking them while

Tortoises. 49

in the act of swallowing, so that all the material of the egg may be saved for food. Snakes are rare in cold and more abundant in warm climates; they are also more numerous in continental than in insular regions.

CHAPTER X.

TORTOISES AND CROCODILES.

27. **Order 3, Chelonia (Tortoises).**—This order consists of those reptiles whose bodies are enclosed in a bony case composed of a dorsal or upper convex shield, called the *carapace* and a flat ventral or under shield, the *plastron*. The carapace is notched in front and behind, and between it and the plastron project the head and neck, the limbs, and the tail. These parts can be retracted under cover of the bony case. Each shield consists of a layer of epidermis or tortoise-shell, and a layer of bone, which in the carapace consists of dermal plates added to the tops of the spines of the vertebræ, the surfaces of the ribs, and a row of marginal bony plates below these. The plastron also consists of nine plates of ossified dermis covered by a symmetrical series of horny laminæ. The skull is short, rounded, and not armed with teeth, which are replaced by horny beak-like jaws. The lower jaw is in one piece in the adult. The shoulder-girdle consists of three bony rods, two in

E

50   *Vertebrata.*

front, and one behind ; these are included within the carapace, as also is the pelvic girdle.

FIG. 21.

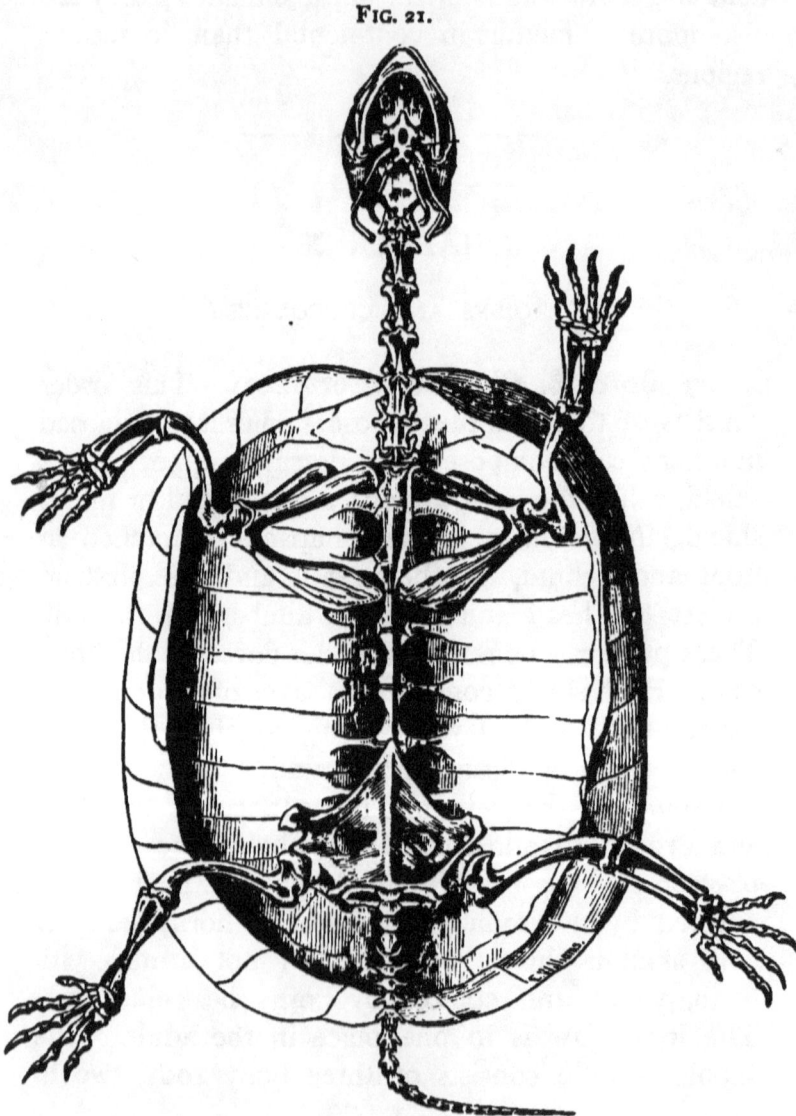

Skeleton of European tortoise, the plastron or under-shell removed.

Crocodiles.

The land forms included under this order are tortoises, such as the common Greek tortoise, which live on land and have stumpy feet with short nails. The aquatic forms or turtles, such as the green turtle used in making turtle soup, and the hawks-bill turtle used for its 'tortoise shell,' are known by their webbed feet. The largest tortoises of the present day only measure a few feet in length, but in ancient days tortoises reached enormous sizes; thus the *Colossochelys*, or giant fossil tortoise of India, sometimes reached a length of over thirteen feet. Tortoises are slow in growth, and attain to extraordinary ages. They are for the most part vegetable feeders, differing in this respect from most other reptiles.

28. **Order 4, Crocodilia.**—These, the highest in organisation of the entire class, are inhabitants of the rivers of tropical countries, and are among the largest of living reptiles. They have a rough, hard, scaly coat of epidermis which is placed dorsally on a dermal bony surface. The vertebral column is provided with ribs, and is composed of vertebræ hollow in front and convex behind. The skull is long, and covered with peculiar sculptured markings. The teeth are seated in sockets in one row, and are renewed several times in succession. The heart has a complete septum or partition in the ventricle dividing it into two distinct cavities, but the aortic arches still communicate with each other at their bases. The feet are webbed and possess strong claws, and there are dermal glands in the throat secreting a peculiar musky material. The forms included are the crocodiles of the Nile and Indian rivers, with their long

tapering snouts, in which the longest teeth of the lower jaw notch the sides of the upper jaw. The alligators of the New World have heads oval or rounded in front, and in all of them the lower jaw teeth are hidden by the edge of the upper, when the mouth is closed. The gavial of the Ganges has a long, slender-pointed head, and is the smallest of the group.

Of all the reptiles the crocodiles are those which in point of structure approach most closely to the birds. They have a gizzard-like stomach, a nictitating membrane in the eye, an immovable joint between the tibia or leg bone and the first bone of the tarsus or ankle, a single carotid or neck-artery, and many other structural peculiarities which show their superiority over other reptiles. Among the orders of the reptile class now extinct, there was one which included bipedal forms which had possibly a kangaroo-like mode of progression, and one of flying reptiles, which indicated a still closer relationship to the birds.

CHAPTER XI.

CLASS IV.—AVES (BIRDS).

29. **General Characters.**—These familiar vertebrates are characterised by possessing an epidermal clothing of feathers, warm blood, a four-chambered heart, no teeth, and in general an adaptation for aerial locomotion. The mode of progression on the earth

Feathers.

is strictly bipedal, as the fore-limbs never touch the ground, being modified into wings. Like reptiles they are oviparous and their eggs are of large size; in most cases also the young are for a certain period under the care of the mother, by whose agency they are provided with food.

30. **Feathers.**— Feathers are epidermal processes secreted by long grooved papillæ and they are of several sorts. The strong distinct feathers, which have a central axis and lateral expansions or vanes, are called contour-feathers, while the smaller soft feathers which clothe the intimate surface of the skin, which have soft or woolly processes and no axis, are called down-feathers. In each contour-feather we notice, firstly, the hole at the base (fig. 22, e) where it is thickened around the base of the papilla; secondly, the slit-like hole, f, marking the region above which the sheath of the papilla has split; thirdly, the rachis, or the square solid axis, b; fourthly, the flat expanded lamina, or vane, c, composed of separate barbs, the margins of each of

Fig. 22.

Contour-feather.
a, barrel; b, rachis; c, vanes; f, upper umbilicus and aftershaft; e, lower umbilicus.

which are joined to their neighbours by numerous hooklets.

In this respect contour-feathers differ from down, in which the barbs are all discontinuous. In young birds the entire plumage consists of simple down-feathers covering the whole surface almost uniformly, and in some birds which do not possess the power of flight, this condition is more or less perpetuated, and thus all the feathers have discontinuous barbs, as in the ostriches. In the great majority of birds, however, this primitive surface clothing is shed and becomes replaced by a second growth of feathers, which differs from the first in that the component feathers are for the most part contour-feathers, arranged in definite tracts, and between these *pterylæ*, or feather tracts, there are spaces quite devoid of contour-feathers. In the course of life, many birds change their feathers several times, the process being called 'moulting.' To defend the feathers from the influence of moisture there is a gland situated on each side of the tail bone which secretes an oily material of use in lubricating the plumage. The largest feathers are those of the wing, and they are grouped into primaries, secondaries, and tertiaries, according as they are borne respectively by the hand, the lower, or the upper end of the forearm; over these are the scapulars, and on the rudimental thumb is the *alula*. The tail feathers are also long, and as they are used in steering they are named *rectrices* to distinguish them from the oar-feathers of the wing.

The papillæ which secrete the feathers are long, vascular, and deeply grooved on the surface; the

Plumage and Skeleton of Birds. 55

protoplasmic matter exuded by the surface of the papillæ is collected into these channels, it then hardens and forms in the first place a hollow cylinder of horny matter, with ridges fitting into the papillary grooves and thin areas between. As growth takes place most actively at the base of the papilla, this horny sheath is pushed off the surface of the papilla, upon which it shrinks still more, and the horny cylinder splits along its thinnest side, whereupon the two lateral laminæ flatten out as the vanes, while the rib which corresponded to the main groove of the papilla becomes the rachis. The feathers of many birds are of brilliant colours, usually brighter in the males than in the females.

31. **Bones.**—The skeleton of birds is well adapted for their aerial existence. The skull is early consolidated, and articulates with the spine by one occipital condyle. The ten or twelve parts of the lower jaw are also early united into a single piece and the front of the jaw is enclosed in a horny sheath; it articulates to the skull by means of a movable quadrate bone which is kept in its place by two rods of bone, one on the outside stretching from the base of the upper beak (the jugal arch), the other on the inside stretching from the palate (the pterygoid arch). The upper mandible, or beak, is also encased in a horny layer at whose base are the nostrils, very often surrounded by a thick leathery skin, which is called the *cere*.

The neck is usually long and exceedingly flexible, made up of from nine to twenty-three vertebræ; its length and that of the bill usually bears some proportion to the length of the legs. The breast-bone bears in front a prominent keel, to which the muscles which elevate and depress the wing are attached, and this is only absent in such birds as do not fly, as the ostrich, emu, and New Zealand ground parrot. The wings are fastened to a very strong shoulder-girdle, which consists of three parts; firstly, of a V-shaped *furculum*, or merrythought, which consists of the two collar-bones united together in the middle line; secondly, of the coracoid bone, a stout bony rod which fits into a groove in the top of the breast-bone and stretches from thence upwards and backwards to the shoulder joint; thirdly, the scapula, or scythe-blade-like bone, which joints with the coracoid at the shoulder, and descends backwards over the dorsal ribs, slung in its place by muscles. The wing bones consist of, firstly, an arm bone, or humerus; secondly, two forearm bones; thirdly, a consolidated hand made up of several (never more than four) united fingers, of which only the thumb in general bears a claw, rarely the thumb and index fingers, as in the cassowary. The ribs are few and are fastened together by lateral spurs, or processes. The portions of the ribs which articulate with the vertebral column are separate from those that unite with the breast bone.

FIG. 23.

Pelvis of bird.
a, sacrum; b, lumbar vertebræ; d, ilium; p, pubis; g, sciatic foramen; k, ischium.

Feet of Birds.

The tail bones are short and compressed, forming a ploughshare-like process; the pelvic bones are long, and stretch along the spine fore and aft to an extent proportionally unmatched in the rest of the sub-kingdom (fig. 23). The two pubic bones do not unite in the middle line in front of the pelvis except in the ostrich, but always remain separate and open. The thigh bones are short. The leg-bone consists of two parts, which in adult birds are indistinguishably united. Of these the largest part is the tibia, or leg-bone proper, the lower end consists of the astragalus, or first bone of the tarsus or ankle. The lower part of the shank of a bird consists of the remaining tarsal and metatarsal bones elongated into a single shaft, and below this are the toes, of which usually four are developed. The innermost of these or the hind toe consists in general of two joints or phalanges, the second (inner) toe is made up of three, the middle or longest toe, of four, and the outermost toe of five phalanges. The shapes and dispositions of the toes vary with the habits of the birds; thus, birds of prey have stout, grasping feet, with sharply hooked claws. Climbers, like woodpeckers and parrots, have the outer and inner toes turned backwards and the other two forwards. In swimmers, all the forward toes are webbed, while in the scraping birds the toes are short, stout, and armed with blunt nails. Many of the bones in the body of a bird are hollow, and instead of containing marrow they are lined by a delicate membrane and contain air, which is conducted into them from the respiratory organs by thin walled canals. This condition is specially exhibited in the birds of most powerful flight, but the bones of very young birds contain marrow.

32. **Muscles and Viscera.**—The muscle or flesh of birds consists of very close fibres, and the sinews or tendons are often converted into bone. There is an enormous muscle on the front of the breast, the great pectoral, whose action is to depress the wing; beneath this is a smaller, or second pectoral muscle with oblique fibres, arranged like the barbs of a feather, and converging to a tendon which, winding round a pulley at the top of the coracoid, is inserted into the top of the humerus and raises the wing; this is the second pectoral. In the legs of many birds there is to be found superficially on the front of the thigh a slender little muscle, which, starting from the front of the pelvis, passes down the upper or front surface of the thigh, winds round to the back of the knee and runs by a tendon into the superficial flexor (or bender) muscle, for the longest toe (*plantaris*); a second muscle (the *peroneus*), from the outside of the leg can generally be traced into the same toe-muscle. These muscles are supposed to be of importance in the action of perching, and as their tendons pass over several joints they probably have a complex action.

The digestive system of birds consists of the following parts: first, the bill or prehensile organ, varying in shape and texture according to the nature of, and mode of obtaining, the food upon which the bird subsists; secondly, the tongue, rarely soft, usually hard and horny, often barbed; thirdly, the long food-passage, or œsophagus, which, above the furculum, usually dilates into a crop (fig. 24, *b*), below which is

Viscera of Birds.

a glandular stomach (*c*) communicating with the gizzard, or true muscular stomach (*c*). This cavity has a thick muscular wall consisting chiefly of two masses of muscle united by a strong tendon, and lined by a rough horny cuticle ; into this birds frequently introduce small stones which assist in triturating or grinding the food, as this organ is chiefly the place where the material of the food is reduced

FIG. 24.

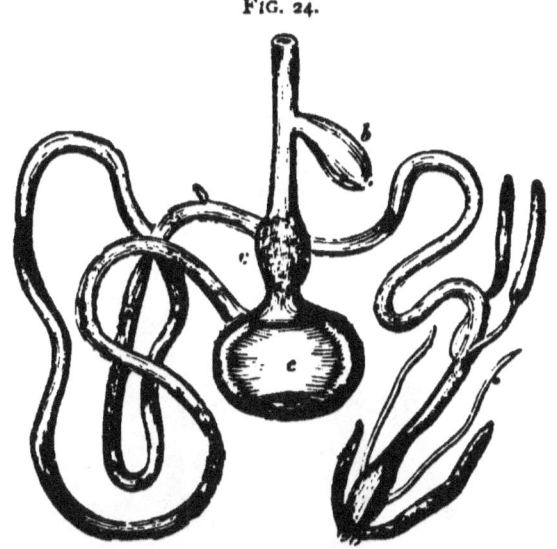

b, crop ; *c, c*, glandular stomach and gizzard.

mechanically to a condition of pulp to prepare it for further digestive changes. The gastric juice secreted in the glandular stomach is here thoroughly mixed up with it, and the food mass is thus prepared for the intestinal canal. The gizzard is especially strong in grain, or fruit-eaters, weak or absent in flesh-eaters.

Birds have two separate ventricles in the strong muscular heart ; one on the right side for propelling

Vertebrata.

the impure or venous blood of the right auricle into the lungs, and the other, or left ventricle, for driving the purified blood after its return from the lungs, through the body; the opening into the right ventricular cavity from the auricle is guarded by a muscular flap. There is only one aortic arch developed in the adult bird, and it arches to the right side, and in many birds there is only one artery developed in the neck for the supply of the head. The lungs are large, and surrounded on their lower surfaces by large air-sacs, into which the bronchial tubes distinctly open; from these cavities pass the membranous canals, which convey the air to the principal bones. There is no muscular layer underlying the lungs for the purpose

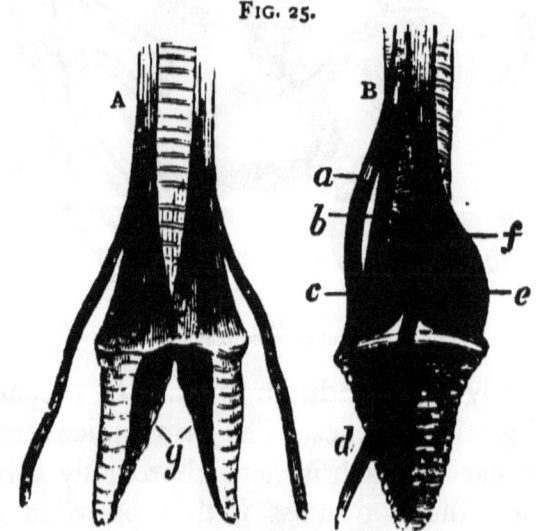

FIG. 25.

Organ of voice of the raven.
A, front view; B, side view showing the muscles of vocalisation.

of directly acting on them in respiration, except in the ostrich and apteryx; but as the sternal and vertebral

Voice and Senses of Birds. 61

ribs can move on each other, the bony wall of the thorax or chest cavity is susceptible of a large range of motion for breathing.

As, from the activity of their motion, birds require a more perfect system of nutrition for their ultimate tissues and organs than reptiles, their respiratory apparatus is very highly developed, and hence their temperature is higher than that of any other group of animals.

An organ of voice is usually developed in the air-passages of birds, most commonly at the point where the windpipe or trachea bifurcates to send an air-tube to each lung (fig. 25). At this spot there is a drum-like cavity or syrinx (g), in which certain tense membranes can be made to vibrate, and can be acted on by muscles (a, b, c, d, e), attached to the windpipe. Thus the organ differs from that in mammals, in which the seat of voice is the larynx or upper end of the windpipe. In the wild swan the long and sinuous windpipe is contained in a hollow which is provided for its reception in the keel of the sternum.

The blood of birds contains small elliptical corpuscles which are nucleated.

The eye of birds is remarkable for possessing bony plates in its 'white,' as well as a curious folded vascular projection at the bottom of the eyeball, which projects forwards towards the crystalline lens. There is also a third eyelid, or nictitating membrane, placed below and within the two ordinary lids, and moved by two little muscles on the back of the eyeball, and there is an additional gland whose secretion keeps this accessory lid moist. The senses of smell and hearing are also largely developed in some birds, notably in vultures and owls, the latter being provided with a distinct external ear.

Most birds have but one oviduct, and that is on the left side; in its lining there are glands which secrete the white of the egg, its membrane, and the shell, during the downward passage of the yolk. The embryonic bird is provided with a rudimental knob on its pre-maxillary bones, which it uses in breaking the egg-shell wherein it is contained.

CHAPTER XII.

CLASSIFICATION OF BIRDS.

33. **Primary Divisions.**—About 8,000 species of birds are known to the naturalist, and these are divided into two primary sub-classes.

The first sub-class is called *Ratidæ*, and includes all those birds which have a sternum without a keel, a rudimentary furculum and wings, feathers with discontinuous barbs and not distributed in feather tracts, and with no oil gland. They are all natives of warm or temperate climates, and strictly limited in their range. Several gigantic forms which existed until recently, are now extinct, such as the moa of New Zealand and the æpyornis of Madagascar. The ostrich of Africa is a familiar instance, and is provided only with two toes. The American ostrich or rhea is smaller, and inhabits South America.

Parrots and Cuckoos.

The cassowary is a native of the East Indian archipelago, and the emu of the Australian continent. The apteryx of New Zealand is the most remarkable of these birds, as it has perfectly rudimentary wings and a long slender bill, and there is a remarkable disproportion between the size of the egg, which is very large, and that of the bird.

The second sub-class of birds is called *Carinatæ* and includes all those birds which have a keel on the breast-bone, a merrythought, usually functional wings, whose feathers are in tracts (except in the penguins) and have the barbs united along their margins. This includes fourteen orders of birds, of many of which there are familiar illustrations easily obtainable.

34. **Order 1, Parrots (Psittaci).**—The most intelligent and most highly organised of birds; easily known by their sharply hooked beaks, both the upper and lower part of which are movable, and by their brightly-coloured feathers. Their feet are prehensile, the outer and inner toes being turned backwards, while the two middle toes are turned forwards, and thus they are enabled to grasp in climbing. The tongue is soft, and the muscles which move it are more distinct than those of most birds, and hence the singular power of mimicking sounds possessed by many of them. They are natives of the

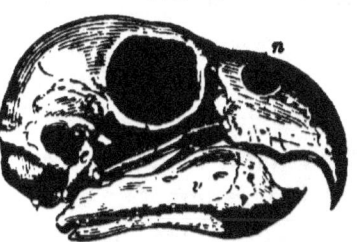

FIG. 26.

Skull of parrot.

n, nostril; *e*, quadrate bone; *v.* lower jaw; *m.* orbit.

tropics, the cockatoos being mostly from the East Indian archipelago, the macaws from South America, the common parrots from Africa and Madagascar. One curious genus, Strigops, the ground parrot of New Zealand, is exceptional in having no keel on its sternum, and some parakeets from Australia have no merrythought. They are vegetable-feeders, principally subsisting on fruits, but often eating honey. Many species live long in confinement, and they are all easily domesticated.

35. **Order 2, Cuckoos, &c. (Coccygomorphæ).**—These are usually long-beaked birds with small flat tongues, having the toes arranged either permanently or temporarily like those of parrots, with the outer and inner turned backwards. The wings have long covering feathers. Some of these birds have enormous beaks thrice as long as the head, like the little toucans of America; in others the beaks are surmounted with great horns, made of spongy bony tissue covered with horn, as in the hornbills of the Eastern tropics. Other examples of this order are the cuckoos, so familiar for their peculiar note and for their habit of laying eggs in the nests of other birds; the kingfishers, bee-eaters, hoopoe, rollers, &c. Some are remarkable for their colours, like the plantain-eaters of Africa. The tongues are hard, often bristled, as in the toucans; few have much vocal power. They are for the most part feeders on insects and animal substances.

36. **Order 3, Woodpeckers (Pici).**— Mostly brightly-coloured birds, with straight, strong, conical beaks, and slender and actively protrusible tongues.

The wings have short coverts. The middle toes are united at the base; the inner toe is small, directed backwards, as is also the outer toe. The tail feathers are short, stiff, and serve as organs of support. These are insect-eating birds like the last group, and they derive their name from their efforts after the capture of their prey. In these the tongue bone is specially elongated, and its lateral processes coiled and disposed to allow of the rapid protrusion of the barbed tongue. Woodpeckers exist everywhere but in Madagascar and Australia.

Fig. 27.

Foot of woodpecker.

37. **Order 4, Swifts and Humming-Birds (Macrochires).**—A small order of birds, mostly of very minute size, and almost all of powerful flight. Some of these, like the swifts, have flattish beaks; others, like the humming-birds, have long tubular bills. In each wing the forearm and hand greatly exceed in length the upper arm, hence the Latin name given to the order. The feet are very weak, scarcely able to support the weight of the body, and the inner toe may in some be turned forwards or backwards. They have a very simple syrinx, and little or no voice. They are mostly tropical birds, and vary much in size, the goatsuckers being the largest, sometimes of comparatively large size; while the swifts are much smaller and somewhat swallow-like. One of these, the Collocalia of the Malay archipelago, secretes, by

means of glands in the throat, a glutinous material of which it constructs its nests, which are the edible birds' nests of Eastern commerce, used as food in China. The humming-birds of Brazil, of which there are very numerous species, are also examples of this order, and include the smallest forms of the entire class of birds; thus *Melisuga minimus,* from the island of San Domingo, only weighs about nine grains, and measures two inches in extreme length; its nest is about the size of a walnut, and it contains two eggs each nearly as large as a pea.

38. **Order 5, Perching birds** (*Passeres.*)—This large order includes all our small birds, with the exception of those hitherto mentioned. They may be recognised by possessing short wing coverts, a tarsus covered in front with seven large scales, and slender toes, of which the first joints of the two outer are united. They have a well-developed syrinx or organ of voice, and many of them can sing. These birds are very numerous, and make up about twenty-one families. The best known of these are the following :—The thrushes, known by their slightly curved bill, with a notch or tooth on each side near the tip, and with bristles at the angles of the gape of the mouth. They are insect-eaters for the most part. The commonest species are the song thrush; the blackbird, known by its yellow bill and eyelid-edge and its black body; the missel thrush, known by its white-tipped three outer tail feathers ; the fieldfare, the redwing.

FIG. 28.

Foot of passerine bird.

Passerine Birds.

To this family belongs the mocking bird of America, which can mimic the song of any other bird. The birds of the wagtail family are recognisable by their slender forms, long legs, long tails, and moderate wings with nine primary feathers. They include the common pied wagtails, the yellow-breasted wagtail; closely allied to which are the hedge-sparrows (*Accentor*) with strong, sub-conical, straight bills, and wings with a very short first quill, the third and fourth primaries being the longest. The warbler family, consisting of small singing birds with awl-shaped beaks flattened at base, are also closely allied; of these the most familiar examples are the nightingales (*Philomela*); robin red-breasts of Europe; red-starts (*Phænicura*); sedge and grasshopper warblers (*Salicaria*); white-throats, black-caps (*Curruca*); and willow-wrens (*Sylvia*). The gold-crested kinglet (*Regulus*) is the smallest American bird of this order, its length being under 4 inches. The pipits (*Anthus*), have awl-shaped bills, keeled at the base above, with two long scapular feathers and long hind claw. In North America the warblers (*Silviidæ*) of Europe are represented by the *Silvicolidæ* or American warblers.

The crow family (*Corvidæ*) constitute a group of much larger birds; they have strong conical bills with no notch, and robust feet. This family includes the jackdaw, crow, raven, jay, and magpie, and the starling is a nearly related form. These have ten primary feathers, while the birds of the conical-billed finch family possess only nine. This family consists of the house-sparrows, hawfinches, linnets, bullfinches, and nearly related are the larks and buntings.

Among the most remarkable tropical forms are the lyre-birds of Australia, the oven-builders of Brazil; the sun-birds, nuthatch, wax-wings, &c.

39. **Order 6, Birds of Prey (Raptores).**—This order consists of eagles, owls and vultures, which feed on animal food, and are armed with strongly hooked bills (fig. 30), and with strong, sharp and curved claws (fig. 29). At the base of the bill is a

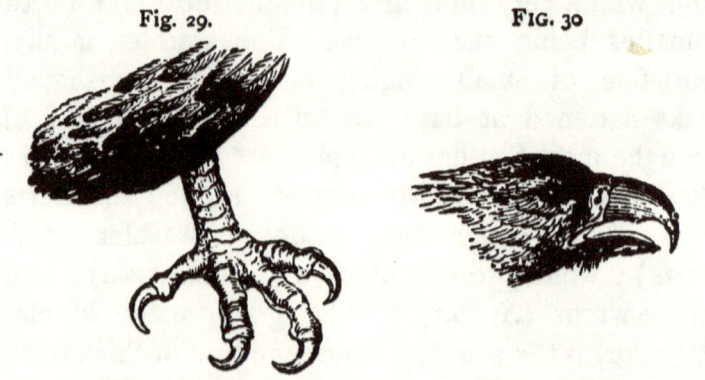

Fig. 29.   Fig. 30.

Foot of eagle.   Head of eagle.

cere or skin, which is pierced by the nostrils. The gizzard is weak, the digestive tract short, the sense organs are acute and powerful. Their strong wings have ten primary feathers, and the tail has twelve rectrices. Owls are mostly nocturnal, round-faced birds, with short beaks, and with eyes directed forwards. They have no crop, and peculiarly soft plumage. Some have tufts of feathers above the ears, such as the horned owls. Vultures are carrion-eaters, most abundant in warm climates, with naked or down-clad head and longer bills. Eagles have feather-clad heads, and short, sharply-hooked bills, and they for the most part feed on prey which they kill for themselves. To this family belong the hawks, kites, buzzards and harriers, as well as the larger eagles, ospreys, and falcons.

CHAPTER XIII.

CLASSIFICATION OF BIRDS CONTINUED.

40. **Order 7, Pigeons (Gyrantes).**—This well-marked group consists of the doves and pigeons, characterised by having a gristly plate covering the base of the upper mandible, pierced in front by the nostrils. They are vegetable-feeders, with a large glandular crop which sometimes secretes a milky fluid with which the parents nourish the young birds. They have a strong gizzard, shielded or feathered tarsi, and four usually free toes all on the same level, with short, slightly-hooked claws. They are mostly birds of powerful flight, and have ten primary quill feathers in their long pointed wings, and twelve or rarely sixteen rectrices. They are mostly social birds, often living in great societies. The pigeons, wood-quests, and doves are familiar instances, as also are the passenger pigeons of North America, which migrate in millions, darkening the air by their flocks. Our common pigeons, in all their varieties, are descended from the rock-dove, *Columba livia*. The curious dodo of Mauritius was an aberrant large pigeon incapable of flight, and hence it was easily

captured by the early voyagers, and was extirpated in the seventeenth century.

41. **Order 8, Scraping birds (Rasores).**—This large and economically important order includes the poultry, turkeys, pheasants, grouse, partridge, &c., heavy plump-bodied birds, with comparatively small rounded wings, weak in flight, and with a moderate length of beak and legs; they have stout blunt claws, the hind toe being raised above the level of the others. The name of the order is derived from the habit common to most of them of scraping in searching for their food in or on the ground. The tarsus often bears spurs, especially in the males, and the plumage is close and often brilliantly coloured, as in the peacocks and pheasants. Many of them have naked areas on the head, where the skin is soft and vascular, forming wattles or crests. As they are mostly grain-eaters, they have large muscular gizzards, capacious crops, and long intestines. Our common domestic fowls are natives of India, as also is the peacock and that most gorgeously coloured bird the Impeyan pheasant, whose plumage has a rich metallic lustre. The golden pheasant is a native of China, the turkey of America. In Australia the order is represented by the mound-birds and brush turkeys, which hatch their eggs in 'hot-beds' formed of large masses of decaying vegetable matters which they heap together for the purpose.

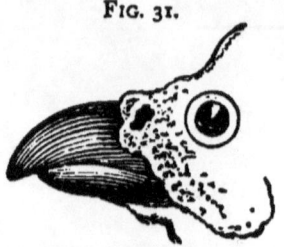

FIG. 31.

Head of Numida.

42. **Order 9, Grallæ.**—This group consists of long-

Storks and Ducks.

legged birds which are often waders in habit, and are characterised by possessing small hind toes and long bills. They feed on worms, molluscs, and fish, rarely on vegetables. The side of the head presents no bare patch between the angle of the mouth and the eye, and the palate exhibits a long cleft between the two lateral halves of the upper jawbones. To this order belong the plovers and peewits, coots and waterhens, corncrakes and snipe, the cranes and bustards, oyster-catchers, herons, and bitterns.

43. **Order 10, Storks (Ciconiæ).**—This group also consists of birds with long legs and bills, which in habit resemble the last, but differ from them essentially in their structure. Thus they have the two

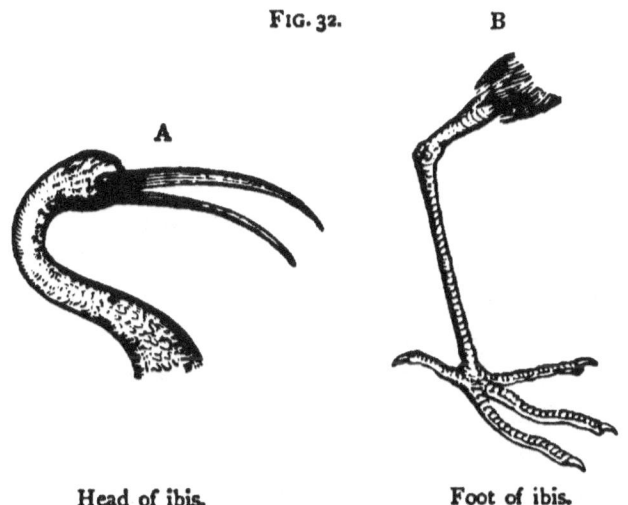

Fig. 32.

Head of ibis.   Foot of ibis.

lateral sides of the upper-jaw united along the middle line of the palate ; the *lore* or space between the angle of the mouth and the eye is bare, and the hind toe is long and functional. The best known examples are the ibises, spoonbills, storks, and jabirus, some of which are distinguished for their brilliant colours, like the scarlet ibis, the straw-necked ibis, and the scarlet spoonbill. The loose feathers of the leptoptilus of India are used for ornamenting bonnets, under the name *Marabou* feathers.

44. **Order 11, Ducks and Geese (Lamellirostres).** —The birds belonging to this order make a very natural assemblage characterised by possessing webbed feet and long flattened bills, which on the under surface of the upper mandible exhibit a series of close transverse lamellæ; these act as sensitive prehensile surfaces in feeding, and large nerves are distributed on them. They have large fleshy tongues, and the hind toe is free and small. The wild swan presents a curious arrangement of its very long and sinuous windpipe, a coil of which lies within the hollow keel of the sternum. The best known forms are the ducks, geese, mergansers, swans, teals, widgeon, &c.

45. **Order 12, Longipennes.**—These are also web-footed marine fish-eating birds, with long pointed wings well fitted for flight. They have long compressed beaks, with the nostrils either slit-like, as in the common gull, or tubular, as in the petrel. The hind toe is free, and usually of small size.

The gulls, terns, petrels are the best known examples, the largest species in the order being the famous albatross, found on the ocean about the equator, which is allied to the small petrels or Mother Cary's chickens.

46. **Order 13, Pelicans (Steganopodes).**—A curious order of water birds which have all the four

toes included in the broad web, hence the feet have a singularly inturned appearance (fig. 33). Many of them have long bills and throat pouches, like the pelicans and frigate birds; other and better known forms are the gannets, cormorants, and long-tailed tropic birds.

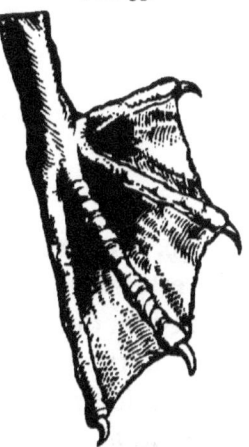

FIG. 33.

Foot of pelican.

47. **Order 14, Pygopodes.**—The last order of birds includes a singular assemblage of seabirds, whose wings are small and sickle-shaped, scarcely fitted for flight, and sometimes with scale-like feathers, as the penguins of the Antarctic Ocean. They have the hind limbs even farther back than in the generality of seabirds, and hence the curious erect position assumed by these birds when standing; they have hard pointed compressed bills, and a small hind toe, the three anterior toes are closely webbed. The auks of the northern seas, the puffins, guillemots, and razorbills of our shores, are the most familiar examples. The great auk of the northern seas, is wingless, and like the dodo has become extinct.

48. **Migration of Birds.**—Among birds, as among fishes, we notice the curious habit of periodical migration; the travelling at regular periods into districts wherein suitable food is abundant, and their return on change of season; thus the swallows, swifts, rice birds and warblers visit the north about the middle of April, breed there, and then return to their winter quarters in the Southern States and the West Indies

on the advent of cold weather, about the first week of October.

CHAPTER XIV.

CLASS 5, MAMMALIA.

49. **General Characters.**—This, the highest class of vertebrate animals, includes all those viviparous, warm-blooded animals which are provided with superficial dermal glands for the purpose of secreting a fluid called milk for the nutrition of the young until they are able to seek out other nutriment for themselves. They are for the most part terrestrial in habit ; they are all provided with epidermal covering in the form of hairs ; and the lower jaw in them articulates directly with the base of the skull, the quadrate bone being very small and included in the ear cavity, so that it is of use only in conveying sound-waves to the nerves of hearing. Man, all quadrupeds, seals, whales, and bats are examples of this class.

The superficial clothing of hairs characteristic of the class may be only transitory, as in whales and some thick-skinned animals, or the hairs may be thick and spine-like, as in the porcupine and hedgehog, or they may be united into scales, as in the manis and armadillo, or on the tail of a rat. Each hair is the epidermal secretion of a single papilla, and is a solid cylinder composed of long cortical or superficial cells, and rounder central cells. The hairs arise

Skeleton of Mammalia. 75

in pits or follicles, and into these follicles there open sebaceous glands, which secrete an oily material for the lubrication of the hairs.

The neck-region of the vertebral column or backbone in all mammals consists of seven vertebræ, except in three cases;[1] the back region consists of about twenty, but the number is more variable; the shoulder girdle is never connected directly to the spine, but the pelvic girdle always is so, and hence there are always certain vertebræ thickened and united for the purpose of supporting the pelvis; these are known as the *sacrum*, and behind this in most mammals is the tail, which varies extremely in length, sometimes, as in the long-tailed manis of Western Africa, having over forty vertebræ, in others, as in some bats, having only three. In man there are four very small rudimental tail vertebræ, and the same number exists in the gorilla, chimpanzee, and orang-outang. In many mammals, as the South American monkeys, opossums, and kinkajous, the tail is prehensile and is used as an additional hand in climbing.

50. **Skeleton.**—The skeleton consists of two classes of bones, some with an interior of spongy cells, others with an internal cavity. In both cases the hollow spaces are filled with marrow. The skull in mammals is a solid box to which the upper jaw is immovably fixed, and it articulates with the first vertebra of the neck by means of two articular knobs or condyles. The lower jaw is composed of two pieces only, one on each side, and it forms a joint directly with the

[1] These are two sloths, one having 9, the other 6 vertebræ, and an aquatic American animal, the manatee, which has 6.

skull, beneath the ear. The shape of the articular surfaces which form this joint is variable, and depends on the nature of the food and the character of the motions which are necessary for mastication. Thus, in flesh-eating animals the lower jaw has a transversely elongated, cylindrical condyle, which can allow only of a vertical motion, while in gnawing animals the lower jaw slides forwards and backwards.

51. **Teeth.**—The jaw arches, and they alone, bear teeth, which are arranged in one row; no accessory teeth are developed on the palate as in reptiles and fishes. The teeth are always in sockets, and are

FIG. 34.

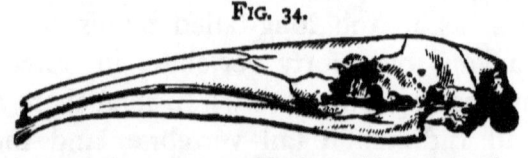

Skull of anteater, a perfectly toothless mammal.

rarely absent, as in the anteaters (fig. 34), though sometimes they are rudimental and disappear early, as in whales. There are usually two sets of teeth; one an early developed or milk set, which soon drop out and are succeeded by a second or permanent set; thus reminding us of what we found in crocodiles, where successively growing teeth follow each other in the one row almost indefinitely as long as growth continues. Those teeth in the upper jaw which are rooted in the foremost bone, or premaxilla, are called incisor teeth, and have usually a cutting edge and a single root. When the first tooth in the maxilla or jaw proper, is placed near the suture or line of contact between that bone and the premaxilla, it is

Teeth of Mammals. 77

generally long and pointed and has but one root. To it the name canine is given, while the other maxillary teeth have in general two or more fangs, and are called grinding teeth or molars. The milk teeth are usually fewer than the permanent teeth, and hence some of these grinders have had predecessors while others have not; those which are secondary are called premolars, while those which are primary (the hindermost), are called molars. Similar names are given to the corresponding teeth in the lower jaw. As the teeth vary in number and size in the different orders of mammals, they afford a good and easy system whereby the different forms can be discriminated; and in order to be able briefly to describe the characteristic dentition of any animal, zoologists are in the habit of tabulating the number and arrangement of the teeth of animals in a set formula; thus

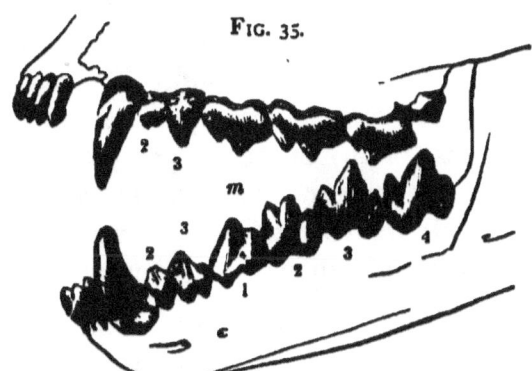

Fig. 35.

Teeth of Tasmanian devil.

to write the dental formula of an animal we first put down the initials of the sets of teeth, and follow each initial by the number of teeth of that sort in the two jaws, those of the upper jaw being written like the numerator of a fraction, while those of the lower are placed as the denominator; thus, in an adult man the dental formula is $I\frac{2-2}{2-2}$, $C\frac{1-1}{1-1}$, $P\frac{2-2}{2-2}$, $M\frac{3-3}{3-3}$; that is, on each side of each jaw there are two incisors, on each side of each jaw one canine, two premolars, and three molars. The jaws are almost always protected by fleshy lips, except in the first order.

52. **Viscera.**—Mammals have well developed brains, and usually acute sense-organs. The lungs and heart are separated from the intestine and other digestive organs by a muscular partition, called the diaphragm, which is an important agent in breathing. The heart consists of four cavities, and the opening between the right auricle and right ventricle is guarded by a membranous valve consisting of three flaps. There is but one aortic arch in the adult, and it arches to the left side; there are two carotid arteries for conveying blood to the brain. The blood contains round, non-nucleated corpuscles, and therein differs from that of any of the foregoing classes.

There are seventeen orders of mammals at present living, but representatives of several additional and most remarkable intermediate orders have been found in a fossil state, especially in the tertiary beds in America.

CHAPTER XV.

CLASSIFICATION OF MAMMALS.

53. **Order 1, Monotremata.**—The first order of mammals is called *Monotremata*, and includes two remarkable Australian forms, the platypus and the spiny anteater. They are both small animals, being about a foot in length. Both have long coracoid bones separate from the shoulder-blade or scapula, which, bird-like, reach as far as the sternum, and the two collar-bones unite into a single T-shaped merrythought-like bone. In both forms there are two long spur-like bones articulated to the front of the pelvis and embedded in the abdominal muscles, and in both the bones of the skull unite at an early period to form a perfectly continuous braincase. They are also characterised by the intestine and excretory organs opening, as in the birds, into a common cloaca (hence the name of the order). The platypus, or *Ornithorhynchus*, is aquatic, and has a duck-like bill and two small, flat, horny teeth in each jaw. The male has a strong hollow spur on the ankle which communicates with the duct of a poison gland and is a weapon of offence. The spiny anteater, or Echidna (fig. 36), is toothless, and has a long slender horny bill, a worm-like tongue, and a dermal covering of strong stout spines. The young of both these forms are born in a very imperfect state of development.

54. **Order 2, Marsupialia.**—The second order of mammals is named *Marsupialia*, and includes kanga-

80   *Vertebrata.*

roos and opossums, and all those other Australian forms in which the females bear on the under surface

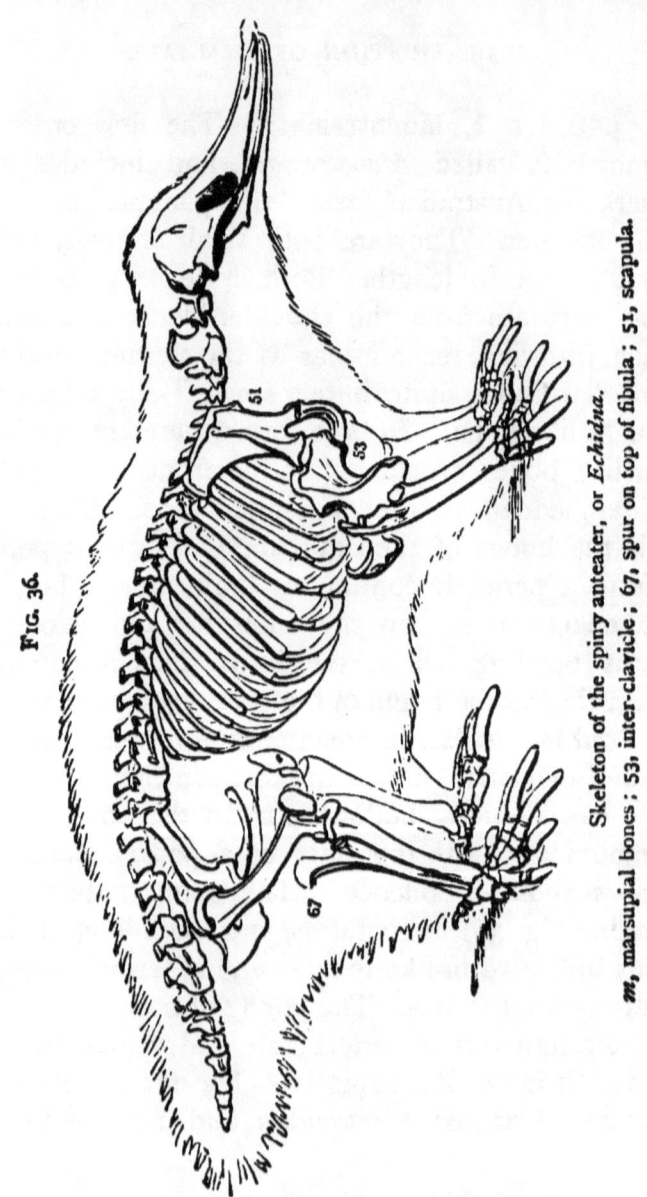

FIG. 36.—Skeleton of the spiny anteater, or *Echidna.*
m, marsupial bones; 53, inter-clavicle; 67, spur on top of fibula; 51, scapula.

Kangaroos.

of the body a pouch wherein the young are received and sheltered after their birth. This pouch is supported by two bones (fig. 37, *m*,) similar to those described in connection with the pelvis of the Monotremes; to these bones the name marsupial bones has been given, but they exist in the pouchless males as well as in the pouch-bearing females. All the marsupials are clad with thick fur, and they are armed with claw-bearing toes, two of which on the hind foot tend to become very small and united within a common web of skin. They exhibit many characters of inferiority to the other mammals; thus the two lateral lobes of the fore-brain are nearly smooth on the surface and are imperfectly united together, and the young are born in an exceedingly rudimental state.

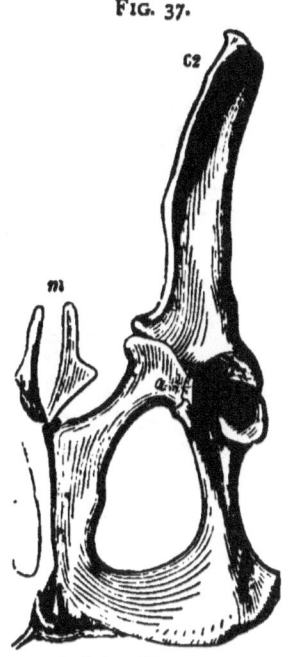

FIG. 37.

Pelvis of kangaroo.
m, marsupial bones; 62, ilium.

The marsupials vary very much in habit, and are modified to suit these habits. Thus, the Tasmanian devil and Tasmanian wolf are flesh-eaters, with sharp claws and sharp strong teeth (fig. 35). The opossums of America are insect-eaters, and have sharp and numerous teeth; they are the only marsupials which live outside the great Australian region, to which all the others are confined, and of which they are almost the sole mammalian inhabitants. Some of

Vertebrata.

the opossums have the pouch rudimental, and the mother carries her young ones on her back, often

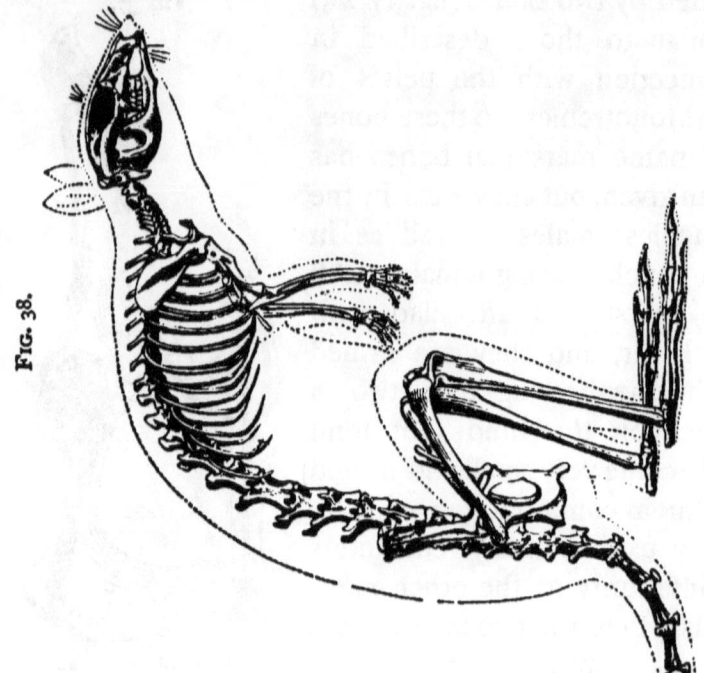

Fig. 38.—Skeleton of kangaroo.

with their prehensile tails coiled round her tail. Others, like the yapock of South America, are amphibious, and have webbed feet.

The kangaroos proper (fig. 38) are characterised by the enormous disproportion of the fore and hind limbs; the former are short, five-fingered, while the latter are very long with long feet, the middle or third toe (which corresponds to our fourth, as they have no great toe) being enormous in length, the fourth being a little smaller, while the first and second are united and excessively

Kangaroos, Phalangers.

slender. The tail is thick and with the hind legs makes a tripod whereupon the animal rests when standing. In feeding, the animal bends down so as to rest on the short forepaws, and in running it progresses by a series of long leaps or bounds in which it uses only its hind legs.

The largest living kangaroos are about five to six feet high when standing; but the majority of the species are small, some being not larger than a rat.

FIG. 39.

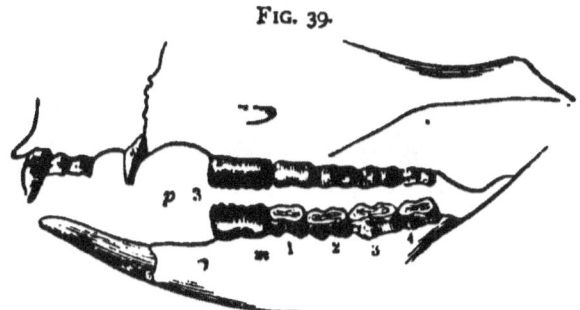

Teeth of kangaroo rat.

These true kangaroos are herbage-feeders, and they have a complexly-pouched stomach to enable them to digest green food. Their teeth generally are :—

$$I\frac{3-3}{1-1},\ C\frac{0}{0},\ \text{or}\ \frac{1}{0},\ P\frac{1-1}{1-1},\ M\frac{4-4}{4-4}.$$

The phalangers, or Australian opossums, are fruit-eaters for the most part, and like the opossums of America they have an opposable thumb on the hind foot, which thus is able to act in grasping like a hand. Some of these phalangers have wing-like side folds of skin stretching from the fore to the hind limbs, whereby they are able to take long flying leaps.

The wombat is a burrowing and gnawing marsupial, whose chisel-shaped incisor and other teeth continue permanently to grow, and thus the waste of tooth-tissue which takes place in the process of grinding the roots and twigs which constitute its food, is restored. This animal is about $2\frac{1}{2}$ feet long, and, like the koala or native bear of Australia, has an accessory gland in the stomach, and a long cæcum or pouch, where the large and small intestines unite. They are both also almost tail-less, and the koala has its thumb and index fingers capable of being opposed to the others.

Some fossil kangaroos, like the Diprotodon, were of great size; one thigh bone of this animal in the museum of the University of Dublin, must have been at least two feet in length when complete. It is also interesting that the earliest fossil mammals which have as yet been discovered are marsupials. The bones of marsupials are, in general, easily recognised; thus the lower jaw has an inflexed angle, whereby it can be distinguished from that of any other mammal. The dentitions of marsupials are very variable, as can be seen from the four subjoined examples :—

Kangaroo (fig. 37) $I\frac{3-3}{1-1}, C\frac{1-1}{0-0}, P\frac{1-1}{1-1}, M\frac{4-4}{4-4}$.

Wombat . . $I\frac{1-1}{1-1}, C\frac{0-0}{0-0}, P\frac{1-1}{1-1}, M\frac{4-4}{4-4}$.

Myrmecobius or banded anteater $\Big\}$ $I\frac{4-4}{3-3}, C\frac{1-1}{1-1}, P\frac{2-2}{3-3}, M\frac{5-5}{6-6}$.

Tasmanian devil (fig. 35) $\Big\}$ $I\frac{4-4}{3-3}, C\frac{1-1}{1-1}, P\frac{2-2}{2-2}, M\frac{4-4}{4-4}$.

CHAPTER XVI.

PLACENTAL MAMMALS.

55. The Placenta.—In all the succeeding orders of mammals the young are not born until their internal organisation has become much more perfectly developed than in the case of the young of the marsupials and monotremes; and in order to provide for their nutrition while they are thus growing, a peculiar vascular organ, called the *placenta*, is developed, whereby blood is supplied to the embryo for its nourishment; hence they are called placental mammals to distinguish them from the marsupials, which are named non-placental mammals.

Order 3, Edentata.—The third mammalian order is known as *Edentata*, and includes the anteaters and armadillos, which are easily recognised by the absence of incisor teeth, at least in the middle of the jaws, so that the front of the long, snout-like mouth appears toothless, hence the name. They are all armed with strong, usually sharp claws, and are clad with coarse hair, or else with hard scales, and feed on insects, small animals, or carrion. The true anteaters are natives of South America, and are quite toothless (fig 34). They have exceedingly long, worm-like tongues, which they can protrude for the purpose of entrapping the insects whereon they feed; and they have an enormous pair of glands in the neck which secrete a glutinous fluid to render the surface of the tongue sticky. This long tongue they can retract rapidly, and in order to enable them to accomplish this, the retractor muscle extends back to the hinder end of the breast-bone, which itself is often enormously elongated. Some anteaters are over five feet in length, others are much smaller. The great Cape anteater of South Africa is closely allied, but has a strap-like tongue and grinding teeth, which are peculiar in their structure, as each tooth consists, not of a single papilla like the teeth of most other animals, but of a closely united bundle of separate papillæ (fig. 40). The pangolins of Africa and Asia are covered with overlapping epidermal scales, and are also toothless and insect-eaters. They all have enormous claws on their hands for tearing open the ant-hills so as to reach their prey.

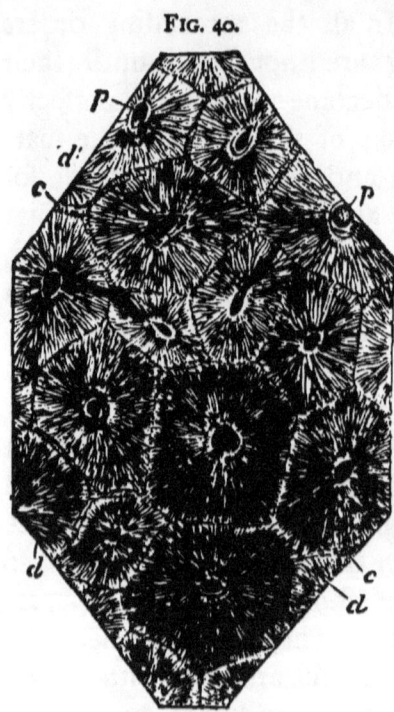

FIG. 40.

Tooth of *Orycterope* or Cape Anteater magnified, showing the separate papillæ, *p*, of which each tooth is made up; *d*, dentine, or toothsubstance; *c*, cement.

The second family, or the armadillos, are South American, scale-covered burrowing animals, with grinding teeth and a short tongue. They feed chiefly on carrion or small animals, and their dermal armour is arranged in transverse girdles or bands which may be movable on each other.

Armadillos.

The Edentates now existing are all of moderate or small size, but from the remains of fossil forms we

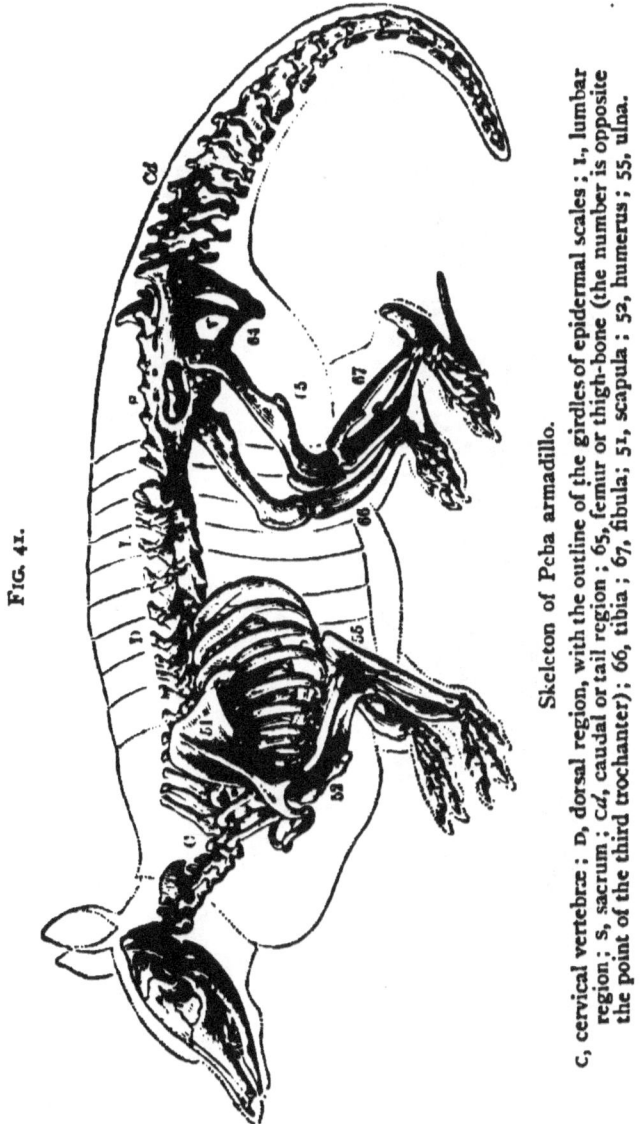

Fig. 41.—Skeleton of Peba armadillo. C, cervical vertebræ; D, dorsal region; L, lumbar region; S, sacrum; Cd, caudal or tail region; 65, femur or thigh-bone (the number is opposite the point of the third trochanter); 66, tibia; 67, fibula; 51, scapula; 52, humerus; 55, ulna.

know that some of them must have been of gigantic proportions.

88   *Vertebrata.*

56. Order 4, Bradypoda, or Sloths.—These are tail-less animals inhabiting South America. They

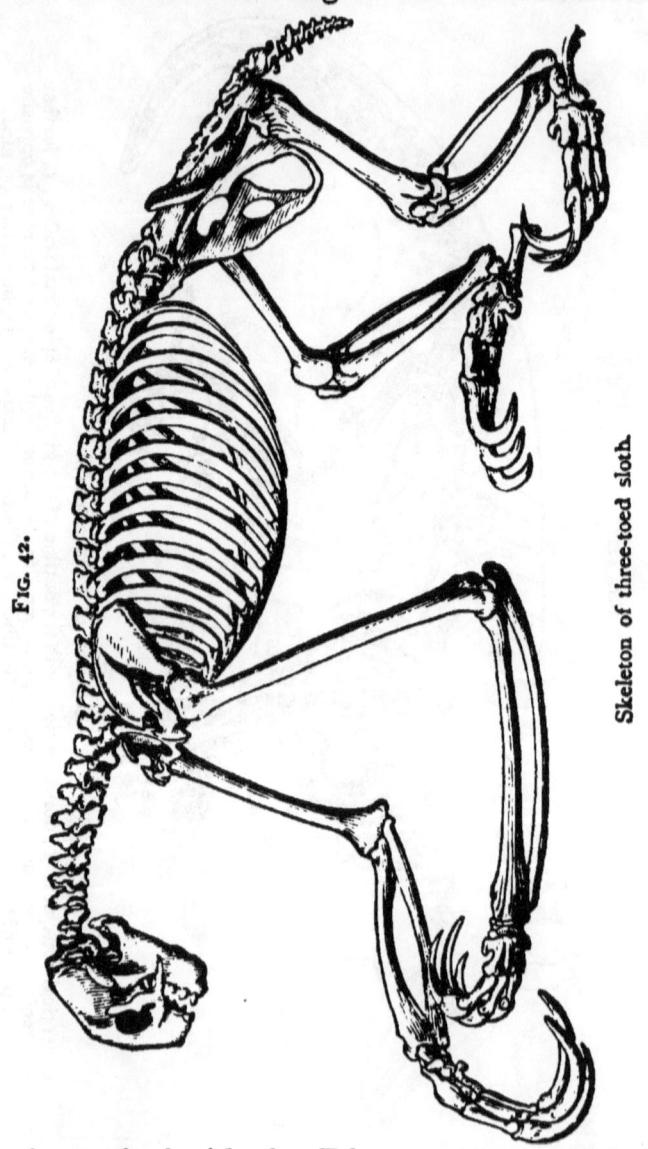

Fig. 42.   Skeleton of three-toed sloth.

are often united with the Edentates, from which they

differ in the possession of short round heads, not prolonged into a snout, with a lower jaw of one piece, even from a very early age, and also by having a very remarkable down-directed process of the malar or cheek-bone. They are strictly vegetable-feeders, and have sacculated stomachs. Their whole organisation is adapted to an arboreal life, and they live suspended from the branches of trees by their long and strong hook-like claws. They are clad with coarse hair of a dirty white or brownish colour, and have two or three toes only. The peculiarity of their neck vertebræ has been alluded to before (§ 49). They have no incisor teeth and $\frac{4-5}{5}$ molars, which are simple and nearly flat-topped.

The Megatherium, a fossil sloth from South America, must have been little less in size than a large hippopotamus. In many respects it and its allies seem like passage forms from the sloths to the armadillos.

57. **Order 5, Sirenia or Manatees**, constitute a small group of sea-weed-eating marine animals, of a somewhat fish-like habit and form, usually found near the mouths of rivers. They have a thick skin, sparsely covered with bristles, and flat-crowned grinding teeth. They have no hind limbs, and the fore-limbs are converted into paddles. The heart in some is deeply cleft, the right and left ventricles being nearly separate from each other (fig. 43). One animal of this group, the Rhytina, which inhabited some islands in Behring's Strait, has become extinct within the last century. Another, the dugong, inhabits the Indian Ocean,

90   *Vertebrata.*

while the manatee or mermaid is a native of the opposite shores of the South Atlantic, extending from South America to Africa. These are often confounded with whales, but can be known therefrom by their

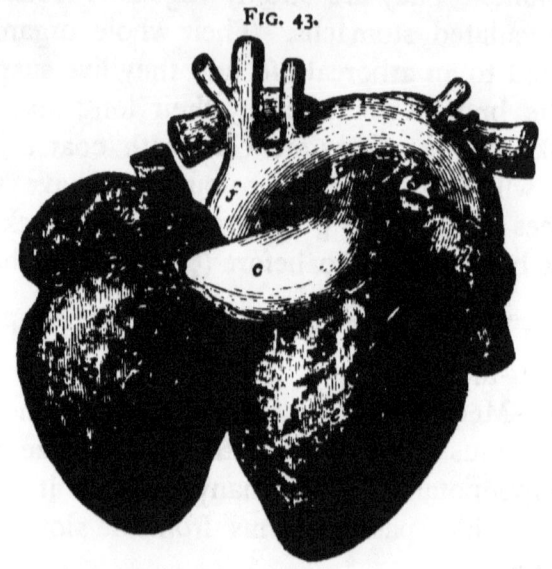

FIG. 43.

Heart of dugong, showing the separation of the ventricles.
a, right auricle ; *d*, left auricle ; *b*, right ventricle ; *e*, left ventricle ; *f*, aorta ; *c*, pulmonary artery.

possessing a neck, a movable elbow-joint, a trace of nails, and nostrils far forward and not at the top of the head. They also, except the extinct Rhytina, possess teeth.

58. **Order 6, Ungulata,** includes all those herbivorous mammals whose extremities are used solely as organs of progression, and not of prehension, and in which each toe ends in a hoof or broad case of horny epidermis. They are usually animals of large size, and they have no collar-bones. Their brains, however, are small in proportion to the bulk of the body, and

the intestinal canal is of very great length. There are two chief sub-orders of these hoofed animals, the first consisting of such as have odd toes on their hind feet, and unsymmetrical toes on the fore feet. Of these odd-toed mammals, there are three living types—horses, tapirs, and rhinoceroses. The horse and ass have only a single toe developed on each limb, which corresponds to the third toe of ordinary mammals. They have also a dentition of

$$I\tfrac{6}{6}, C\tfrac{1-1}{1-1}, P\tfrac{4-4}{4-4}, M\tfrac{3-3}{3-3}.$$

The two best known forms are the horse and the ass; the former is characterised by its tail, hairy from its base, and by the wart-like callosities on the inner surface of its legs. Remains of horses are found in the bone caves of Britain and of South America, as well as in those of Continental Europe. The striped races of the genus *Equus* are confined to Africa; they are the zebra, the quagga, the dauw, &c., and are scarcely tameable. The wild asses inhabit Western Asia. Fossil horses are known, exhibiting all the intermediate grades of development of feet from the single hoof of the common horse to the *Eohippus* with four functional toes and a fifth rudimentary one on the fore feet, and three toes behind.

The tapirs, natives of Malaya and of South America, are also uneven-toed ungulates, possessing three toes on their hinder, and four (but laterally unsymmetrical) toes on their fore feet. They are characterised by possessing a proboscis-like snout, and rather long legs. In number the teeth are equal to those in a horse.

92   *Vertebrata.*

The rhinoceros (fig. 44) is the third type of this sub-order, and is a native of Africa and the Malay

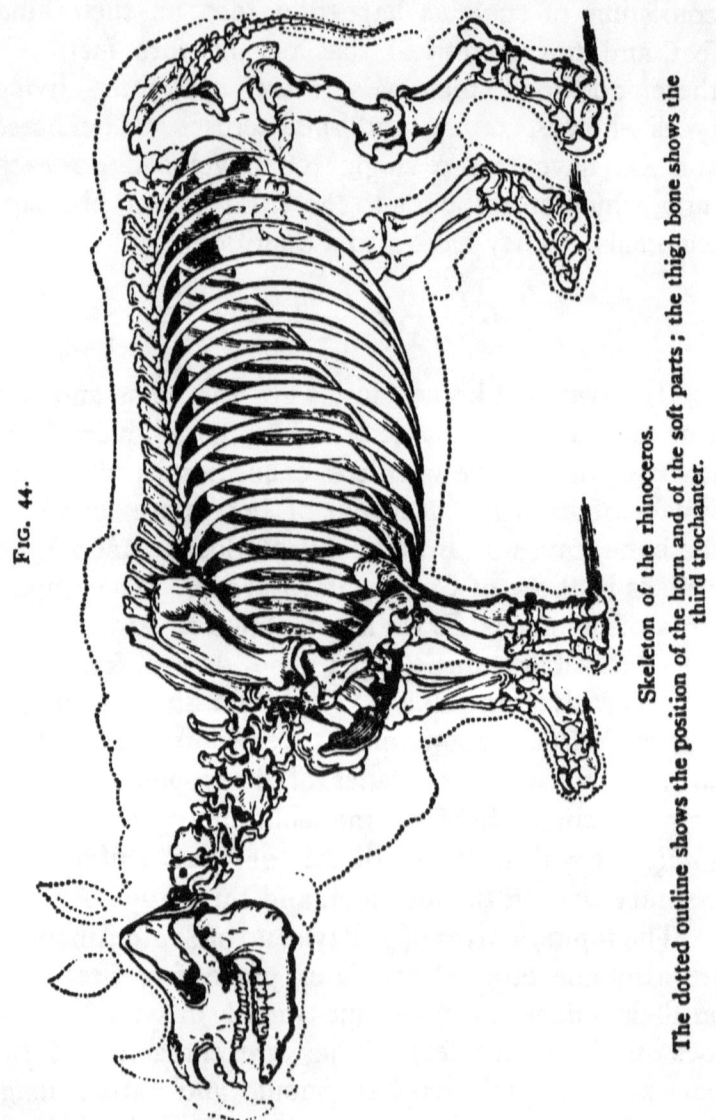

Fig. 44.—Skeleton of the rhinoceros. The dotted outline shows the position of the horn and of the soft parts; the thigh bone shows the third trochanter.

archipelago; the foot is three-toed, and the skin of

enormous thickness and often folded. The leading characteristic is the long epidermal horn which is rooted in the dermis on the upper surface of the nose. This in structure consists of a tuft of confluent hairs, and sometimes grows to several feet in length, and is of great hardness; the horn is always medial, and usually single, when two exist they are placed one in front of the other. At one time a species of rhinoceros clothed with a woolly coating inhabited Great Britain and the northern parts of Europe and Asia, but it became extinct in prehistoric times.

All these odd-toed ungulates have at least twenty-two vertebræ in their trunk, interposed between the neck and the sacrum, and they all have a bony knob or third trochanter on the outside of the shaft of the thigh bone for the attachment of muscles. See fig. 44, also fig. 41.

The second sub-order of hoofed animals includes those whose toes are. in even numbers, two or four, and are laterally symmetrical (when there are four, two are in front and two behind). They have for the most part nineteen dorso-lumbar vertebræ, and none of them have the protuberance on the thigh-bone referred to above. Many of them have horns, but these are always on the forehead, and one on each side, never median as in the rhinoceros.

59. **Swine and Hippopotami.**—There are two very well-marked divisions of these even-toed ungulates. In one of these the animals have simple stomachs, and the grinding teeth have little knobs or protuberances on their surfaces, hence these are called *Bunodonts*; in the other group the stomachs are complex,

and the hardest layer of the teeth (the enamel), is arranged in crescents; these are known as *Ruminants.* Of the bunodonts the pigs are the most familiar examples. Our domestic pigs are derived from the wild boars of Southern Europe and Asia, animals which formerly inhabited Great Britain in a wild state. The babyroussa of the Malay Islands is a singular pig whose upper canine teeth grow upwards and arch backwards so as to reach the forehead where they end in a curled point. Most of the pigs have large tusk-like canines, and their teeth are usually represented by the formula

FIG. 45.
Crown of the tooth of a deer, showing the enamel crescents.

$$I\frac{3-3}{3-3},\ C\frac{1-1}{1-1},\ P\frac{3-3}{3-3},\ M\frac{3-3}{3-3}.$$

The hippopotamus of the rivers of Africa is an enormous pig-like creature, with very short legs and a heavy body, and with long tusk-like incisors, two in each jaw; it sometimes reaches a length of nine feet.

60. **Ruminants.**—The ruminants are so called because they chew the cud, that is, they subject their food to a second chewing after it has been swallowed. They are, for the most part, large soft-fleshed animals, the favourite prey of large carnivores, and as the food which they require for their nourishment is bulky, being green herbage, and only to be obtained in open places of pasturage, where they would be exposed without shelter to the assaults of their enemies, it becomes a matter of vital importance for their well-

being that the process of mastication, a long and tedious one in the case of such food, should be kept over until the animal has laid in its store of provisions

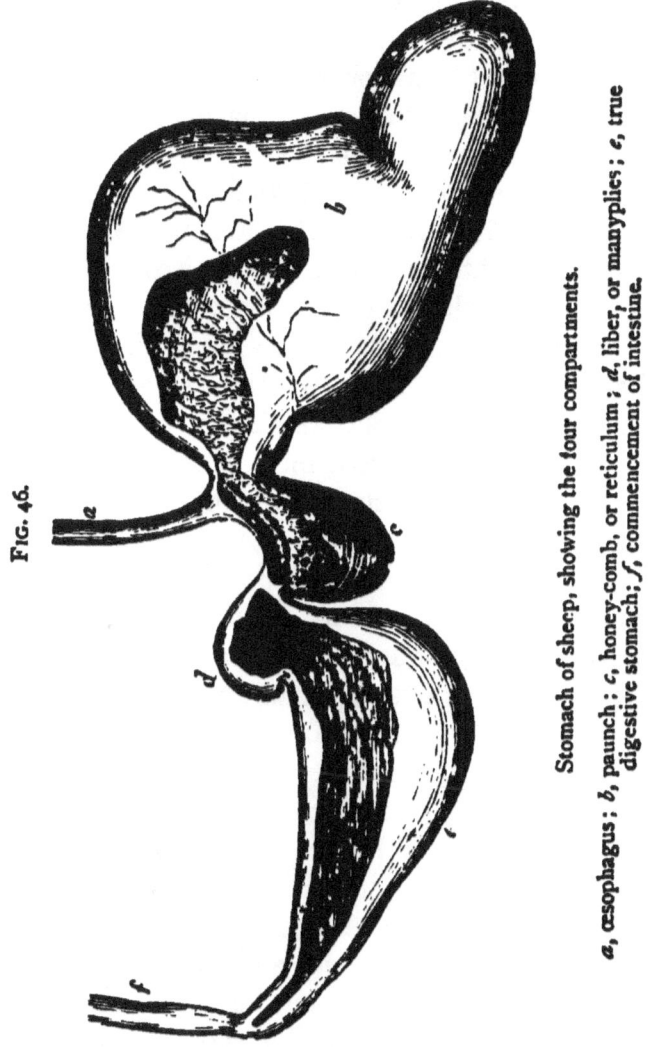

Fig. 46.—Stomach of sheep, showing the four compartments. *a*, œsophagus; *b*, paunch; *c*, honey-comb, or reticulum; *d*, liber, or manyplies; *e*, true digestive stomach; *f*, commencement of intestine.

and retired to a sheltered hiding-place. Accordingly the stomach of a ruminant is divided into four compartments, and into the first of these (called the *paunch*) the food is taken when first swallowed; then it passes into the second division, which consists of many large hexagonal cells or little chambers; here it becomes divided into masses for re-chewing, and these pass up the œsophagus back into the mouth, where it is carefully and slowly masticated, and mixed with saliva, after which it is re-swallowed, but this time as a semi-fluid soft material, which on reaching the stomach is conducted along a gutter made by a mucous fold, into the third stomach or liber, which consists of many layers of mucous membrane arranged like the leaves of a book. Here the materials are still farther mixed up with the secretions of gastric glands, and pass on into the fourth stomach, where digestion finally takes place. The camels of Arabia and Africa differ from the other ruminants in having no third stomach, in possessing canine teeth in each jaw, and two lateral incisor teeth in the upper jaw. They have also nails rather than hoofs on their large and well-padded toes. The hump on the camel's back consists of fat and cellular tissue. There is a single hump on the dromedary, but there are two on the back of the Arabian or Bactrian camel. The second stomach of the camel has deep cells or compartments, which has given origin to the fables about the capacity of camels to store water in their stomachs.

The llamas of the Andes in South America are closely allied to the camels, and agree with them in most of their peculiarities, but have no humps. The musk-deer, which inhabit the mountainous regions between the Himalaya and the Altai mountains, have

The Cow.

also canine teeth, and are distinguished by the presence of a pair of odour-secreting musk-glands.

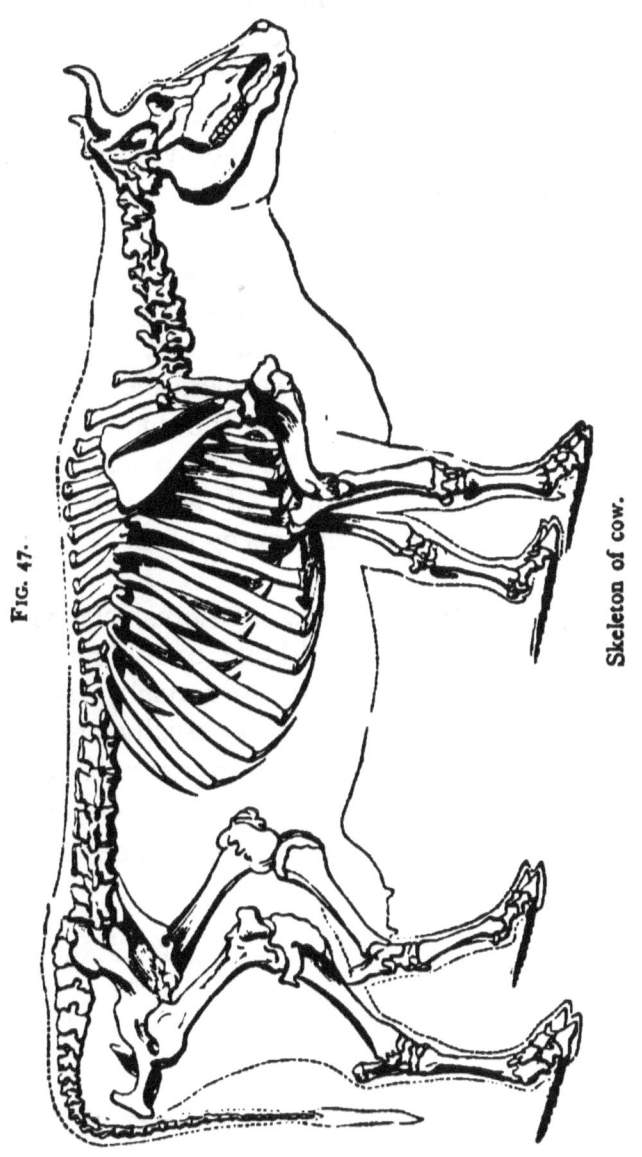

Fig. 47.—Skeleton of cow.

The other ruminants have neither canine nor incisor teeth in the upper jaw, and most of them possess horns. In the giraffe, the tallest and longest-necked of the mammals, these horns are short processes of the frontal bone covered with hairy skin. In the cows, antelopes, goats and sheep, these horns are made up of an outer hard, horny sheath, placed over a bony core or process of the frontal or forehead bone. In the ox and cow group, the horns are directed forwards, and are smooth, while in the antelopes, which are mostly natives of Africa, the horns are directed backwards, and are often ringed or waved. One American species, the pronghorn, sheds its horns periodically like the true deer. The goats and sheep have compressed angular wrinkled horns, often coiled. Our domestic sheep are possibly derived from the mountain sheep of South Europe and Asia.

The deer family possess solid horns composed of bony processes of the frontal bone, often branched in various ways. These antlers are annually shed and renewed, each new growth being usually larger than its predecessor. The best known examples are the Virginian deer, the fallow deer, and the roebuck. In most of these ruminants the dentition is represented by the formula

$$I \frac{0-0}{3-3}, C \frac{0-0}{1-1}, P \frac{3-3}{3-3}, M \frac{3-3}{3-3}.$$

CHAPTER XVII.

CLASSIFICATION OF MAMMALS—*continued*.

61. **Order 7, Cetacea (Whales).**—These, like the Sirenia, are marine mammals with no hind limbs, and having the fore limbs converted into fins. They are fish-like in shape, without necks, and have a smooth thick skin beneath which is a thick layer of fat known as blubber. The nostrils are situated on the upper surface of the head, and are called blow-holes, and are well protected by dermal folds so as to prevent the entrance of water into the air-passages while the whale is beneath the surface of the sea. These animals require to rise to the surface to breathe, and on doing so they forcibly eject a shower of spray, consisting of the mucus secreted by the membrane of the nasal passages, the vapour of the breath, and whatever sea water lurks in the crevices about the nostril; this process is called blowing, and it is in reality somewhat like a forcible sneeze preparatory to a deep inspiration. The sense of smell is almost or altogether absent. There are seven cervical vertebræ, but they are usually united together so as, in old whales, to form one bone.

The tail in whales consists of two lateral, horizontally-placed lobes consisting of folds of skin and connective tissue appended to the end of the vertebral column; this is the chief instrument of locomotion.

The mouth in true whales is of enormous capacity, and as their food is mostly small fish, cuttlefishes and molluscs, they require to take in very large quantities of this material for their nourishment, which they do in the following way. The jaw arches are covered all around their edges with horny plates of 'whalebone,' fringed with bristles in place of teeth, and these act as strainers. In feeding, the animal opening its mouth, takes in a mouthful of sea-water and its animal

FIG. 48.

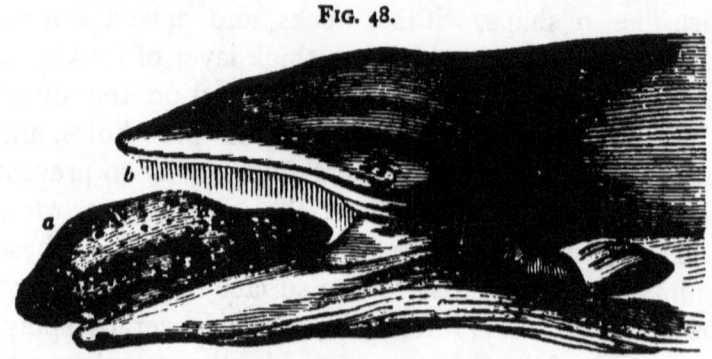

Head and tongue of whale.
a, tongue (represented much too large); *b*, whalebone plates.

contents, and then by closing the jaws and pressing the tongue against the palate, expels the water through the slits between the whalebone plates, which by their opposition and by their bristly margin retain the solid materials to be subsequently swallowed.

In some whales there are exceedingly minute rudiments of the hind limbs, in the form of small ischia or pelvic bones, embedded in the muscles of the abdomen, and not visible on the surface.

Whales have usually complex stomachs, often with four chambers; they have also a moderately long alimentary canal, large and tortuous networks of blood-vessels along the ribs, and a thick fleshy diaphragm.

Seals and Walruses.

The large-headed sperm whales are often as much as sixty to eighty feet long. One third of the whole length is formed by the head, whose anterior bones, enormously dilated, are hollowed into a chamber which contains the substance called *spermaceti*, used in making ointments and cosmetics. These whales possess from fifty to sixty large conical teeth in the lower jaw, and therein differ from the baleen whales, which in some cases possess small embryonic teeth that disappear early and are replaced by the whalebone plates. The common porpoises, bottle-noses, and dolphins have numerous simple teeth in both jaws, and the narwhal has one enormous front tooth which sometimes grows to a length of $5\frac{1}{2}$ or 6 feet, forming a horizontal tusk. Whales are the largest of animals, and have been seen over ninety feet in length.

62. **Order 8, Pinnipedia.**—This small order consists of the seals and walruses, and forms a connecting link between the whales on the one hand and the bears on the other. They are aquatic, fish-eating, hair-clad mammals, with four fin-like limbs, each provided with five webbed digits. The hind-limbs are stretched horizontally backwards on the same line as the tail, to which they are very closely united. They have roundish heads provided with numerous sensitive bristles, large eyes, and loosely united facial bones. They have valvular nostrils, no external ears, simple stomachs, and large venous cavities to hold the impure blood while respiration is suspended during diving.

Most seals are marine, but some live in freshwater lakes as in Lake Baikal. Our common seal is inoffensive and easily tamed. The walrus, known by its huge tusks or canine teeth, used for digging up the molluscs on which it feeds, sometimes reaches twenty feet in length. The fur seals, whose beautiful skins are of such commercial importance, are natives of the Southern Atlantic and Pacific Oceans. The dentition of the common seal is

$$I \frac{3-3}{2-2}, C \frac{1-1}{1-1}, P \frac{3-3}{3-3}, M \frac{3-3}{2-2}.$$

63. Order 9, Carnivora.—The flesh-eating mammals are the cats, dogs, weasels and bears, known by possessing sharp claws, long pointed canine teeth, a simple stomach, and a short intestine. The lower jaw is constructed to move only in the vertical plane up and down, having no lateral motion, the condyle

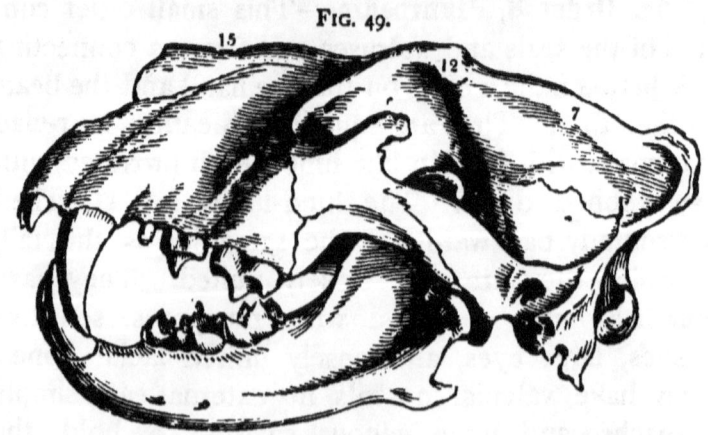

FIG. 49.

Skull of lion.
7, median temporal crest; 12, post-orbital process; 15, nasal bone.

being transversely lengthened. The molar teeth are ridged and sharp, so as to be fitted for dividing flesh.

They never have collar-bones. The skull of a carnivore can be easily known by the prominent medial crest for the attachment of the powerful muscles which move the lower jaw (fig. 49, 7).

The dog is a typical carnivore, whose teeth are represented by the formula

$$I \frac{3-3}{3-3}, C \frac{1-1}{1-1}, P \frac{4-4}{4-4}, M \frac{2-2}{3-3}.$$

In progression dogs are digitigrades, that is they only rest on the last joint of their toes in walking, and their claws are blunt, not capable of being retracted. The numerous races of dogs cannot be sharply marked off from each other, nor can some of the varieties of the dog be sharply differentiated from wolves. The wolf has usually erect ears and larger teeth, but no absolute point of difference can be relied upon. The fox has an oval pupil and a more bushy tail. All the true dogs have comparatively smooth tongues.

The family *Felidæ*, or cats, are also digitigrade carnivores, but they differ from the *Canidæ*, or dogs, in having the claws capable of retraction when not in use, and thus they are preserved from undue friction and are sharp; the retraction is accomplished by means of lateral elastic ligaments. The cats are more purely flesh-eaters than the dogs, and usually hunt and kill their prey; their dentition is

$$I \frac{3-3}{3-3}, C \frac{1-1}{1-1}, P \frac{3-3}{2-2}, M \frac{1-1}{1-1}.$$

The lion is a native of Africa and Asia, the tiger, the

strongest of the carnivores, is confined to Asia. Other forms are the panthers and leopards, the ounce, the jaguar or American leopard, the puma or American lion, the tiger-cats, ocelots, lynx, and domestic cats. This last-named is probably the descendant of the wild cat of Abyssinia tamed by the ancient Egyptians. The wild cat of this country (*Lynx canadensis*), ranges over the entire continent south of the Arctic circle. The cheetah, or hunting leopard of India, has only partially retractile claws. The cats have all rough tongues armed with numerous sharp, recurved papillæ.

The hyænas are intermediate in some respects between the dogs and the cats. They have the dentition and rough tongues of the cats, with a more doglike form and non-retractile claws. They are nocturnal, and can be known by the peculiarly low hind-quarters in comparison with the fore.

Civets and mongooses make another family called *Viverridæ*, which usually possess odorous glands, rough tongues, short legs, and a semi-plantigrade mode of progression. The weasel and otter family, *Mustelidæ*, differ from these in their shorter, rounder heads, smooth tongues, and longer bodies. Many of these are sought for on account of their skins, such as the vison, ermine, sable, mink, &c. Others, like the weasel, skunk and pole-cat, are well-known vermin; the *Mustela foina*, or marten, was the domestic cat of the classic authors.

The plantigrade carnivores are those that bring their whole foot-sole to the ground when walking; they are bears, badgers, and kinkajous. The badgers

Bears, Badgers, Kinkajous. 105

have scent glands, whereby they are easily distinguished. The kinkajou, a native of South America,

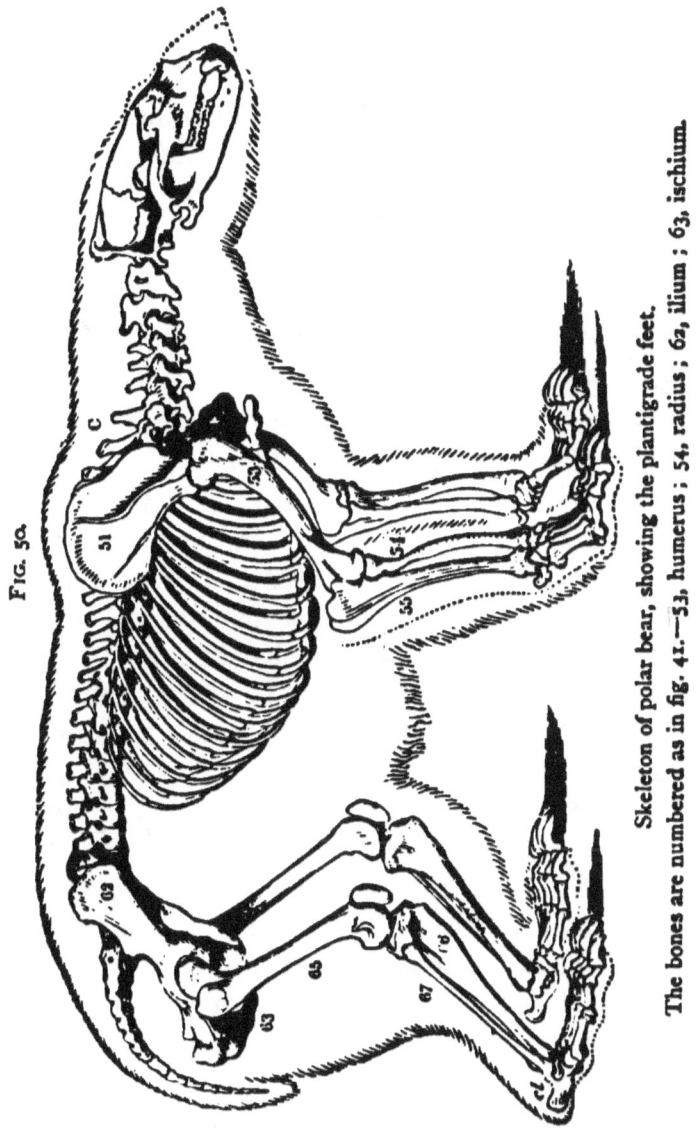

Fig. 50.—Skeleton of polar bear, showing the plantigrade feet. The bones are numbered as in fig. 41.—53, humerus; 54, radius; 62, ilium; 63, ischium.

has a prehensile tail and retractile claws. The best

known of the bears are the polar or white bear of the Arctic regions, the black bear of America, the brown bear of Europe, and the grizzly bear of the Rocky Mountains, possibly the same as the giant cave bear, now extinct in these countries. The brown bear formerly inhabited the British Islands, but was extirpated in Scotland in the eleventh century.

The bears differ from the other carnivores in the possession of tubercled teeth which can be used for masticating vegetable matters, and many of them are capable of partaking of a mixed diet.

64. **Order 10, Hyracoidea.**—A small order including a few little tail-less animals, natives of Africa and Syria, one of which is the cony, mentioned in the Bible. They are somewhat rabbit-like in habit, with four toes on the fore feet, and three on the hinder, each toe being armed with a flat nail. The molar teeth have been compared in pattern to those of the rhinoceros, and there are no canines. They have sacculated stomachs and no collar-bones.

65. **Order 11, Rodentia.**—Gnawing animals, the largest order in the entire class, including the rats, mice, squirrels, &c. They are all small and claw-bearing, and have a most remarkable dentition. There is usually but one incisor on each side of each jaw, and this tooth is chisel-shaped; it consists of two materials, one a hard substance or enamel on the outside or front, the other a softer dentine or bone-like substance behind. In their growth the upper and lower teeth oppose each other, and the constant friction during feeding wears away the surface of the tooth, which however is constantly growing, but as the soft dentine

wears away more quickly than the harder enamel, the tooth is kept constantly sharp; hence when one incisor in a rodent is broken, the one that should

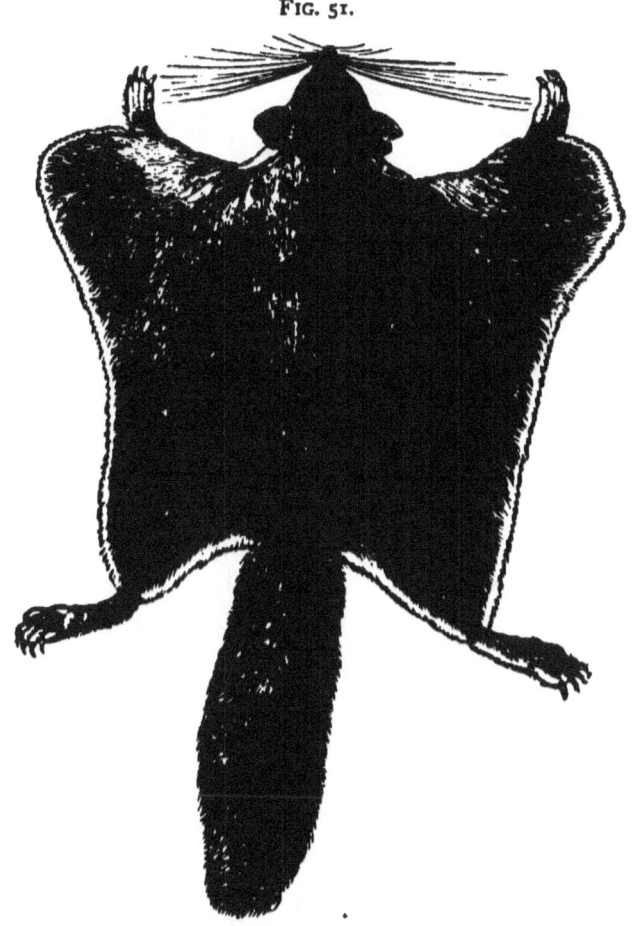

FIG. 51.

Flying squirrel.

oppose it grows on continuously, and sometimes this mode of growth locks the jaws together.

There are no canine teeth in rodents, and the

molars are separated from the incisors by a long interspace. The lower jaw is large, and its condyle is so articulated as to permit it to slide backwards and forwards in mastication, thus giving the power of gnawing.

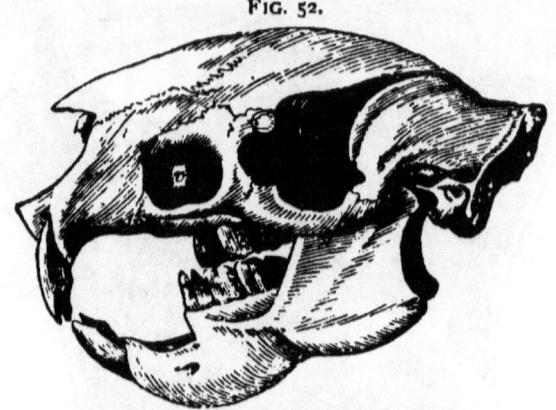

FIG. 52.

Skull of porcupine, showing *v*, the large infra-orbital cavity.

Rodents have small, smooth brains, usually a simple or saccular stomach, and a long cæcum or blind pouch from the intestine (except in dormice). Some genera, like guinea-pigs, hares, and rabbits, have no collar-bones, others, like squirrels and beavers, have these bones well marked. The hares and rabbits have a thin layer of enamel surrounding the backing of dentine on the incisor teeth, and have two small incisors behind the large ordinary pair in the upper jaw.

The squirrel family are usually long-tailed elegant creatures, and in one genus, the flying squirrel (fig. 51), there is a lateral parachute of skin stretching from the fore to the hind limbs. The beavers have flat scaly tails and webbed hind feet. The rats and mice

Gnawing Animals. 109

are known by their long cylindrical scaly tails, and usually rooted teeth (except in the voles). The common grey rat, introduced from the banks of the

Fig. 53.

The spalax, or blind rat.

Volga in 1727 into Western Europe, has now nearly exterminated the black rat. Spalax (fig. 53), the rat-mole of SE. Europe and NW. Asia, has rudimental eyes covered by the skin, and Dipus, the jerboa of the East, has long, kangaroo-like hind legs and very small fore legs. The porcupines have a covering of quill-like hairs, and have an enormous hole in the front of the skull wall, directly under the eye (fig. 52), which is partly occupied by a muscle of mastication. The chinchillas, coypu, &c. which are sought for their fur, are also examples of this order.

Hybernation.—Many rodents, like some mammals of other orders, bears, bats, &c., spend their winter in a condition of sleep: this process is called hybernation. Previous to retiring to this rest, these animals store up fat in different regions of the body, especially in a large gland called the thymus, placed in the thorax, or cavity of the chest, in front of the heart. This fat is absorbed during the winter, and the animal arises next spring lean and hungry. The lemmings extend far north into the Arctic regions, some having been captured at the winter quarters of the 'Alert' in 1875, in N. latitude 82°.

66. **Order 12, Proboscidea (Elephants).**— No groups of mammals appear more diverse from each other, in size at least, than do the rodents and the elephants, and yet the latter are structurally more

FIG. 54.

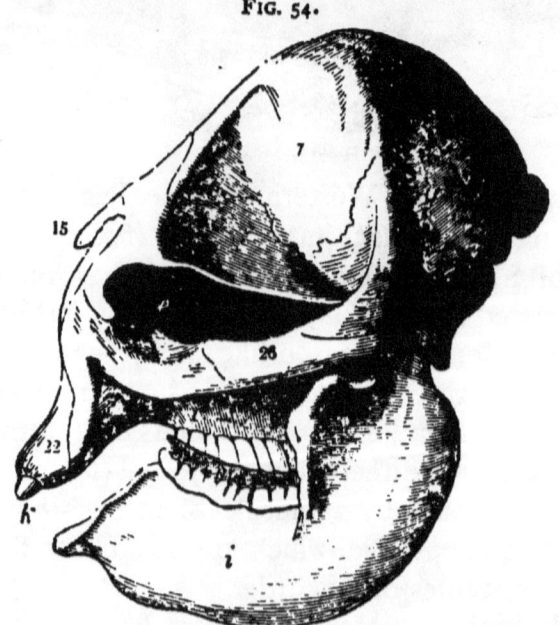

Skull of young elephant.

22, the premaxillary bone, containing the root of the tusk k; 15, nasal bone; 7, tempora region; 26, zygomatic arch; i, lower jaw; c, upper jaw.

closely allied to the former than to any other order of mammals. The elephants are the giants among

Elephants.

living land animals of the tropics, and are covered with a thick naked, or sparsely haired skin. They have five hoof-covered toes on each foot, though sometimes two toes are included in one hoof. The proboscis, or trunk, is a muscular and exceedingly movable double-barrelled tube appended to the nose,

FIG 55.

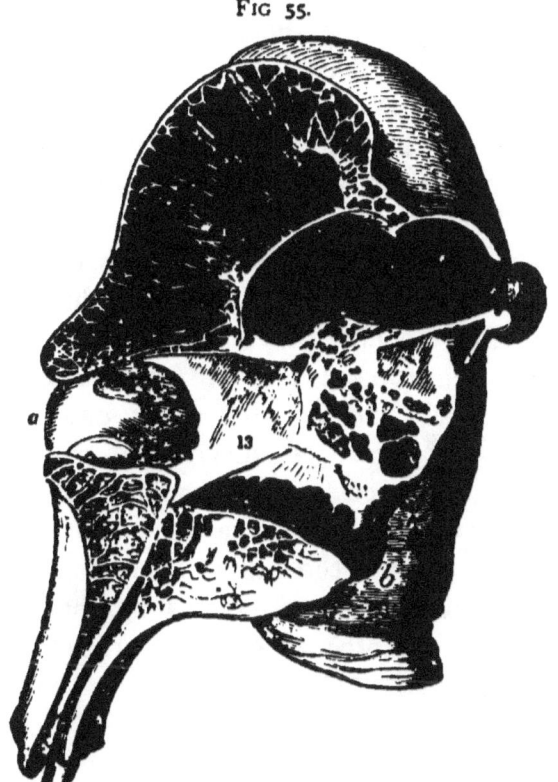

Section of the skull of the elephant, showing the small size of the brain-case, *e*, and the large size of the air spaces.

b, marks the posterior nostrils; 13, the cavity of the nose; *a*, the front opening of the bony nostrils to the edge of which the trunk is attached.

in fact an extension of that organ, which, by means of a finger-like appendage at the tip, can pick up even exceedingly small objects. The teeth of an elephant consist of two tusks or incisors in the upper jaw, which grow continuously, sometimes to enormous sizes, and furnish the ivory of commerce. There are no incisors in the lower jaw, but there are on each side of each jaw two large, rough-crowned, quadrate teeth, whose crowns are marked by transverse enamel ridges, used in grinding the twigs and shoots of trees on which these animals feed. There is a constant succession of these molars, seven of which are developed during the life of the animal on each side of each jaw, but never more than two, or at most three, are laterally functional at one time. The skull is enormous, most of its bulk consisting of huge air-cells, and the brain is large and convoluted on the surface. Two species of elephants are now living, confined to the tropics: one in Africa, known by its convex forehead and flapping ears; one in India, which has a concave forehead and smaller ears. Formerly several species of elephants lived in Europe, and remains of one form have been abundantly met with in some parts of the British Islands. In Siberia, also, there exist numerous remains of a hair-clad elephant, the mammoth, which had probably existed down to a comparatively modern time.

CHAPTER XVIII.

LEMURS, MOLES, AND BATS.

67. **Order 13, Prosimii.**—The lemurs, which constitute this little order, are monkey-like animals, chiefly confined to the Island of Madagascar, and to other islands in the Indian Ocean. They are arboreal, fruit- or insect-eating animals, with an opposable thumb on the fore foot, and sometimes on the hind foot as well, the second toe of which always bears a long claw, while all the others usually have flat-nails like those on the human fingers. In some respects the animals resemble the sloths of the New World, and many of them are nocturnal. Their teeth are always of the four kinds, and are more numerous than those of man. They are clad in an exceedingly soft and thick fur, and many of them have bushy tails, while others, like the Loris, or slow lemurs, are perfectly tailless. The largest forms measure about three feet in length, but some are much smaller, being only a few inches long. Many zoologists regard them, on account of their opposable thumbs, as closely allied to the monkeys; but in their simple brains and in the structure of some of their internal organs, they represent a much lower grade of organisation than that of the monkeys. The aye-aye of Madagascar, a strange little animal, about the size of a rabbit, has nails only on its thumbs, and claws on the other fingers. One singular genus from the Philippine and

Malay Islands, Tarsius, has the tarsus or ankle-bones of the foot exceedingly long, like the corresponding bones in the frog, so that it appears to have two ankle joints.

68. Order 14, Insectivora.—This order of mammals consists of the shrews, moles, and hedgehogs, which, as their name implies, feed on insects and worms, and other small animals. They are all of small size, and possess strong claws, long tapering snouts, and numerous sharply pointed teeth, the canines being small or absent. They all possess complete collar bones, a character which distinguishes them from Carnivores, and gives to the fore-limbs a fixity and definiteness of action that would be otherwise wanting. Their brains are usually small and smooth, not unlike those of rodents. In habit they are plantigrade, terrestrial, and usually active. The moles are familiar instances, and present in the highest degree the character of a fossorial or digging animal; the paddle-like hand the square arm-bone or humerus (fig. 56, 53), and the enormous muscularity of the fore-limb enable it to dig with wonderful celerity in pursuit of the worms and insects on which it feeds, while the

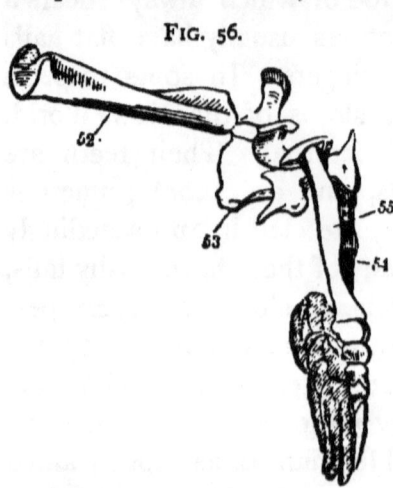

FIG. 56.

Bones of fore-limb of mole.
52, scapula; 53, humerus; 54, 55, fore-arm bones.

Moles and Bats.

velvety skin, and the rudimental eyes and outer ears, give it the greatest degree of fitness for its subterranean life. Moles are common in America and Great Britain, but are absent from Ireland. The shrew-mouse and the hedgehog are equally common types; the former can be easily distinguished from the true mice by the structure of the teeth. The pigmy shrew of S.E. Europe is the smallest known mammal, being only about two inches long. The flying lemurs of the East Indian archipelago, which form the last family of this order, have a wide parachute-like membrane stretching from the fore-limbs to the hind, and thence to the tail. They form a connecting link between this order and the next.

69. **Order 15, Cheiroptera (Bats).**—This curious group of mammals includes the only forms in the entire class which have any true powers of flight, the so-called flying phalangers, flying squirrels, and flying lemurs having only the power of taking long leaps, In the bats the fore-limbs are very long, the fingers are enormously lengthened, and are united together by an extensive and thin membrane, which stretches from finger-tip to finger-tip, and from thence to the hind limb; the thumb alone is free, and it is always armed with a claw. The outline of this membrane is shown by the dotted line in fig. 57. They are mostly nocturnal, with smooth brains and feeble powers of sight, and are rarely of large size. To move the wings they are provided with powerful pectoral, or breast muscles, and there is often an imperfect keel on the sternum, for muscular attachment. They have also long and strong clavicles. Their hind

116 *Vertebrata.*

limbs are turned outwards in a peculiar manner, so that the knees bend backwards, and the great toes are

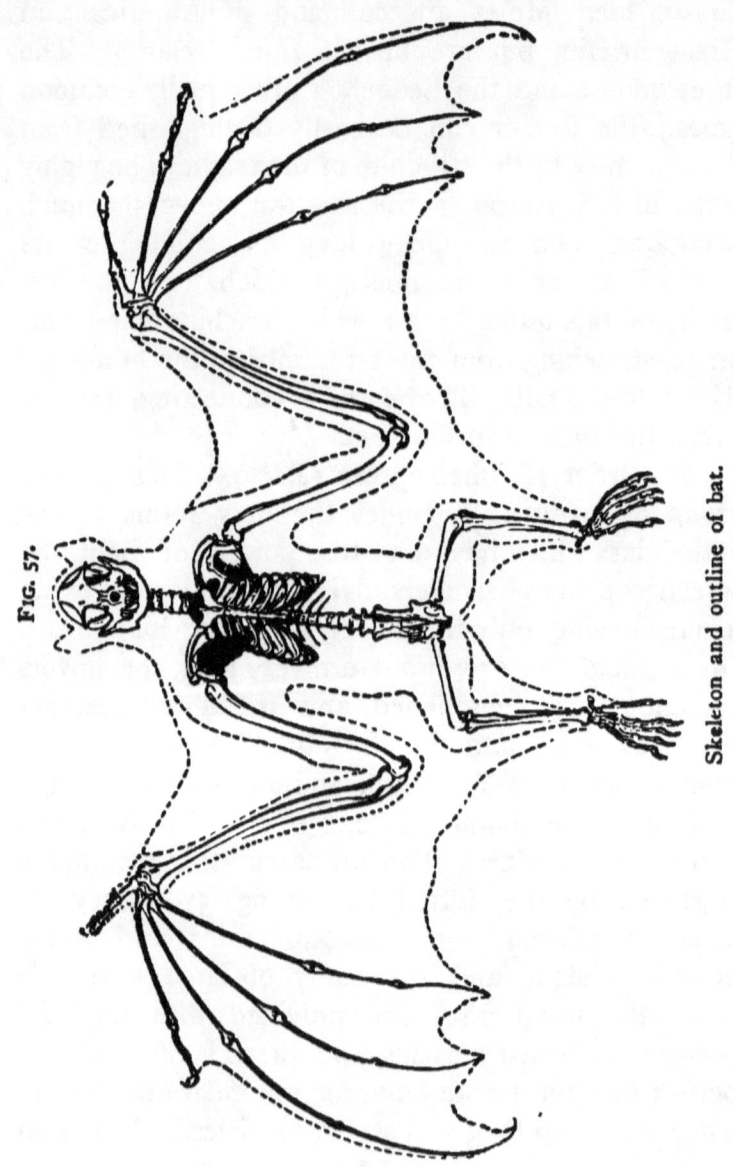

Fig. 57.—Skeleton and outline of bat.

thus twisted to the outer side of the foot, which has five equal claw-bearing toes. Many bats have enormous ears, others, like the vampires of South America, have sensitive leaf-like organs on their noses, made up of complicated folds of skin overlying processes of gristle. The body is covered with soft hairs whose surface presents a peculiar and characteristic scaly appearance under the microscope, and the fronts of the wings are extremely sensitive. They rest by hooking on to branches or ledges by the curved claws of their hind toes, and many of them thus feed with their heads downwards. They are extremely awkward in progression on the ground, and rarely resort to this method of locomotion. Most of the bats of temperate climates hybernate, and these are almost all insectivorous, having sharp-pointed teeth like those of the Insectivora. In warmer regions of the New World there are numerous large species, such as the vampires, which are suctorial in habit, sucking the blood of large animals, for which purpose they have sharp lancet-like teeth, and a long suctorial stomach. In the tropics of the Old World there are the largest individuals of the order, the fruit bats or Pteropi, which inhabit the Asiatic and insular shores of the Indian Ocean. They have blunt teeth, moderate ears, and, in one species, the distance from tip to tip of the wings is often as much as five feet. They are sometimes called flying foxes, from their prevailing colour and the shape of their heads.

CHAPTER XIX.

MONKEYS. MAN.

70. Order 16, Primates.—This, the last and highest order of mammals, includes the most highly organised members of the entire animal kingdom—the monkeys, apes, and mankind. They all possess opposable thumbs on some of the extremities, and (except among the marmosets) flat nails in place of claws. The face is mostly naked though fringed with hairs. The teeth are of three kinds and thirty-two in number, the formula being usually

$$I\frac{2-2}{2-2},\ C\frac{1-1}{1-1},\ P\frac{2-2}{2-2},\ M\frac{3-3}{3-3}.$$

They have the highest proportional development of brain of all animals, and the fore-limbs are chiefly set apart to wait on the head. There are four sub-orders included:—

1. The marmosets of South America, gregarious small monkeys of a squirrel-like habit, which have sharply tubercled teeth, claw-like nails on all the digits, except the great toe, which alone bears a flat nail. The long fur-clad tail is incapable of grasping, and the thumb is scarcely opposable.

2. The American monkeys, which differ from all others in having an additional premolar tooth on each side of each jaw $\left(P\frac{3-3}{3-3}\right)$. They have for the most part prehensile tails, and the thumb of the

Monkeys.

hand is not well developed, or is absent as in the spider monkeys: on all their fingers they have thick convex nails. Most of these live in the woods of Brazil, and are found in troops. The howling monkeys have a drum-like enlargement of the tongue bone at the top of the larynx or organ of voice, and with it they can produce a loud booming sound, audible for nearly a mile. In all the American monkeys the nostrils are separated by a very broad partition, their ear-drums or tympanic bones in the skull have also wide oval mouths.

3. The Old World monkeys and apes are characterised by having a narrow nasal septum, and the ear-drums have a long tubular mouth. The dentition is similar to that of man, the premolars being $\frac{2-2}{2-2}$. They have almost always an opposable thumb on the hand as well as on the foot, though it is rarely as perfect, and the muscle which bends it is never separate from the common flexor muscle of the other fingers. The baboon family may be known by possessing cheek pouches, and callous patches whereon they sit, as well as by their elongated jaws. The true baboons have dog-like muzzles and very short tails; they are confined to Africa and Arabia, and some of them have curiously coloured faces; thus the mandrill, with its blue, deeply-grooved cheeks, its brilliant scarlet lips and nostrils, and its white beard, is a most striking-looking creature. Some, like the Barbary ape, the only species which now lives in Europe, have no visible tails; others, like the cercopitheci or green monkeys, have long tails, but these organs are

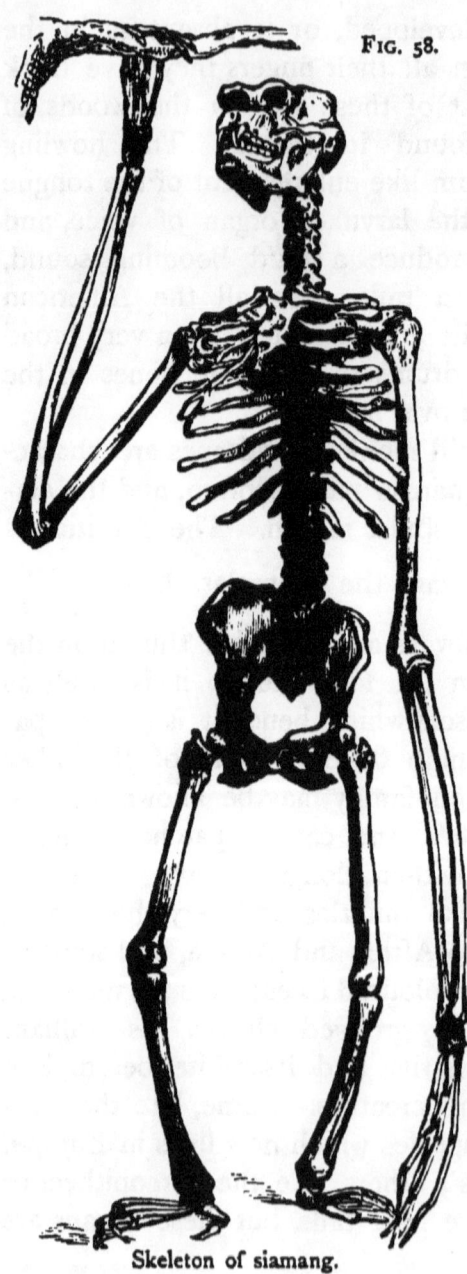

Fig. 58.

Skeleton of siamang.

never prehensile. Many, like the macaques of Eastern Asia, have long and prominent canine teeth, but these are weapons of offence, not indicative of a carnivorous diet. The sacred monkey of India (*Semnopithecus*), and the thumb-less Colobus of Africa, have no cheek-pouches, but possess long tails and callosities, while the highest group of the sub-order, the so-called anthropoids, have no tails, callosities, nor cheek pouches. The chimpanzee is a black-haired ape, a native of Guinea, which sometimes reaches a height of five feet. The orang-utan, a larger brown-haired species, with longer arms and a larger, rounder head, is found in Borneo and Sumatra. The gorilla, the largest of the anthropoids, is a native of Senegambia, and is nearly as tall as, but much stouter than, a man. The gibbons of Southern Asia differ from the anthropoids in having callosities, and resemble the orangs in the enormous length of their arms (fig. 58).

4. Man is the last and highest type included in the order, and though in an anatomical point of view there are not a sufficiently numerous series of differences of kind to lead us to form of him a separate order, yet there are enormous differences of degree, even of such kinds as are cognisable by the zoologist, who, from the difficulties incident thereto, cannot easily take psychological considerations into account in constructing a classification.

Man has a rudimentary (though an almost complete) hair clothing, and a perfectly opposable thumb on the hand, moved by independent muscles, while the great toe is only capable of grasping by approximation, not by opposition, and even this power, though great in some savage tribes, is almost destroyed, in civilised races, by the habit of wearing shoes. The arms in man are shorter, and the hind limbs longer and stronger than in any of the apes. Progression is bipedal, and the feet are plantigrade, while the arms are specially and solely set apart for waiting upon the head. The muscles which keep the body erect, such as those of the back, the extensors of the hip-joint, and the muscles of the calf are enormously greater than are the corresponding parts of monkeys, while the spinal column exhibits a series of curves so constructed that the centre of gravity falls between the feet. The brain of man is larger in relative size and complexity than that of any other animal, being on an average fifty ounces in weight, while that of the orang-utan weighs only about sixteen ounces. Man is also capable of articulate speech, and, psychologically, man is susceptible of education, which, in kind as well as in degree, is utterly unknown among the lower animals.

Man also is capable of fitting himself for residence in any climate, and having been thus long scattered over the face of the earth, the single human species presents to us numerous varieties, none of which, however, exhibit any approach to true specific distinctness. These varieties may be classed as follows:

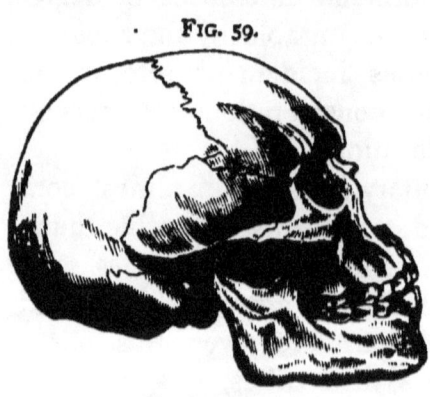

FIG. 59.

Skull of negro.

1. Woolly-haired races, such as the Negroes, Andamanese, and the Negritos of the Malay Archipelago.

2. Straight-haired races, which may be,

a. Australioid or dark-skinned, small-headed races, such as the aborigines of Australia, the aboriginal or hill tribes of India and Ceylon, possibly the ancient Egyptians, and the aboriginal races of the stone age.

b. Turanian races, yellow or red-skinned, mostly broad-headed races, like the Mongols, Chinese, the American Indians, &c.

c. Iranian or Indo-Germanic races, pale or olive races, usually bearded, and usually with longer heads and straighter features.

INDEX AND GLOSSARY.

ABO

ABOMASUS, the fourth stomach in ruminants, 96
Acanthopteri, spiny-finned fishes, 30
Accessory eyes in Scopeline fishes, 29
Acrania, headless vertebrates, 5
Æpyornis, a gigantic extinct bird of Madagascar, 62
African mud-fishes, 14-33
Aftershaft, 53
Air in bones of birds, 57
Albatross, 72
Allantois, a membrane surrounding the young of reptiles, birds, and mammals before birth.
Alligators, 52
Alula, the bastard wing, or feathers borne on the thumb in birds, 54
Alveoli, the sockets of the teeth in vertebrate animals.
Amblyopsis, or blind-fish, 29
American monkeys, 118
Amphibia, 34
— blood of, 36
Amphicœlous vertebræ, bones of the vertebral column which are hollow on both surfaces, 15
Amphioxus lanceolatus, 4
Amphiuma, one of the amphibia, 39
Anacanthini, soft-finned fishes with no swimming bladder, 29
Anal fin, 14
Anatomy of amphioxus, 4
Anguis fragilis, 43
Animals, vertebrate, characters of, 1
Anteaters, 80-85
Antelopes 100
Anthropoid apes, 120

BAB

Anura, tailless amphibians, such as frogs, 39
Aorta, the large bloodvessel which conveys the pure blood from the heart, 21
Aortic arches, 9; in reptiles, 40; in birds, 60; in mammalia, 78
Aplacentalia, such mammals as have no placentæ.
Apteryx, wingless bird of New Zealand, 63
Arch, neural, 3
Arch, hyoid, 8
Arches, aortic, 9
— branchial or gill, 18
— visceral, 7
Armadillos, 86
— scales of, 74
Arterial cone in fishes, 2
Arteries, branchial, 21
Articulation, a joint between two bones.
Artiodactyla, even-toed hoofed animals, 93
Asymmetry of flat-fishes, 31
Atlas, the first bone of the vertebral column, which supports the head.
Atrium in amphioxus, 4
Auricle of heart, 9
Australioid races of man, 122
Aves, birds. 52
Axolotl, a Mexican amphibian, 40
Aye Aye, 113

BABOONS, 119
Babyroussa, a kind of pig from the Malay Islands, 94

Index and Glossary.

BAD

Badger, 104
Barbary ape, 119
Barbel, a river fish, 28
Basking shark, 25
Bats, 115
Bears, 104
Beavers, 108
Bee-eaters, 64
Bile, 9
Birds, 52
Bitterns, 71
Blackbird, 66
Blackcap, 67
Blennies, 31
Blind amphibians, 37
— fishes, 29
— rats, 109
— worms, 43
Blood of amphibians, 36
— of fishes, 21
— — vertebrates, 9
— corpuscles of fishes, 22
— — of birds, 61
— vessels of birds, 60
— — of fish-gills, 20
Blowing and blowholes of whales, 99
Boa, 8, 46
Body of vertebrate animal, 2
Bones, formation of, 17
Bony pike of California (Lepidosteus), 27
Bony skull, 7, 17
Bottlenose whales, 101
Box fishes, 32
Bradypoda, the sloth family, 88
Brain of cod, 19
— — craniota, 19
— — fishes, 19
Branchial, pertaining to the gills.
— arteries of fishes, 21
Breathing, 10-35
Bullfinch, 67
Bullhead, 31
Bunodonts, hoofed animals with tuberculated teeth, 93
Bustard, 71
Buzzard, 69

CADUCOUS gills, gills which fall off before the animals reach maturity.
Cæcum, the first part of the large intestine.
Cæcilians, worm-like amphibians, 37

COB

Calamoichthys, African reed fish, 27
Callophis, snake, poison gland of, 48
Camels, 96
Canine teeth, the eye-tooth, the foremost tooth in the maxillary bone, when it is single-fanged, and the corresponding tooth in the lower jaw.
Carapace, the upper shield of a tortoise, 49
Carnivora, flesh-eating mammals, 102
Carp, 28
Carinate birds, those with a keel on the breast-bone, 63
Carotid arteries, neck bloodvessels, 78
Carpus, the bones of the wrist-joint.
Cartilage bones, such as begin their existence as masses of gristle, 17
Cassowary, 62
Catarrhine monkeys, old world monkeys with a narrow partition between the nostrils, 119
Cats, 103
Cave amphibians, 38
Cave bear, 106
Cavities in the vertebrate body, 2
Cebus, South American monkeys, 118
Cephalic, pertaining to the head.
Cephalisation, subordination in function of limbs to the head, 11
Ceratodus, Australian fish, 34
Cercopithecus, green monkeys, 119
Cere, soft skin at the base of the horny beak in birds, 68
Cerebrum, the greater or anterior lobes of the brain, 20
Cetacea, whales, 99
Chamæleons, 44
Cheetah, hunting leopard of India, 104
Cheiroptera, 115
Chelonia, tortoises and turtles, 49
Chewing the cud, 95
Chimpanzee, 120
Chinchilla, 109
Ciconiæ, storks, 74
Circulation in fishes, 20
Civets, 104
Clavicle, the collar-bone.
Claws of cats, 103
Cloaca, the cavity into which the intestine and excretory organs open, 79
Cobra, hooded snake, asp, 48

Index and Glossary.

COC

Coccygomorphæ, the cuckoo order of birds, 64
Coccyx, the rudimental tail in the higher mammals.
Cockatoos, 64
Cod, 17, 18, 29
Collocalia, the swallow which secretes the 'edible bird's nest,' 65
Colobus, 120
Colossochelys, a giant extinct tortoise, 51
Colubrine snakes (non-poisonous), 46
Concentration of segments characteristic of vertebrates, 10
Condyles, knobs of bone by which one bone forms a joint with another, 36
Contour feathers, the strong quill-feathers on the surface of a bird, 53
Coots, 71
Coracoid bone, one of the bones of the fore part of the shoulder-girdle, 56, 79
Coral snake, 48
Cormorants, 73
Corncrake, 71
Corpuscles, microscopical bodies found floating in blood.
— of blood in amphib.a, 36
— — — — birds, 61
— — — — fishes, 22
Corvidæ, the crow family, 67
Cows, 97
Coypu, 109
Cranes, 71
Craniota, skull-bearing vertebrates, 5
Cranium, the skull of a vertebrate animal, 7
Crocodilia, 51
Crows, 67
Ctenoid scales, fish-scales with a comb-like hinder edge, 14
Cuckoos, 64
Curruca, black-caps, 67
Cuticle, the outer layer of the skin.
Cycloid scales, thin bony fish-scales with a smooth rounded margin, 13

D

*D*AB, flat-fish, 30
Dasypeltis, snake, teeth in the gullet of, 48
Dasyurus, Tasmanian devil, 81

EEL

Dasypus, armadillo, 87
Deer, 98
Dental formulæ, 77
— formula of cat, 103
— — — dog, 103
— — — horse, 91
— — — kangaroo, 84
— — — man, 78
— — — marsupials, 84
— — — pig, 94
— — — ruminants, 98
— — — seal, 102
— — — sloths, 89
— — — Tasmanian devil, 77
Dentine, the ivory substance of teeth, 13, 25
Dentition, the arrangement of teeth in an animal.
Dermis, or true skin, of fishes, 12
— — — — reptiles, 40
Diaphragm, the muscular partition between the cavity of the chest and that of the abdomen, 60, 78
Digestive system of birds, 58
— — — frogs and tadpoles, 36
— — — sharks, 25
Diphycercal tails, tails in fishes with an even marginal fringe of fin rays.
Dipnoi, fishes whose swimming bladder acts as a breathing organ, 33
Diprotodon, giant fossil kangaroo, 84
Dipus, the jerboas, or jumping rats, 109
Dodo, the extinct gigantic pigeon of Madagascar, 69
Dog, 103
Dog-fishes, 15, 26
Dolphin, 101
Domestic fowl, 70
Dormouse, 108
Dorsal fin, 14
Doves, 69
Dragon, 43
Ducks. 72
Dugong, 89

E

*E*AGLES, 68
Ear passage, nature of, 8
Echidna, the spiny anteater of Australia, 79
Edentata, toothless mammals, 85
Edible birds' nests, 65
Eels, 28

EGG

Egg cases of sharks, 25
Egg pouches of pipe fishes, 32
Eggs of birds, 65
— — fishes, 22
Elasmobranchs, sharks so called from their laminar gills, 23
Electric organ of gymnotus, the electric eel, 28
— — — malapterurus, 28
— — — mormyrus, 28
— — — torpedo, 26
Elephants, 110
Embryonic characters in vertebral column of sharks, 24
Embryos of flat fishes, 30
Emus, 62
Enamel, the hardest portion of a tooth, formed by the calcification of the outer layer or epidermis of the tooth papilla.
Epidermis, or surface layer of the skin of fishes, 12
— of reptiles, 40
Equus, the horse and ass genus, 91
Ermine, 104
Erythacus, robin redbreast, 67
Exoskeleton, bony deposits in the skin or surface tissues, 14
Extensor, a muscle which straightens a joint.
External gills in sharks and amphibians, 39
Extinct reptiles, 52
Eye of amphioxus, 5
Eyes of birds, 61
— — snakes, 46

FALCONS, 69
Fallow-deer, 98
Fauna, the collective name applied to the animals of a country or district.
Feathers, 53
Feeding of whales, 100
Feet of birds, 59
Felidæ, 103
Femur, the thigh-bone.
Fieldfare, 66
Fierasfer (a parasitic fish), 30
Filefishes, 32
Finches, 67
Fin rays, the bony filaments and spines which are included in the fins of fishes.
Fins of fishes, 14-19
Fish, epidermis of, 12

GIL

Fish, gills of, 8
— head of, 17, 18
— lateral line of, 15
— notochord in, 17
— scales of, 12
— shape of, 12
— tail of, 12-15
Fistularia, or tobacco-pipe fish, 3
Flat fishes, 30
Flounders, 30
Flying fishes, 32
— foxes, 117
— lemurs, 115
— squirrels, 107
Forelimbs, 114
Fossil amphibians, 37
— edentates, 87
— elephants, 112
— fishes, 27
— horses, 91
— mammals, 78
— reptiles, 52
Fowls, domestic, 70
Fox, 103
Freshwater and marine fishes contrasted, 22
— seals, 101
Frigate birds, 73
Frilled lizards, 43
Fruit bats, 117
Fry of salmon, tail of, 15
Functional, capable of performing any duty, or of being useful in the economy.
Furculum, the merrythought of birds, 56
Fur seals, 102

GANGLIA, masses of nerve matter, 19
Gannets, 73
Ganoid fishes, fishes with burnished scales, 27
Gar pike, 32
Gavials, 52
Geckos, 43
Geese, 72
Gibbons, long-armed apes, 121
Gill arches, 8-18
— cover, 19
Gills of amphibians, 41
— — fishes, 20-21
— — ganoids, 27
— — lampreys, 24
— — pipe-fishes, 32
— — sharks, 25

Index and Glossary.

GIL

Gills of teleosts, 29
Giraffes, 98
Girdles of limbs, 8
Gizzard, the muscular stomach of birds, 39
Globe fishes, 32
Glutinous hag, 23
Gnawing animals, 106
Goat, 98
Goatsucker, 65
Gobies, 31
Golden pheasant, 70
Goldfish, 28
Gorilla, 121
Grallæ, wading birds, such as cranes and herons, 70
Greek tortoise, 51
Grey rat, 109
Grizzly bear, 106
Grouse, 70
Guillemots, 73
Guinea pig, 108
Gulls, 72
Gurnards, 31
Gymnophiona, cæcilians, or blind amphibians, 37
Gymnotus, the electric eel, 28
Gyrantes, the name given to the pigeon order, 69

HADDOCK, 29
Hag, glutinous, 23
Hair, 74
Halibut, 30
Hallux, the great toe
Hammer-headed shark, 26
Hares, 108
Harrier, 69
Hawfinch, 67
Hawk, 67
Hawksbill turtle, 51
Head, 11
Hearing, organ of, 6
Heart of amphioxus, 4
— — birds, 59
— — crocodiles, 51
— — dipnoi, 33
— — fishes, 21
— — ganoids, 27
— — mammals, 78
— — manatees, 90
— — reptiles, 41
— — sharks, 25
— — teleosts, 27
Heat of birds, 61
Hedgehog, 114

JAW

Helen's eel, 28
Hemisphere of brain, 20
Herons, 71
Herring, viscera of, 28
Heterocercal tails, fishes' tails in which the vertebral column is prolonged into the upper lobe of the tail, 15-25
Hind limbs, 8-18
Hippopotamus, 94
Hollow horns, 98
Holothurians, sea cucumbers, inhabited by fishes, 30
Homocercal, evenly bilobed fishes' tails, 15
Honeycomb, the second stomach of ruminants, 96
Hoopoe, 64
Hornbills, 64
Horned owls, 68
Horns in mammals, 98
Horse, 91
House sparrow, 67
Howling ape, 119
Humerus, the bone of the arm.
Humming birds, 66
Hump of camel, 96
Hybernation, winter sleep, 109
Hyenas, 104
Hyoid bone, the bone which supports the base of the tongue.
Hyracoidea, the order to which the coney belongs, 106
Hyrax, coney, 106

IBIS, 71
Ide, a carp-like fish, 28
Iguana, group of American lizards, 43
Ilium, the haunch bone or side of the pelvis.
Impeyan pheasant, 70
Incisor teeth, 76
Insectivora, 114
Insessores, perching or sparrow-like birds, 66
Internal gills, 39
Intestine of shark, 25
Iranian races of man, 123
Isinglass, 27

JABIRU, 71
Jackdaw, 67
Jaguar, 103
Jaw arches, 7

K

Index and Glossary.

JAW

Jaws of fishes, 18
— — mammals, 76
— — marsupials, 84
— — sharks, 24
Jay, 67
Jerboa, 109
John Dory, 30
Jugal arch, bony arch in the skull from the outside of the upper jaw to the base of the joint of the lower jaw with the skull.
Jugular, pertaining to the throat.

KANGAROO, 82
Kidney, 10
Kingfishers, 64
Kinkajou, 105
Koala, the native bear of Australia, 84

LABYRINTHODONTS, fossil amphibians with complex teeth, 37
Lacertilia, lizards, 42
Lamellirostres, ducks and geese, 72
Lamprey, 17, 23
Lancelet, 3
Larks, 67
Larynx, the organ of voice, placed at the top of the windpipe.
Lateral line in fishes, 15
Leg of birds, 57
Leiotrichous, straight haired, 122
Lemmings, 110
Lemur, 113
Leopard, 104
Lepadogaster, 31
Lepidosiren, mud fish, 17, 31
Lepidosteus, the bony pike of California, 27
Leptoptilus, the bird which yields the Marabou feathers, 72
Liber, the third stomach of ruminants, 96
Limb girdles, 8, 75
Limbs of boas, 8
— — frogs, 39
— — whales, 100
Linnets, 67
Lion, 102, 103
Liver, 3-9
Lithe, 29
Lizards, 8, 42

MER

Llamas, 96
Longipennes gulls and terns, 72
Lophobranchii, pipe-fishes having tufted gills, 32
Lore, the space between the eye and the angle of the mouth in birds and reptiles, 71
Loris, 113
Lump fish, 31
Lung, 31, 35, 37
Lynx, 104
Lyre-birds, 68

MACACUS, macaques, or bonnet and rhesus monkeys, 120
Macaws, 64
Mackerel, 31
Macrochires, long-handed birds, such as swifts and humming birds, 65
Magpie, 67
Malapterurus, electric organ of, 28
Malar bone. *See* jugal arch, 89
Mammalia, animals that suckle their young, 74
Man, 121
— tail of, 75
— teeth of, 78
Manatee, 75-89
Mandible, the lower jaw, 55
Mandrill, 119
Manis, the scaly anteater or pangolin of the Eastern tropics, 85
Manyplies, the third stomach of a ruminant, 96
Marabou, the stork which yields ornamental feathers, 72
Marine fishes, 32
Marmosets or Oustitis, 118
Marsipobranchii, fishes with pouched gills, as lampreys, 23
Marsupialia, pouched mammals, kangaroos, 80
Marsupial bone, 81
Maxilla, the bone which forms the chief part of the upper jaw, 76
Megatherium, gigantic fossil sloth, 89
Melisuga, 66
Membrane bones, 17
Menopoma, American gill-bearing amphibians, 39
Merganser, 72
Mermaid's purses, 25
Mermaids 89

Index and Glossary.

MER

Merrythought, 56
Metamorphosis of tadpoles, 35
— changes in form taking place during the processes of growth.
Migration of birds, 73
Milk, 74
— teeth, 77
Mink, 104
Minnow, 28
Missel-thrush, 66
Moa, 62
Mocking-birds, 67
Molar teeth, 77
Mole, 114
Moloch, spiny lizard, 43
Mongoose, 104
Monitor, 43
Monotremata, an order of mammals having a cloaca, 79
Mormyrus, electric organ of, 29
Mother Cary's chickens, 72
Moulting, the process of the periodical shedding of feathers, 54
Mound birds, 70
Mouse, 108
Mouth of whales, 100
— — vertebrates, 3
Mud eels, 38
— fishes, 15, 33
Mullets, 31
Muscles of birds, 58
Musk, 96
— deer, 96
— glands of crocodiles, 51
Mustela foina, or marten, 104
Myrmecobius, the banded ant-eater of Australia, 84

NARWHAL, 101
Nature of sense organs, 6
Neck, 9, 75
Neural arch, 3
Newts, 39
New Zealand parrots, 64
Nightingale, 67
Nitrogenised waste, 10
Nostrils of lamprey, 23
Notochord, the gristly rod which exists as the first form of backbone in the earliest stage of all vertebrates, 2, 17, 28
Numida, head of, 70
Nuthatch, 68

PEN

OCCIPITAL bone, the bone which forms the back of the skull.
Ocelot, 104
Œsophagus, the gullet or food-passage from the mouth to the stomach, 3, 59
Old world monkeys, 119
Operculum, the gill cover in fishes, 19, 28
Ophidia, snakes, 44
Opisthocœlous, vertebrate bodies which are concave behind and convex in front.
Opossums, 81
Optic lobes, 20
Orang-utan, 121
Ornithorhynchus, the platypus or duck-mole of Australia, 79
Orycteropus, Cape ant-eater, 86
Osprey, 72
Ostrich, 58, 60, 64, 66
Otter, 104
Ounce, 103
Oven-building birds, 68
Oviparous, reproducing by the aying of eggs,
Ovoviviparous, retaining eggs within the body until they are hatched
Owls, 68   Ox, 97
Oyster-catchers, 71

PANTHER, 103
Pangolin, 86
Papilla, a wart-like projection of the dermis.
— feather, 54
Paradise, birds of, 68
Parasitic fishes, 30
Parasphenoid bone, the long bone at the base of the skull in fishes, 36
Parrots, 63
Parrot fishes, 32
Partridges, 70
Patella, the small bone or 'cap' of the knee-joint.
Paunch, 96
Peacocks, 70
Pecten, a structure in the eye of bird, 61
Pectoral fins, 19-26
— muscles of bird, 58
Peewit, 71
Pelias, the viper, 47
Pelicans, 73
Pelvis, 56, 81
Penguins, 66, 72

Index and Glossary.

PER

Perch, 31
Perching birds, 66
Perennibranchiate amphibians, 40
Peroneus muscle in leg of birds, 58
Petrels, 72
Phalanges, the b nes of th fingers and toes.
Pharyngognathi, wrasses, fishes with united pharyngeal bones, 32
Pharynx, the uppermost part of the digestive canal, 3
Pheasants, 70
Philomela, nightingale, 67
Phœnicura, redstart, 67
Physostomi, fishes with a swimming bladder, 28
Pici, woodpeckers, 64
Pig, 93
Pigeon, 69
Pike, 28
Pinnipedia, seals, 101
Pipa, South American toads which carry the young on their backs, 40
Pipe fishes, 32
Pipits, 67
Pisces, fishes, 11
Placenta, 85
Placoid scales, 12
Plaice, 30
Plantain eaters, 64
Plantaris muscle in the bird's leg, 58
Plantigrade, a term applied to animals which in walking place the entire surface of the sole of the foot on the ground.
Plastron, the under shield of a turtle or tortoise, 49
Platypus, 79
Platyrrhine, American monkeys with a wide nasal septum, 119
Plectognathi, sunfishes whose upper jaw-bones are soldered together, 32
Pleuronectidæ, flat-fishes, such as the plaice, &c., 30
Plovers, 71
Poison-fangs, 47
Poisonous snakes, 47
Polypterus, Nile ganoid fish, 27
Porcupine, 109
Porpoises, 101
Pouch in marsupials, 81
Prehensile tails, 75
Premaxilla, teeth in, 77
Premolar teeth, 77
Prey, birds of, 68

ROA

Primates, 118
Proboscidea, elephants, 110
Pronghorn antelope, 98
Prosimii, 113
Proteus, 38
Protopterus, the African mud-fish, 33
Psittaci, parrots, 63
Pteropus, fruit bats, 117
Pterygoid arch, 55
Pterylæ, tracts of strong feathers in birds, 54
Puffin, 73
Puma, 103
Purses, mermaids', 25
Pygopodes, penguins, 73
Python, 6, 46

QUADRATE bone, 74
Quagga, 91

RABBIT, 108
Rachis, the central axis of a feather, 53
Radius, the outer bone in the forearm, 40
Raptores, birds of prey, 68
Rasores, scraping birds, poultry, 70
Rat, 108
Ratidæ, running birds with no keel on the breast-bone, 62
Rat-mole, 109
Rattlesnake, 47
Raven, 67
Rays, 26
Razorbill, 73
Rectrices, the strong tail-feathers, 54
Red deer, 98
Redstart, 67
Reed-fish of Africa, 27
Regulus, wrens, 67
Remora, sucking-fish, 31
Rennet, 96
Reptiles, 40
Respiration, 3, 22
Restoration of lost parts in reptiles, 42
Reticulum, 96
Rhea, 62
Rhinoceros, 92
Rhinodon, gigantic shark, 26
Rhytina, extinct sea-cow, 89
Ribs, 9
Roach, 28

Index and Glossary.   133

Robin, 69
Rodentia, 106
Roebuck, 98
Rollers, 64
Rook, 67
Ruminantia, animals which chew the cud, 94
Ruminating, 95

SABLE, 104
 Sacrum, the united vertebræ which enter into the pelvis, 75
Saith, fish, 29
Salamander, 38
Salicaria, warblers, 67
Salmon, 28
Sawfish, 26
Scales of amphibians, 39
— — fishes, 12, 25, 28, 29, 32
— — reptiles, 43
Scapulars, feathers on the shoulder, 54
Sclerotic plates, 61
Scopelidæ, accessory eyes of, 29
Scraping birds, 70
Screw propeller, principle of, 12
Sea-cows, 89
Sea-horses, 32
Seals, 101
Sebaceous glands, 74
Segments of skull, 7
— — body, 10
Segmental ducts, 10
Selachia, sharks, 24
Semnopitheci, 120
Sense organs in tadpoles, 36
— — 6, 15
Shape of fishes, 12
Sharks, 7, 13, 17, 24, 25
— external gills of, 39
Sheep, 98
Shrews, 115
Sieboldia, giant salamander, 39
Siren, mud-eel, 38
Sirenia, sea-cows, 89
Skate, 26
Skeleton of bird, 55
— — frog, 37
— — lepidosiren, 16
— — mammals, 75
— — sole, 15
— — tortoise, 50
Skin, action of, in respiration, 10
— of amphibia, 34
Skull, 6
— of amphibian, 36

Skull of bird, 55
— — elephant, 110
— — fishes, 17, 18
— — mammal, 75
— — reptile, 41
Skunk, 104
Slits, visceral, 3–6
Sloth, 75, 88
Smell, 20
Snake-like lizards, 43
Snakes, 44
Snipe, 72
Sole, 15–29
Song thrush, 66
Spalax, the blind rat-mole of S. Europe, 109
Sparrow, 67
Species of fish, number of, 22
Spermaceti, 101
Sperm whales, 101
Spider monkeys, 119
Spiral valve in shark's intestine, 25
Spoonbills, 72
Squirrels, 108
Stag, 98
Starling, 67
Steganopodes, pelicans and cormorants, whose fourth toe is included in the web, 72
Stickleback, 31
Stomach of camel, 96
— — ruminant, 95
— — sheep, 95
— — whales, 100
Storks, 71
Strigops, the New Zealand ground parrot, 64
Sturgeons, 17, 27
Sucking fishes, 31
Sunbirds, 68
Sunfish, 32
Swans, 72
Swifts, 65
Swimming bladder in fishes, 22, 29
Swordfish, 33
Sylvia, wood warblers, 67
Syrinx, the organ of voice in birds, 61

TADPOLE, 36–38
 Tails, 9, 15, 19, 78, 101
Tapirs, 91
Tarsius, 114
Tasmanian devil, 77, 81
— wolf, 81
Teal, 74

134   *Index and Glossary.*

TEE

Teeth, 10–14
— of elephant, 111
— — lamprey, 23
— — mammals, 76
— — rodents, 107
— — snakes, 46
Teguexins, 47
Teleostei, bony fishes, 27
Tench, 28
Terns, 72
Thorax, the cavity of the chest, 8
Thrushes, 67
Thymus gland, 110
Tiger, 103
Titmouse, 67
Toads, 39
Toes, 57, 82, 91
Tongue, 8, 44, 45, 58, 79
Torpedo, 27
Tortoises, 49
Toucans, 64
Trabeculæ, processes of gristle at the base of the embryo skull, 7
Trachinus, weaver fishes, 31
Tree frogs, 40
Tropic birds, 73
Tropidonotus, the ringed snake, 46
Trout, 28
Trumpet fish, 31
Trunk of elephant, 111
Tunicated worms, relation of to vertebrates, 2
Turanian races of mankind, 123
Turkey, 70
Turtles, 49

ULNA, the inner bone of the forearm, 40
Ulotrichi, woolly haired races of man, 122
Umbilicus of feather, 53
Ungulates, hoof-bearing mammals, 90
Urodela, tailed amphibians, 38

VAMPIRES, 117
Vanes of feathers, 53
Veins of the liver, 3
Vena portæ, the vein that carries the blood from the intestines to the liver, 3

ZEB

Venomous snakes, 47
Ventral fins, 19
Ventricles of heart, 9
Vertebra, one of the detached elements of the backbone, 3
Vertebral column, 24, 29, 36, 41, 45
Vertebrata, characters of, 1
Vipers, 47
Visceral arches and slits, 3, 19
Viscera, organs of the body.
Vison, 104
Viverridæ, 104
Voice in birds, 60, 61
Voles, 108
Vultures, 68

WAGTAILS, 67
Walrus, 102
Warbler, 67
Waste of living bodies, 10
Water hens, 71
Water snakes, 48
Wattles, 70
Waxwings, 68
Weasels, 104
Weevers, 31
Whalebone, 100
Whales, 99
— limbs of, 100
— teeth of, 76
Wheatears, 67
Whinchat, 67
Whiting, 29
Widgeon, 72
Wild cat, 104
Wild swan, windpipe of, 72
Wings of bats, 117
Wolf, 103
Wombat, 84
Woodpecker, 64
Woodquest, 76
Wrasse, 32
Wren, 69

YAPOCK, 82

ZEBRA, 91

www.ingramcontent.com/pod-product-compliance
Lightning Source LLC
Chambersburg PA
CBHW032048230426
43672CB00009B/1519